THE EXPLOSIVE TRUE STORY OF JAY-Z'S LIFE

THE DRUG DEALER!
THE AWARD-WINNING RAPPER!
THE RECORD COMPANY EXECUTIVE!

"He didn't come into the game to learn; he came to teach…the card-deck-thick money stacks, all rubber banded up, foreshadow the personal fortune (which now exceeds $50 million) he would amass…He told us in '96 that he came to take this nuts, and he did."

—Vibe Magazine

A MUST READ!!!

"Few hip-hop artists can balance staying true to the streets and go platinum at the same time; Jay-Z happens to be one of them. …satisfies both his street and suburb audiences. Jay-Z sells records, not his soul."

—Daily News

"This is his strongest album to date, with music that's filled with catchy hooks, rump-shaking beats and lyrics fueled by Jay's hustler's vigilance…Jay has become a better architect of songs."

—Rolling Stone Magazine

INTENSE!   POWERFUL!

FOR ANYONE WHO WANTS TO KNOW THE INTIMATE DETAILS OF HIP HOP'S LEADING MAN. IT'S ALL HERE!

JAY-Z

...and the Roc-A-Fella Dynasty

by Jake Brown

Colossus Books

Phoenix
New York   Los Angeles

JAY-Z ....and the Roc-A-Fella Dynasty

by Jake Brown

Published by:
Colossus Books
A Division of Amber Communications Group, Inc.
1334 East Chandler Boulevard, Suite 5-D67
Phoenix, Z 85048
amberbk@aol.com
WWW.AMBERBOOKS.COM

Tony Rose, Publisher/Editorial Director   Samuel P. Peabody, Associate Publisher
Yvonne Rose, Senior Editor   The Printed Page, Interior & Cover Design

© Copyright 2005 by Jake Brown and Colossus Books
ISBN#: 0-9749779-1-8

Library of Congress Cataloging-in-Publication Data
Brown, Jake.
Jay Z—and the Roc-A-Fella dynasty / by Jake Brown.
   p. cm.
   ISBN 0-9749779-1-8 (pbk. : alk. paper) 1. Jay-Z, 1970- 2. Rap musicians—United States—Biography. 3. Roc-A-Fella Records (Firm) I. Title.
   ML420.J29B76 2005
                          2005043666

Dedication

This book is dedicated to my wonderfully loving family of Aunts and Uncles—Debbie Koob, Sharon Schweiss-Neff, Vickie Kearns, Heather Thieme, Carol Thieme, Jeff Thieme, Steven Thieme, Paul Brown (RIP), Bob Brown (RIP), Jim Kearns. This is a story of perseverance of the tallest order, and you have all been great examples of this in my lifetime in your own influential ways.

About The Author

Jake Brown resides in Nashville, Tennessee. An avid writer, Jake has penned several books, including the best-sellers: *SUGE KNIGHT — The Rise, Fall & Rise of Death Row Records*; *Your Body's Calling Me: The Life and Times of Robert "R" Kelly — Music Love, Sex & Money* and *Ready to Die: The Story of Biggie — Notorious B.I.G.* Upcoming titles on Colossus Books are: *50 Cent: No Holds Barred* and *Tupac SHAKUR (2-PAC) in the Studio: The Studio Years (1987-1996)*.

Contents

Prologue

Hip-hop is the most competitive enterprise within the record business today, running against the very grain that the music industry's traditionally relaxed bible preaches. Rap's sermon is governed by a street code of conduct that operates largely absent of conventional moralities, and lends itself, instead, to a bottom-line mentality focused on survival and the pursuit of money, and an inherently cut-throat work ethic to accompany that pursuit.

Things aren't much different in Corporate America's heartless, dog-eat-dog atmosphere; still, hip-hop has a human side, wherein its sound reflects and communicates the real struggles and plights of a historically oppressed and economically brutalized race of people, and inspires hope where Corporate America certainly never has. Where Fortune 500 corporations give millions of dollars a year to charity, their underlying motive is almost always in the interest of the tax write-off as much as it ever is doing any real good.

The hip-hop community, conversely, is genuine by nature, championing a foundation of "keeping it real", and within that context, is capable of extreme generosity within its own ranks, as much as it is of extreme violence.

Violence is second-nature in the rap industry, just as it is on the street, and the parent companies who have established extremely profitable joint-ventures with hip-hop independents like Roc-A-

Fella, Death Row Records, No Limit Records, and Cash Money Records, have caught on and up quickly in their education on and tolerance of the inherently violent nature of rap music. As a result, hip-hop's elite stars- from Jay-Z to P. Diddy and DMX to Snoop Dogg, 50 Cent to Eminem, and even Biggie and Tupac- have seen to it they had the same legal protection as anyone of great importance within the whose-who of the financial community.

The bottom line is money talks, such that, Jay-Z for example, was given 3 years probation after pleading guilty to stabbing a rival record executive at a record release party- a crime which would have netted the average violator a minimum of a year in prison. Because Jay-Z employed an attorney who was friendly with both the judge and the prosecutor, the rapper was given what most view as preferential treatment. He even had the audacity to show up 15 minutes late to sentencing, and wore a Roc-A-Fella Custom-tailored sweat suit. Still, he'd have worn that sweat suit out on the corner.

All of the aforementioned have had run-ins with the law despite their corporate positions and personal wealth, simply because they never left the street, nor its hustler mentality—not in the course of achieving the privileged positions they did, nor in staying atop of the game once they had made the climb. This was principally because all were following the cardinal street edict of never forgetting the neighborhood you came from, nor its implied code of conduct.

Jay-Z began as a street pusher, and it can be convincingly argued that he never strayed far from that mentality once he left Marcy Projects for Park Avenue—from selling drugs to selling records. Adapting his business acumen from the street to the boardroom once Jay-Z had made the transition from illegal to legitimate entrepreneurs was, therein, almost natural. As a result, the transition was almost seamless, largely because nothing had really changed but the product they were pushing. The personalities were still the same, the cliques, the jealousy i.e. "player-hating", the inherent potential for ego clashes that could jump off at any moment, no matter the stakes, the potential lives or fortunes lost. Most importantly, was the reality that this sort of uncertainty as a constant was required to keep the senses sharp, the competition fierce, and the record buyers interested.

Late hip-hop icon Biggie Smalls, a.k.a. the Notorious B.I.G. explained the latter from the dual point of view of a street hustler, explaining how the two were synonymous by way of pointing out in rhyme that "if I wasn't in the rap game, I'd probably have a key, knee deep in the crack game, cause the streets is a short stop, you're either slangin' crack rock or you got a wicked jump shot."

Only the rap game offered the parallels of instant material gratification and heightened rush of adrenaline that the crack game could, the rap star and neighborhood drug lord were analogous to one another on a street level—both celebrated and rivaled, feared and loved—and often interchangeable as many of today's most popular and successful hip-hop stars began as street hustlers with nothing in mind but the real. No shorts. No room for second place, on the street or the chart.

The phenomenon of the hip-hop renaissance man (i.e. rap star, C.E.O. of his own label, clothing line, restaurant chain, etc.) then seems almost natural, or at the very least accepted as such, even if it wasn't commonplace as recently as a decade ago. Statistically there are more independent labels operating inside of hip-hop than in any other genre in the record industry today. Its second nature for a hip-hop star to desire to be his own boss, to see the most money possible, to cut out the middle man, go directly to the source.

Just as the crack hustler ambitiously desires to take over as many spots as possible, the hip-hop entrepreneur is no different in nature, nor very often in tactic or technique. Hence the tolerance, and almost expectation, of criminal activity within the world of hip-hop, even on the corporate level.

Suge Knight rationalized it best when he explained back in Death Row Records' heyday that "as long as you have money coming in, (the major labels) will deal with you." No one can deny the dollars that hip-hop brings in, and as any big business is ruthless by nature, the dog-eat-dog world of rap in a corporate context is no different. An overriding theme of shared confidence seems to exist among moguls that they would have made it to the top in the end regardless of the means, be it as crack dealer or rap star/C.E.O.

Roc-A-Fella Records co-owner Jay-Z echoed the afore-mentioned conviction in a rap off his 2001, multi-platinum selling BluePrint album, explaining that you could place him "anywhere on God's green earth, I'll triple my worth, I sell Ice in the winter, I sell fire in hell, I am a hustler baby, I'll sell water to a well…I smartened up, opened the market up." While the methodologies may differ- i.e. no one is encouraging a corporate raider to hold the C.E.O. of a company he desires to buy out the window of his office till he agrees to sell, or perhaps come down in price- there is still much to understand in terms of the underlying principles, formulas, practices, and applications specific to the business of creating and running a rap label from the ground up.

Hip-Hip as an industry has grown from an independent business into a billion-dollar conglomerate, owned and operated not by Harvard M.B.A.'s but by former crack dealers who applied and innovated the same business models their Ivy-league counterparts did to achieve the corporate status and respect they have in the new millennium. In the beginning, young, hungry African American males were the principal students of Hip Hop Business Fundamentals 101.

In the present day, we all study the phenomenon of hip-hop's continued vitality as a business, especially given the current recession within the record industry at large. While overall industry sales were down over 11% in 2002, with record buyers picking up 597.4 million albums in 2003, compared with 669.7 million in

2001, according to USA Today. 2004 and 2005 respectively showed no signs of slowing, and with the rap game constantly reinventing itself in real time, no one can keep up anymore with hip-hop's innovations as an empire. Nor with its moguls, unless they themselves are players in the game.

As hip-hop's earnings continue to grow exponentially above the billion dollar mark, no one can really predict its future, beyond the reality that, as Master P's corporate namesake so aptly implies, there truly is no limit to where rap as a corporate entity can go, so long as there is money to be made.

Hip-hop's expedited growth as an industry is consistent with the very nature of the hustler's lifestyle—fast money, fast living—for today, for the moment, still in an unusually premeditated, predatory manner that suggests years of planning were invested in a takeover that cornered the market in what appeared to be almost an overnight manner. Perhaps the nature of hip-hop's bankability is synonymous to a Las Vegas Casino, by design the house always wins, but promotes an atmosphere where anything can happen, fortunes can be gained and lost in the roll of a dice—much in the same way a hustler takes a gamble with his life every time he steps out on the corner to make a transaction—but it is almost guaranteed that someone is making money, regardless of the individual expendability of a player in the game, the franchise will survive.

In this context, it then becomes the goal of the drug runner to rise to the status of (dealer) and ultimately through the ranks to lord, and as quickly as possible. Equally, a rap star, being a hustler by his very nature, desires to rise from label artist to label C.E.O. as quickly as possible, both because of basic mathematics and survival. Where the average rock star worries about staying high, the average rap star focuses on becoming the dealer of the product, rather than the user.

Rarely do we watch behind-the-music episodes about rap stars recovering from heroine or cocaine addictions, but we're as likely to hear about their surviving a jail stint or attempt on their life in the course of rising to the status where a hip-hop star would even be the subject of such a career-spanning documentary. The lesson we're meant to take is they had no choice but to take the chances took on the streets in the game to get to the top—as the competitive nature of both businesses are parallel to one another in terms of their cut-throat temperament.

Big rewards traditionally involve even bigger risks to begin with, and in the high-stakes game of gangsta rap, an ambitious entrepreneur isn't just risking the loss of his shirt, but his very life. Where this might give other enterprisers pause, it only emboldens hip-hop hustlers in their all-or-nothing pursuit of the brass ring. There are many motivations—among them payback for the generations of racism which stunted every chance for growth blacks ever had hope for, short-changed their every success, and sought to cut off their chances at mainstream success before they ever really got off and running.

The success of hip-hop stands in defiance of that entire history, and is in its very essence a celebration of African American culture and history, both the positive and negative sides of its story. Jay-Z, the co-founder and owner of Roc-A-Fella Records, in addition to being one of the world's biggest rap superstars, and with a net-worth of just over $350 million, laid the basic blue-print for hip-hop's takeover, the methodology and reasoning behind it, and justification for it in one of his most popular hits, "H-to-the-Izzo", explaining that "I do this for my culture, to let 'em know what a nigga look like...when a nigga in a roaster, Show 'em how to move in a room full 'o vultures, Industry shady it need to be taken over, Label owners hate me I'm raisin' the status quo up, I'm overchargin' niggaz for what they did to the Cold Crush, Pay us like you owe us for all the years that you hoe'd us, We can talk, but money talks so talk mo' bucks."

It's because of the full-circle come-about of hip-hop as a billion-dollar industry that Jay-Z was even able to contemplate such power plays, set such terms, and actually exact them. Otherwise, he would be rapping about his plans to do so, rather than actually carrying them out. Jay-Z is a fundamental example of the hip-hop renaissance man, and a pioneer of the model—street hustler to rap star to rap mogul in his own right, as he has co-ownership stakes in his label and master recordings, his clothing line, his restaurant, and film company.

Every pioneering independent entrepreneur in the last decade of hip-hop has title on a singular innovation that helped the entire genre to grow—Russell Simmons introduced the concept of the black-run record label and the joint-venture with a parent company; Suge Knight's was ownership of your own Master Recordings in the course of a distribution deal, Sean 'P. Diddy' Combs' was the hip-hop clothing industry, Master P's was independently-financed and distributed rap movies starring his label's artists, but Jay-Z and Damon Dash's, in the course of Roc-A-Fella, was pooling them all.

No greater collective success has been achieved on any of the aforementioned fronts that in the case of Roc-A-Fella Records. In 2004, Fortune Magazine came out with their Richest Americans under 40, and not surprisingly, Shawn 'Jay-Z' Carter came in at # 16 with $286 million as Co-founder/owner of Roc-A-Fella Enterprises. Each of the company's divisions is competitive if not the elite of its peers, Roc-A-Wear grosses on par or in excess of Sean Jean annually, Roc-A-Fella Records in the millennium has annually out-grossed Death Row Records, Bad Boy Entertainment, No Limit Records, and even its partner label, Def Jam, in the context of Def Jam's directly signed acts vs. Roc-A-Fella's.

Damon Dash's passion, Roc-A-Fella Films has a steady release schedule and profit margin based on the cost of production and distribution, and virtually all of Roc-A-Fella Films' releases have a respectable per-screen average, as well as DVD sales. The company has also diversified its investments beyond the immediate scope of the aforementioned, hip-hop's by-now traditional marketing/ retail ground to include US-ownership and distribution rights to the Scottish-based Armadale vodka brand, among other ventures.

Dash and Jay-Z co-founded Roc-A-Fella Records in 1996, wherein Dash would map out a more ambitious game plan for the then-fledgling Roc-A-Fella Records than any of its predecessors ever could have envisioned at the time. Utilizing Knight's blue-print for a street label, but expanding on that concept, Dash had in mind the aim of "making a big conglomerate out of Roc-A-Fella...We're coming out with a magazine, we're doing a movie, and we're also (planning) a clothing line...The bottom line is that the major labels are putting out music that is made from the street...And we're the closest to the street, so we know how to do it better."

The C.E.O.'s comments six years later on the future of Roc-A-Fella, in 2002, after his label had achieved the status of hip-hop's premier independent empire—exactly as Dash had mapped out in the label's infancy—marked true growth in the very definition of the hip-hop mogul. Namely in that the greater the success Dash had, the more he desired, in true hustler form, explaining that "Unless you got more money than me, I don't see how anybody could be relaxing. And even if they have more money they shouldn't be relaxing with it. If you don't have what I have, and I am still putting in the work, I don't see how someone else still is (relaxing). Now, my thing is, I am going to get all of the money if you let me; y'all might as well get some of it. And even at this point and time, my attitude is that I am still starving. So if I feel like I am starving and you are not feeling that same way, then something is very, very wrong."

Dash further qualified the latter by citing his own addiction to stacking paper as a key motivator in what drive's hip-hop's corporate machinery to continue to perform above and beyond par, "I'm a cakeaholic. I thirst for money, I love to make money, I love to spend money, I love to stack money. If there's money out there it may be a problem because I want it. Everybody better get on top of their game 'cause if you leave anything I'm going to get it."

By 2003, the label's success had made Dash so confident that he spoke openly of his desire to leave Def Jam and go completely independent, with both the production, and marketing/ distribution of his label's releases, which is unheard of even today given the costs of distributing records at the level of an artist like Jay-Z. Only major labels like Warner Brothers or Universal Music Group have enough capital to support their own distribution networks, both in terms of the physical pressing and placement of label releases.

Still, given Roc-A-Fella's seemingly limitless success, as well as because of what was at the time an ongoing beef between Dash and his major label partner, Island/Def Jam Record Group, he lashed out at the notion that his label no longer owed an allegiance to the parent label, despite the fact that they had provided Roc-A-Fella its start-up capital. Given the fact that Dash felt his label had outgrown the benefits of its partnership with Def Jam, specifically in terms of shared earnings, the next logical step inevitably was to cut out the middle man all together in favor of greater potential financial return.

In spite of the risks associated with the untested ground such a move would be attempted upon, it made sense according to the street hustler edict that Dash had followed throughout his career. Further, the fact that Dash displayed a complete lack of loyalty to the label that had helped him get to mogul-status seemed almost natural in the face of the age-old bottom line of making money, "There is no more Def Jam, Def Jam got sold. Def Jam is nothing but a logo, right now Lyor Cohen is the Chairman of Island/Def Jam.

He gets a salary. He runs Island/Def Jam, which has the ROC department. We're under that umbrella, but we're not down with

Def Jam...It's Roc-A-Fella/Island Def Jam. We are a 50/50 joint venture. That's a separate entity, it's not Def Jam, it's not Damon Dash, it's Roc-A-Fella/Island/Def Jam.... Like right now, I haven't gotten the opportunity to address the distribution issue in the music industry because it would take a lot of energy and effort. I will probably get back to that when I can. It is important that I do. I am happy that I got to make money my way, but when you get into distribution, it gets a little gangster, you know what I'm saying?... You've got to be really serious about going for distribution and getting it done."

If anyone was up for the job, it certainly appeared to be Dash. Dash founded Roc-A-Fella Films, which partnered with movie studios like Dimension films and Miramax, for the theatrically-released features "Paid In Full", "Backstage", "State Property", and "Death of a Dynasty", which, among other Roc-A-Fella features, have brought the film division net earnings of $50 to $100 million, according to Dash.

Roc-A-Fella Records took their business expansion to new heights, turning the establishment's head in a new direction in 2003 with the decision on both Damon Dash and Jay-Z's part to purchase US-distribution rights to Armadale, an 80-proof super premium vodka, which they distribute in partnership with Scotland-based William Grant & Sons, in a move Dash simply rationalized as a natural extension of the influence the label and its artists already had over hip-hop culture, "We know what kind of influence we have over our demographic, and we like to capitalize on every opportunity...Unless someone is paying me a billion dollars or offering equity (in a product endorsement deal), we don't play that."

Roc-A-Fella has become a household name over the last decade because Damon Dash and Co. have worked to introduce the company's brand into so many different, diversified areas of American pop culture, from music to film to clothing to liquor and popular media, and it is a truly singular achievement for hip-hop as a brand. Any true study of Roc-A-Fella Enterprises success must extend beyond a study of Jay-Z, and include Damon Dash, who as a C.E.O., is a true renaissance man.

Jay-Z may have taken a business dispute as far as stabbing a bootlegger for pirating his albums, but metaphorically, Dash would likely have cut his throat. Unreservedly ruthless, Dash took Roc-A-Fella Enterprises as a company to the next level, then the one thereafter, and so on until he was so many stories above the competition, that Dash, Jay-Z and their silent partner, "Mr. Biggs", were looking out over an empire that extended into virtually every market available in hip-hop and into beyond.

This was Dash's vision, to race so far past the competition that Roc-A-Fella's only competitor was its own last platinum record. Dash and Co were that hungry, and eventually ended up achieving a level of success that led Jay-Z to feel, with a net worth of just under $300 million, that he had attained all the landmarks he could, both as an independent entrepreneur, in hip-hop, such that he decided to retire as an artist from rap.

For an entrepreneur so busy making moves that he didn't even have the time to stop and WRITE DOWN HIS RAPS, preferring instead to drop them from memory on the spot when recording—Jay-Z had to have attained a wealth of material (both in terms of catalog and wealth) by that point so massive that he felt he couldn't do any more to eclipse it. As such, Jay-Z released his final solo album (for the moment), The Black Album, in November of 2004, which quickly sold 2 million copies, and secretly began negotiating with Def Jam Records to become President of the label.

Far from a vanity position, Jay-Z had proved his savvy in the boardroom enough to impress the suits that he could run the day-to-day operations of the label, which ironically could have put him in the potential position to be Dash's boss, rather than business partner. Not in the nature of either man or their label in terms of what it stood for to each entrepreneur personally, in January of 2005, Jay-Z, Dash and Biggs decided to sell their remaining 50% stake in Roc-A-Fella Records to Def Jam/Island for what was a widely misreported $10 million.

The true figure (including the current and calculated future worth of the label's catalog) was closer to $50 million (including a $10 million CASH Payout at the time of sale, along with substantial stock options in Def Jam/Island, and retained ownership of the Roc-A-Fella brand name outside of the label, among other incentives of the deal.) By February, 2005, Jay-Z had officially been announced the new President of Def Jam Records-another first in the history of hip-hop—and had begun the next era in his legend…

Introduction
Shawn Carter—Hip Hop's Enigma

What is a hip-hop enigma? A subterraneous society rooted in Harriet Tubman who never gave up their blueprints to the underground railroad, or maybe just a code for the ways of the streets passed between generations of hustlers, taking care of their own. This code is passed on in modern day through the slang of rap music, the soundscape of a ghetto that is societally locked down, with no law-abiding means of escape. Its inhabitants are like survivors from some post-apocalyptic world that found a way to live on, to flourish from the underground into a mainstream revolution, just as hip-hop did for inner-city African-America.

Hip-hop is that chain broken, the light being seen for the first time by these prisoners freed, and shining for the first time upon the world they were forced to survive along the way to that liberation. A brutal existence that the white suburbs would only see in a movie, urban warfare seen only on CNN in places like downtown Baghdad. Movies like *Boyz in the Hood* gave a tidy overview that touched on all the themes of the ghetto survival, or *Menace to Society*, which showed there was hardly ever a way out, even in a movie.

Those soldiers within the game, portrayed through characters like O-Dog and Doughboy, are brought to life in our mainstream not by actors, but by real survivors, real soldiers who lived to lyrically tell about it. They were allowed to survive for a reason, because they had a story to tell, a message to deliver as emcees. Some, like Tupac and Biggie, would die for their cause, while others, like Jay-Z, lived on to carry the torch into and for the next generation of urban prophets. Jay-Z is a true soldier, because he came up through the ranks, from private as a fledgling emcee, to Sergeant as a platinum rapper, to Colonel as a multi-platinum icon, to his current rank of General as a retired field soldier who now commands his own army of emcees as President of Def Jam Records. While he asked on his last record, "What more can I say?" This is his story...

Part I:
The Life and Times of Shawn Carter, A.K.A. JAY-Z—1970-1996

Chapter 1
Hip-Hop Illuminati—The Seed of Rap's First Dynasty is Planted:

The Birth and Childhood of Shawn Carter, December 4, 1968

If Tupac was hip-hop's John Lennon, and Biggie Smalls' its Frank Sinatra, Jay-Z—the trilogy in hip-hop's legendry—is rap's Michael Corleone. Tupac was hip-hop's soul, and politically its first true intellectual, giving society's systematic repression of African Americans modern day perspective, calling out attention to the plight of the inner-city with a poignancy and accuracy that hadn't existed since the height of the 1960s civil rights movement in terms of how society embraced his narrative culturally.

Biggie gave a human face to the player/hustler psyche of the hip-hop everyman going through the aforementioned endeavor, offering a survival guide to that struggle, and a soundtrack for life within the street culture of Queens, Brooklyn, Manhattan, and the Bronx, and thematically throughout America's inner cities. Still, Biggie was only ever living better, he left the earth with business unfinished in financial terms. Jay-Z took both men's revenge in the course of his own career: in the spirit of Pac, he broke down all the barriers the latter legend was still fighting—or at best, had just begun—to defy when he died; and for Biggie, he got over so large monetarily that no one could deny Jay his place at the grown-ups table. Where Tupac and Biggie had legend, Jay-Z has achieved legacy.

Most great legacies in American illuminati can be traced back to humble beginnings, from the Kennedy's to the Rockefellers. All of the aforementioned made their first generation of wealth via highly unethical or outright illicit means—it was bootlegging for the Kennedy's. For the Rockefellers, it was oil—when the company at one point controlled 90% of the country's oil at the turn of the 20th century, and routinely bribed politicians to secure the company's market share and under-bidding competitors out of the business. Respective to the latter, though no one would have dared ever refer to the Rockefellers' position in the oil industry as a cartel, the implications are obvious in that they were undeniably a monopoly.

If Roc-A-Fella Enterprises, in 2005, is truly hip-hop's first dynasty, then the parallels are endless between the criminal means utilized to the great financial ends any of America's cornerstone white dynasty to attain their generational power and position, and those which Jay-Z and company undertook to buy their way out of the irrefutably systematic, economic despotism which imprisons America's inner cities. Jay-Z selling crack to finance his way out of the ghetto is no different from Joe Kennedy bootlegging to buy his way into American politics, or John Rockefeller bribing politicians to corner the oil market—period. Only institutional, class-based racism could cite a difference, and attempt to defend it.

Because John D. Rockefeller was America's first recorded billionaire, it was clear what Jay-Z and Damon Dash had in mind thematically when they first decided to found their company, as it could be argued they shaped their company's ambitions after Rockefeller's successes—to become hip-hop's first dynasty, and in 8 short years they would achieve just that. Setting hip-hop entrepreneurialism on a new axis at the dawn of the millennium, what Jay-Z and Damon Dash achieved with Roc-A-Fella was perhaps the first all-African American old boys network. They may have dealt with white corporate America as they had to, but in the Hip-Hop <u>Skull and Bones</u> club, the principal difference may have been the fact that there were real dead bodies within a mini-generation of the that dynasty's founding, not personally on the part of Jay-Z or Damon Dash, but within the general context of both men's' environments and surroundings coming up in the game.

That Roc-A-Fella would earn Jay-Z a net worth of just under $300 million in 10 years is never something even his own mother, Gloria Carter, would have envisioned his great grand-children achieving...based on her own generation's standing societally and economically in December of 1969, the month when her fourth child, Shawn Corey Carter, was born. Recalling that "Shawn was born on December 4th, weighing in at 10 pounds, 8 ounces. He was the last of my 4 children, and the only one who didn't give me any pain when I gave birth to him. That's why I knew he was a special child."

Jay's story began like any other for an African American male growing up in the 1970s and 1980s in the crime-ridden, war zone of the Marcy Projects, located in the (Ft. Greene) section of the borough of Brooklyn, New York.

As Jay-Z remembered his upbringing in the Marcy projects, he recalls "a poor neighborhood, but (one where) you learned loyalty and integrity. You learned to respect other people, because it was a minefield. If you disrespect somebody, or act dishonorable, you get hurt. Somebody puts you in your place. So I learned integrity. It's a beautiful place to grow up, as far as having honor...It wasn't safe. Everyone there was poor and trying to get ahead. There was not much hope. You put all those ingredients together, you have people who are willing to do anything at any time."

"What am I going to do, lose my life? What is my life worth, anyway? That can't be a safe environment. In each of the buildings, there's six floors, four families on each floor, three buildings connected together. Everyone's on top of everybody else. That's a powder keg. Then crack hit around 1985. You had so many people strung out. I mean, everybody. It was an epidemic." In some ways, Jay-Z learned his self worth as he earned his net worth.

Though he grew up in a home filled with the love of many women—namely his mother and sisters—the lack of male presence in his life sent him to the streets in search of a father figure. While he would later find that role model to some degree in the hustlers holding down Marcy Projects' thriving drug trade, from his pre-teen years, the loss of his father played heavily into the rapper's hardened emotional exterior growing into adulthood in the inner city. Elaborating on the latter, Jay explained that "there's no worse pain (than growing up without a father.) That's why a lot of things didn't affect me growing up…I had long-term relationships with three beautiful women who loved me to death, but I had always been holding back. I had never been in love, because my heart was still broken from my father (leaving.)"

Jay's mother, Gloria, recalled that "Shawn was a very shy child growing up, he was into sports. At four, he taught himself how to ride a bike, a 2-wheel at that. But I noticed a change in him when me and my husband broke up." Jay, elaborating on his mother's memory, recalled for his part that "one day when I was four years old…I rode this ten-speed. It was really high, but I put my foot through the top bar, so I'm ridin' the bike kinda weird, like sideways, and the whole block is like, 'Oh, God!' They couldn't believe this little boy ridin' that big bike like that. That was my first feelin' of bein' famous right there. And I liked it. Felt good."

As a child, music was always a part of Jay's home life, recalling that "These people shared everything…but not (our) records. It was like, 'This is my son and your son. This is my house and your house. But this is my record.' That's just to show you how much they loved their music…After a while, I just started tryin' to write rhymes. I used to be at the table every day for hours. I had this green notebook with no lines in it, and I used to write all crooked. I wrote every damn day. Then I started running around in the streets, and that's how not writing came about. I was comin' up with these ideas, and I'd write 'em on a paper bag, and I had all these paper bags in my pocket, and I hate a lot of things in my pocket, so I started memorizing and holding it."

In school, Jay was a bright student, explaining that "I was crazy happy (when in 6th grade I tested at a 12th grade reading level)… When the test scores came back, that was the first moment I realized I was smart. I always liked to read. I still do."

While Jay's relationship with his mother kept him centered, the poverty his family endured as a result of his father's absence… both emotionally, but more importantly financially…led the rapper, from a young age, to appreciate the role money played in compensating for the former with the latter. As Jay explained years later looking back from the top back down on his family's financial troubles, he reasoned that "(Money's) pretty important; I mean, it changed my people's lives, all their living conditions—my sisters, my mom, my nephews. It enabled my mom to retire, which is one of the highlights right now in my life. She just did it, she had a retirement party two weeks ago. It was beautiful. I almost cried…"

"For 29 years she had kids, so she had to walk on eggshells. (She works in) investment banking…She works in the office. She's a supervising clerk…She can't lose her job. She didn't have two weeks to look for another one like some people do. When you're a working person, you're inside of a box, and the minute you get off-track, you have to start playing catch-up. You never gonna catch up. If you livin' paycheque to paycheque, once one of those paycheques is off, you off. It's a mad scramble…I don't even remember her not working. She worked from the time my soul came into my body, when my memory—when I was aware of my surroundings, until I had to really convince her to retire. She wouldn't retire for a while because she was so used to doing for herself, like she was so—she never, ever depended on anybody, ever. So it was really hard just to get her to retire...I've seen her tireless effort."

"She was unbelievable, she still is unbelievable...She's crazy (proud of me.)...That was the best thing (I've done with my success)... the fact that I was able to have her retire, and she was working for so long and the pay was nothing. And when she finally accepted, you know, the fact that she could retire, it was just the best thing I could do for her."

Jay's relationship with his siblings—brother Eric, and sisters Annie and Mickey was always close, particularly with his sister Andrea, who he calls "Annie. That's how the Annie sample came about. When I seen that on TV, I was like, 'Annie?' And then. I watched the movie...(I have) two sisters, one brother. I'm the youngest (child)...My brother lives in upstate New York. He always cut hair, so he's tying to get a barbershop. My sisters, they got different jobs."

Jay may have been the baby of the family, but he grew up fast on the streets surrounding Marcy Projects once his father had abandoned the family. Leaving mother Gloria as the sole bread winner, Jay learned fast how to make green on his own out on the Brooklyn corners of his Ft. Greene neighborhood. His natural desensitization to violence—not only in witnessing it, but also inflicting it when required—came as naturally to Jay as hustling did, such that, at one point, "I uh, shot my brother (Eric) in the shoulder (with) a little gun, like a Dillinger...It was a very stupid thing. He was messed up at that time. He'd took a ring of mine. It was very, very foolish, you know, like a two ringer, but way back then...and it was like a certain thing leading up to these events. I acted outta anger."

"Since that incident, I've never lost it like that…That story's even worse. I was 12…The person who gave me the gun had to be 20 or 21—you're an adult. Damn, why would you do that? How could you even…I don't understand. But I can't blame nobody but myself…(It was) terrible…That's the one thing to this day I regret." While Jay may have experienced discord with his brother, his relationship with his mother was "beautiful. Like brother and sister…If I get an idea, a flashback, I'll call her. Three in the morning': 'You remember when I was four years old, and I learned how to ride a bike, and…' She'll get right into the conversation…I'm like my mom's husband…I'm a very good friend to her…I'm really the dude in the family…And I wanna be that."

"I take care of everybody, and they love me and respect me for that. But they don't kiss my ass or treat me any different because of it. That's the beauty of it." Jay's bond with his mother allowed him to better see, at least through a temporary lens, why his father had abandoned the family, explaining that "if your parents divorced or broke up when you were a kid, it's hard to imagine them as two young people who once fell in love, who had dreams for their family and good times and fights, and were basically human."

In discussing his relationship with his father Atnis Reeves—where there was one—Jay, reflectively, has explained that while he could never forgive his father for walking out on him, he eventually found the strength to be the bigger man and forgive him, explaining that "(My dad left when I was) 12, 11, 12, right…He works odd jobs…My pops did anything from cabdriver to truck driver to working at the phone company…After I was 12, I never knew where he was working. I never kept up with him…(So) like the year before he died, I guess I would say maybe six months before he died (we finally met)."

"And I'm one of those people, a person, I believe that everything happens for a reason. So, because I'm like why then, out of all these years, why would we meet up the year that he died? You know, it was just so we can get out, you know, me, I can release all that anger and all that hostility that I had pent up, and tell him how I felt and how I felt about, you know, him not being around. Even if him and my mom had split up, you know, I'm his son. You're supposed to be there for me…You know, I got to tell him all these things…"

"I hadn't seen my father in almost 20 years when my mom started talking about setting up a meeting with us. At first, I didn't see the point, and I told her that. She felt that, with all my success there was still this huge part missing from my life. She didn't think we should reunite as much as reconcile. I didn't think I was walking around being angry at the guy, but my mother saw some of the comments I'd made about him on records as me still holding on to the pain from my childhood…In hindsight, I was hard on (my dad) in a lot of songs. At that time, everyone was leaving. They was leaving before the kid was born. He wasn't totally a scumbag—not totally."

"After those songs, I told my mom I wanted to talk to him. I can't keep living in the past. My mom got in touch with him. The first time he was supposed to come to my house, he didn't come. I figured it was embarrassing for him, going to his son's house. I got mad again. Like, 'All right, forget it, then! I ain't reaching out no more!'…She was really working both ends, because my father hadn't gone to her to set up a meeting; he was too proud. He didn't want me to think that he was trying to get at me because I was a millionaire or famous rapper. I get that from him. I'm not like that so much now, but I definitely can be proud and stubborn."

"So my mother set up this meeting where he would come to my home. We sent a car to pick him up and everything, but I knew in my heart he wasn't going to show, and he didn't…He couldn't break my heart twice. That first time he left, that was my biggest and only heartbreak in life. I've never let anyone hurt me, definitely not twice…I look just like the guy…You wanna walk like him, talk like him. That's your superman right there. And then there's no more contact with him. The scorn, the resentment, all the feelings from that —as you see, I'm a grown-ass man and it's still there with me."

Despite Jay's understandable protests to being walked out on a second time, he explained that "my mother was real serious; she knew how alcoholism had eaten away most of his organs and how little time he was actually working with. So she pushed again… The second time we set it up, he came. He was crazy uncomfortable. My house is where all my family gets together. We have Saturday meals, and my chef or my mom and sisters cook for my nieces and nephews, and when he came in, he felt completely left out. He was in my home, and we were still a family, and it probably killed him to see that we had survived his leaving—we were still whole."

"I didn't come out of my room. My mother kept offering him food, anything to make him comfortable. Finally, she brought out some Gummi Bears I had stashed away for the kids, and he took those. When my mother brought him to my room, she acted like she was depositing him and leaving us to talk, but she went around to the exercise room connected to my bedroom and eavesdropped on our conversation…"

"When he was there in front of me, it was like looking in a mirror. I'm tall like him, slim-we looked exactly alike. I didn't have much to say, only a question. I just wanted him to tell me how he could leave his son-one who looked exactly like him—to raise himself. Whatever drama my mother had, she never tried to keep us from him. He's the one who decided it would be the way it was…(My mom) Don Kinged that whole situation when he came to my house. I just really got the chance to air it out. Tell him everything that I felt."

"Yo, my pop is stubborn. I see where I get it from. When I was talking to him I was like…I understand why I am the way I am. I got the chance to tell him how I was affected by him leaving and things like that. Then I was cool with it. That's what that verse (on 'Moment of Clarity') was about. I'm like, 'Yo, it wasn't your fault.' All the things that I was blaming him for through my career and through the albums, as I grew I realized it wasn't all his fault...I was just really glad we got the chance to talk...I knew it was coming."

"It's almost like somebody is ready to punch you in the face and you know it and it's coming really slow. It's almost frustrating. I wish you'd punch me in the face already. I don't want you to think that I was happy that he passed away, but it was almost a relief... He tried to hit me with excuses. He said my sister Annie knew where he was, that my brother, Eric, had been to visit him. He was still being proud. I told him that I was a child. I wasn't supposed to look you up, you were supposed to be looking me up."

"He finally broke down and admitted he was wrong. He said he was sorry. Really sorry...I told him everything that was on my mind. And we shook hands, like men...I'm sure that was something he'd wanted to say to me for years. I know that I'd wanted to ask that question my whole life. It's rhetorical. There is no answer. But having the opportunity to look him in his face and ask that question was a gift from my mother to me...I don't think anyone can be a dad to me at this point. I learned how to go inside my own mind, to figure it out, to learn as I go along...And he listened, and he understood what I was saying and where I was coming from."

"And then I was in the process of getting him an apartment, and you know, making sure that he was comfortable, because he was really sick in his liver, his liver was really bad. So I was making sure he was comfortable. And while I was in the process of doing that, he went back in the hospital and he came out for a minute, and then he just passed away...He passed a month or two after we talked...I looked at it more as being a powerful day than being a sad day for me. I was like, 'Why did we meet then, this year?' There must have been something to learn from that. I was able to tell (my father) how I felt and put those negative feelings to rest. I was in the process of getting him a place, buying furniture when he passed. His liver was messed up, and they told him not to drink, but he continued to drink until he expired…I felt unblocked after that conversation… The only way that I can be open completely even now is because of (the) timing (of it all). Because I buried my father with (that) understanding between us."

While Jay-Z naturally harbored regret at missing out on emotional comfort, he sailed free of sorrow over the financial hardship that extended naturally from his father's absence. As the rapper rationalized it, growing up starving kept him hungry well past when he'd even started seeing plentiful bread, as the memory alone of growing up without made him desire a financial stockpile that would last generations even beyond his own, reasoning that "I wouldn't want to grow up no other way. It shaped me, taught me integrity. There's a lot of people in the music business that didn't come from the streets. That's why it's tough for people like us to get along with music executives. We coming from a place where there's integrity, there's honor. There are unwritten rules that people all know…You've got kids that inherited stuff from their parents They don't appreciate it because it was no work; there's no A to Z, it's just Z. To me, you need somewhere to start, somewhere to be like, 'Man, I ain't never going back to not being able to pay my light bill, my stomach growling, eating cereal at night, peanut butter and jelly off the spoon, mayonnaise sandwiches.' This is real. I'm talking from a place where if groceries came and we got to put bananas on the cereal, it was a treat. That was the shit that you can't fathom."

Jay-Z's outlook on the latter also works to shed more light on his desire to start out his career in hip-hop on an independent label, rather than corporate, because there was such a vast difference in mentality between boardroom and street-based hip-hop executives. Years before he'd made the transition from hustler to rap star, Jay knew he had both the innate audacity and talent, recalling that "I was 4 years old, but I remember that morning clearly. As my mom left for work, she told me to wait 'till she got home to practice riding my bike. My uncle had promised to put training wheels on the secondhand bike I'd received from my cousin, but he hadn't gotten around to it. Me, being the youngest of four kids, I was determined to be independent and not spoiled. (Although my family will tell you I am the latter.) I took the bike outside, and from 10 a.m. to 5 p.m. taught myself how to ride without training wheels. Because I was so small, my whole block in Brooklyn was watching in amazement. It was my first feelings of being famous."

"Getting that same buzz as a rapper wasn't all that different, really...There was one green notebook from when I was young (I used to keep my rhymes in). I don't know where it's at (now). It's a shame. Years ago, we were at my grandma's house on Thanksgiving and I had my first demo tape. I was so proud of it. At that time, LL Cool J was really hot. I told my uncle, 'I think I'm better than LL.' He said, 'Get out of here. Never.' To come all the way from that to be considered one of the greatest writers is a huge compliment." Jay's mother, Gloria recalled her son's hip-hop formative years as ones where "Shawn used to be in the kitchen, beating on the table, and rapping at the wee hours of the morning. Then I bought him a boom box, and his sisters and brother said he would drive them nuts. But that was my way to keep him close to me and out of trouble."

Sadly for Gloria, soon enough Jay was out on the streets, a road warrior among a crew that packed more heat than Mad Max, and ran their bombed-out ghetto project like a business. While Jay-Z was a team player in his hustling years, focusing on the bottom line of profits, he also had the love of a crew that made up—to some measure—for the lack of father figure in his life. Explaining the importance of any team taking care of its players—whether sports, hip-hop, or hustlers—Jay explained his philosophy—even years and millions of dollars removed from the poverty that forced him into drug dealing to begin with, that "(even today, the projects haven't changed.) There's no lawyers, no doctors, no psychiatrists.

Everyone that makes money moves out. They just go. I want to tell kids, 'Yo, I'm Jay-Z.' Not even Jay-Z. 'I'm Shawn Carter, from 5C. I lived in that building right there, the one you live in now. And it can happen for you. I don't know what it is that you want to do, but something will happen for you.'...I could name the ones who did (have fathers). There were about three in the whole project...(Growing up without fathers, a boy) learns how to be a man in the streets. Everyone needs that role model, that blueprint, to guide you through...(For me, that was hustling) because rap was the real gamble; hustling was the sure thing...Depending on your environment, it could be a bad thing." For Jay-Z, at first, it was, because rather than just rapping in third person about hustlers in the hood putting in work, he was busy doing just that.

"(I was) a resourceful person who puts himself on the line to improve his condition…I experienced celebrity even before rap…People knew me on the street. They knew what I was doing. It was legend."

—Jay-Z

Chapter 2
The Hustlin' Years

When America talks about drugs, its always in black and white—blacks are the ones who sell it, and whites are the ones who become addicted—even when they do so as a majority in rural parts of America where the african american population is almost non-existent. Still, somehow african americans are to blame, or Latin Americans because the majority of cocaine originates from South America.

Rarely—if ever—does the media focus on the minorities addicted to crack throughout the inner cities of America, for the same reason pot holes downtown never get repaired, while in the suburbs, the roads run smooth. For the same reason that inner cities have check cashing spots and suburbs have banks. For the same reason the only growth enterprise in the ghetto is the drug trade, both because the police do very little but go through the motions in trying to prevent it, as the inner-city crack plague does little to affect the suburban communities they go home to at night; and because the problem is not 'out of control' as long as its contained to the inner city, where the war on drugs—as suburban CNN and Fox News viewers see it—is not a war on drugs, but a WAR ON BLACKS who just won't "stay in line."

Its the same mentality that drove Governor Orville Faubus to dispatch the Arkansas National Guard to prevent nine black students from entering Little Rock Central High School following the Supreme Court's Brown vs. the Board of Education decision which desegregated public schools. The same mentality which inspired Governor George Wallace to block the doors to the University of Alabama in 1963, proclaiming "segregation now, segregation tomorrow, segregation forever!" The same mentality that drove Ronald Regan to paint the racist portrait of the black, crack-addicted welfare mother as the face of the welfare state in the 1980s while White America prospered under trickle-down economics.

The same mentality that made Trent Lott think it was okay in 2002 to suggest on national television that the country would have been better off if Strom Thurmond, a former Ku Klux Klans-man and Dixiecrat Party candidate—had won the Presidency in 1948, remarking that "I want to say this about my state: When Strom Thurmond ran for president, we voted for him. We're proud of it. And if the rest of the country had followed our lead, we wouldn't have had all these problems over all these years, either." Lott, so aloof to his own prejudice, even went as far as defending his blatantly racist voting record in an interview with BET's anchor Ed Gordon thereafter, defending his decision to vote against the Civil Rights Act in 1990, and against the Martin Luther King holiday in 1983, commenting that "I'm not sure we in America, certainly not white America and the people in the South, fully understood who this man was, the impact he was having on the fabric of this country." (In 1983, come on Trent!) The bottom line is Racism and America's drug epidemic go hand in hand because this country doesn't want to make the connection, its that simple.

If we acknowledged the link between inner-city poverty, the fact that its fueled by a lack of jobs, and therein, that those who use drugs do so to cope with their living conditions (YES, THEY ARE THAT BAD), and that those who sell crack do so because it's often their only viable means by which to pay the same bills suburban Americans have to pay. BABY PAMPERS cost the same in the inner city as they do in the suburbs. So does liquor, and toothpaste, and toilet paper, and clothing, electric and phone bills, car payments and insurance, and so on and so forth. Why do you think they never show this side of domestic life in most African-American themed movies about life in the inner city?

Ice Cube has done so in films like *Friday* and *Barbershop*, and John Singleton touched on it in *Baby Boy*, but by and large, movies about life in the inner city perform best when the main black characters are villains—drug dealers, pimps, gang bangers. Rarely do we see a movie about a black Plumber working to support his family, but we've seen a million movies about the white American farmer struggling to do just that. Rarely in the aforementioned movies do filmmakers—even black ones—make the connection between the fact that many African American males who do sell drugs are doing so for one of two primary reasons—to feed children, or pay for studio time. These are statistically supported truths, but we rarely hear about them. If we did, it would put a different spin on drug dealers, most times small timers—but of course never how they are portrayed in Hollywood films.

Think about it—in the post-Clinton welfare reform era, it is a suburban American myth that African American women can have child after child and be endlessly subsidized by the government every time. Most have a 5 year cap on benefits, and after 2 children, benefits become severely limited. As such, how are these young parents supposed to support their children? Well, there's the $5.95 an hour minimum-wage job at McDonalds, which we all can agree doesn't even pay the rent, or selling crack for the baby's father. Its that simple. In doing so, isn't that young, black male being responsible because much of his drug proceeds go to support his child? NOOOOO. That would defy another popular suburban American myth that young, black males are largely absentee fathers.

White America loves to watch Maury Povich's wildly-popular paternity tests. When its proven that the male on the show is the baby's father, they never address in a follow-up how he's paying for that child. Especially if he has more than one, which unfortunately the show guests usually do. Does the end then justify the means, if crack profits go to pay child support? What about if a small-time corner dealer—who despite popular rap album/Hollywood movie myth, does NOT drive a Mercedes Benz, nor could he afford to be making what he does selling what he does—uses that money instead to pay for studio time in the course of recording a demo of his own music.

Contrary to popular belief, basketball is not a wide-spread way out of the ghetto, neither is rap. But young, black males sure put their heart into trying either. Now why would they do that if they preferred selling crack? Simply, they wouldn't. The average suburban family grows up hearing the sound of lawn mowers in the air. The average inner-city family grows up hearing gun shots and police sirens instead. What about the 'WHY DON'T THEY JUST GET A JOB' mentality so popular and pervasive in white suburban America? That's exactly what crack dealing is to a young, black male in the inner-city. And often, the only industry hiring. Certainly, among the only growth industries.

The fact is, most African American males who sell crack are doing so as a means toward other ends—to GET OUT of the ghetto. Ironically, from a corporate template, they are ideal hiree's—self-starters, motivated, profit-driven, fiercely competitive, willing to do whatever is necessary to get ahead. But because they're wearing sweatsuits instead of button-down suits, crack dealers are a million times worse the criminal than a crooked stock trader or Enron executive. The hypocrisy is more frightening than the media portrait of the young, black male could ever be—and that currently is white America's nightmare.

In the course of his rise in hip-hop, Jay-Z as en emcee, and former crack dealer became an overnight corporate executive. His transition had been transparent and almost seamless, among the only differences being the product peddled. In his new position, Jay would seek to point out the latter in clear and irrefutable terms. Its not as though Nike or Timberland—industries whose profits thrive as much from inner-city sales as they do from suburban shopping malls—would ever hire a former crack dealer even though he might be just as talented a salesman and numbers man as a Harvard graduate. The record industry, up until the hip-hop entrepreneurial renaissance in the later 1990s, was the only industry ballsy enough to give hustlers the latter opportunity.

And the risk paid off, almost every time, in spades. As a dollars-driven industry—more cut throat than Wall Street could ever dream to be—labels like Interscope in the early 1990s gave Death Row the chance to prove itself as a template for hip-hop what Motown had been for Pop Music. P. Diddy, via Bad Boy, would take the baton and run into even newer territory with Sean Jean Clothing, and by the time Roc-A-Fella came to prominence in the late 1990s, the takeover was on. Damon Dash and Jay-Z not only sought to own their masters, design and own the clothes on their back, but also to manufacture the liquor they drank, the shoes they wore, and the cell phones they spoke on.

By the time Jay-Z's net worth was listed at $286 million in 2004 by *Forbes Magazine*, the game was over. African Americans had finally won a piece of the pie, albeit a small and thankfully growing one. Where Jay-Z may have been African-America's John D.

Rockefeller, the next generation of legitimate entrepreneurs on his level would be on the level of Bill Gates—and only because he has become among the forefathers of modern black wealth. The bottom line, as far as Roc-A-Fella Records would be concerned, was that Jay-Z and company had BEATEN THE SYSTEM!

As the rapper reasoned, "we root for villains—the Scarfaces of the world—(because they are) placed in a situation of underdog, and they have some type of success, (albeit) it short-lived. We never pay attention to the ending, just the good parts. Anybody that comes from that situation and rises above that, we're with them. Think about that. From Marcy Projects to owning your own company? Any person that goes from ashy to classy or, you know, is from orphanage or the projects-it's pretty similar. Instead of treated we get tricked, instead of kisses are get kicked—that's how every ghetto person feels. Like nothing good is gonna ever happen to you." The concept of black-owned anything scares the SHIT out of white America, and its only because of the ever-present institutional racism in America that it does. What is there to honestly be threatened by?

Back on the block as a teenage hustler years earlier in the early 1980s, Jay-Z had plenty to feel endangered by—the threat of jail time, or of losing his life completely. Corroborating the aforementioned narrative, and explaining why he first got involved in the thriving Marcy Projects crack trade, Jay reasoned that "(back when I started selling, it was at the height of the crack epidemic, and a) pretty rough time for everyone, like in—especially—I mean, the neighborhood, it was a—it was a plague in that neighborhood. It was just everywhere, in the hallways. You could smell it in the hallways...Back then it was like—it was—I would say it was like two things. Like, it was either you was doing it or you was moving it..."

"I had a girl out in Long Island, and you know in Long Island they've got houses and trees; she had a nice little situation. I used to go over there and eat cereal, cookies and milk, have little snacks, and go back home. I didn't have no money, so one time I took some food with me. She put it in a bag, which was a little embarrassing. When I got back, my friend was like, 'Yo, you got any more of those cookies?' I was like, 'Nah.'…Cookies! I'm talking about cookies, and this is my man. We did things together. But I was like, 'Nah, I ain't got any more cookies.'"

"So he went next door, and I poured the milk all the way up to the top, got the cookies, sat down in front of the TV. As soon as I looked up, he was standing there, just shaking his head. He was like, 'We gotta get right.'…(Because of that, I became) what you'd consider a hustler…I was never a worker, and that's not even being arrogant. I was just never a worker…I've never worked ever. I've never had a job. It's enlightening…The will to win and not going back to where I was at (motivated me.)"

The effects of the crack epidemic hit Jay as personally as it could hit anybody living in the midst of the hell that was the inner city in the 1980s, explaining that "I never used crack (but) I'd seen my brother. After my father, that was the next person I looked up to. He had all the girls, he played basketball. Then he was a whole different person (once he started using.)" Jay never sold to his brother, though he did shoot his brother once for stealing a ring to support his habit, a striking example of how harsh the environment he grew up in truly was, explaining that "My brother was a really, really, really tough person to get along with. He was messed up on drugs really bad…I shot him when I was 12 with a little Dillinger…I didn't know better. (I apologized) right away, and that made it worse (because he forgave me.)"

Naturally, Jay kept his dealing from his mother, who worked so much she couldn't have likely noticed if she'd wanted to, reasoning for his part that "she had a lot of trust in me. She gave me a long leash, and she let me, you know, learn on my own." For her part, Gloria Carter, in hindsight, has accepted her son's past, explaining that "that's a reality. That's a reality, and that's the kind of society that we live in as far as these people—these kids are concerned…(I worried for Shawn over) the elements (he was involved with)."

As Jay got deeper into the game, he did so—ironically—out of an addiction of his own, to the money he was making off his customers' addiction to crack, explaining the progression as a natural one in which "it starts off as one thing, then it becomes another. In the beginning it's 'I gotta take care of my family', but you can't keep saying that, because in your first month, you've changed their whole situation around. Once you start living The Life it's just no stopping…It's like making the money, the sound of the money machines clicking-for some people the sensation of the coke under their nails, like dirt for construction workers-the constant hustle, everything from living to the actual work. It's completely addictive…I was getting more money than most of the cats-than all of the cats I was with."

Confirming Jay's player-on-the-rise status, fellow New York emcee and former robber of drug dealers, Capone, who hailed from the same Ft. Greene, Brooklyn hood as Jay, remembered that "Jay always had a nice big something. One of them niggas icing his shit up in '85. I never tried to catch him for nothing, though. He got respect-Marcy (Projects) and shit."

Among Jay's early hustler influences was a local Ft. Green legend known as Danny-Dan, who also grew up in the Marcy projects. A mentor to Jay, the rapper recalled, "Danny Dan was a cat with in the projects, coming up…He was very influential in my life, but from afar. Holmes was doing it. He'd always put something away, not touch it. I was like, I need to be doing that…He always said he'd die in a car crash and he did…Coming back from D.C. on I-95." Danny Dan was allegedly buried with over $100,000 worth of ice on, and Jay was rumored to have taken over his Virginia selling territory after Dan's passing.

Even before Dan's passing and his expansion to Virginia, Jay had moved from the corners of Marcy outward to New Jersey, flexing his talent for product marketing, and innovating the game in such a way that "I went out of town, not far, to Jersey. Me and my man. We was pioneering some shit. I was never around the Calvin Kleins,' because to be around them you would have to be under them. You weren't going to be over them. That would have been conflict...I've never been someone who has a headliner. I've always been a coach or a team leader. Even in Trenton, when I started hustling. I used to wear a rubber band on my wrist, like a ghetto money clip. The little dudes who were working with me had to earn their rubber bands. They had to make a certain quota for the week to get the rubberbands. If they did something that wasn't thorough, like lost work or put someone on the team at risk, they got their rubberband popped."

Moving out even further in time beyond the regional market place, Jay expanded into the South, explaining that he broke into markets foreign to his own by utilizing the power of the p-u-s-s-y, such that "everything that has ever happened has to do with a girl...You ain't going in nobody's town, just settin up. You meet somebody and befriend her. You need her and the most thorough nigga in town. Because girls yap, she'll tell you who that is, who has money. You meet him; you've got something for him-better prices. He'll bring everybody else in line."

Where there was friction over his move into small-town hustling turf, Jay categorized the beef "alot of little fires. But in small towns you ain't wildin' out. You'll go to jail. This shit is like a Commonwealth; they'll lock you up for cursing. It takes a special nigga to do a small town. Anybody can do D.C. You strong-arm D.C. Y'all can shoot at each other every weekend...It was sweet for minute, then New York niggas fucked up.

A lot of shit happened 'cause of bitches...You gotta believe that. You go into a nigga's town, you shining and you messing with all their broads. You go into their town; drive whatever you want. Shine, fine. But don't fuck my baby's mother, man. And my man's baby's mother and his man's baby's mother. 'Cause now we sitting at Sizzler like this nigga fucked all your baby's mothers. Now it's a problem."

For all of Jay's success materially, there were ups and downs at this point in his life—mostly personally—as a by-product of his profession. Chief among them was a constant anxiety rooted in paranoia over being busted...even when he wasn't on the clock— because the game so thoroughly absorbed his life and identity. Elaborating on the insecurities of a hustler's persona, Jay explained that "you never gonna know this feeling, but you could just be driving, absolutely doing nothing, but if you see a cop in the rearview, because you live your life so...You do so much dirt every day that you don't even know what's on you. That feeling right there, I hate. I don't ever want to fear another man, ever, ever. But with those cops in the rearview—the lights don't even have to be on."

Years later, looking back on all he survived in the course of his life hustling, Jay admits that "sometimes I sit on the edge of my bed for like an hour. I'll be in a zone, and I'll just think about...just everything. But then I shake it off you know? Well, no, I don't...I live with it. Wit this whole thing, you don't recruit, people come to you, wanting to work begging you to be out on. We all know what the consequences are-jail or death...(I'd only go back to it) if I was put in a situation of hopelessness..."

"Yesterday I was at a restaurant at 145th and Broadway, and the cops came in. It was the best shit in the world. This cop was fumbling with his hat because he was so nervous to meet me. I was like, 'Goddamn,' you know? Ten years ago he woulda been in my rearview mirror and my heart woulda been beating. But right now he walks in this restaurant He was a great guy, but the fact that he was so nervous to meet me that he dropped his hat on the floor—it was the most amazing shit ever."

Jay is convinced moments like the latter were possible because the man upstairs had bigger plans in mind for him, such that Jay's hustling was merely a means to a much larger end, with the rapper reasoning that "I think God protects anyone with a good heart. People say, 'That's a comfort blanket so you can do whatever the fuck you want.' But my intention was good. I was in a place where there's no hope. It was like, Fuck, man, I ain't going to continue to live like this. I've got to do something. Then I got addicted to that life. It was fun. It helped my situation, helped everyone around me."

"I had no aspirations, no plans, no goals, no back-up goals."

—Jay-Z

Chapter 3
Shawn Carter becomes Jay-Z

Even while hustling, Jay was always aware of the voice whispering rhymes quietly in the back of his mind, his artistic angel battling back and forth with the hustler angel—he former beckoning Jay to give music a shot, while the latter told him to focus on the dollars. For his own part, Jay explained that he first started flirting more seriously with the prospect of rapping full time in "the late '80s. At Gordy Groove's house, Big Daddy Kane, Jaz, and myself are about to put vocals on a tape (not a CD, a tape), a freestyle over a beat Gordy created. Jaz goes first, I go second, Kane goes last. I still remember Kane's rhyme: 'Setting it off/Letting it off/Beginning/rough to the ending.'"

"I was inspired and went directly home to write a thousand new and improved rhymes. During the next few months, the tape circulated and the feedback was positive 'the second kid who rapped.' I was taught in my family to believe that anything worth having you had to work extremely hard for. But rap came easy for me. I wouldn't say I took it for granted, but I didn't realize I had a gift until I made that tape."

Jay's mentor at the time, fellow Marcy project native Jaz-O, was attempting his come-up at the same time Jay was first discovering he had a talent for rapping. As such, the two became partners in rhyme, so much so that Jay first developed his stage name out of the friendship, explaining that "I've always been more observant than talkative…That's how I got the name Jay-Z from Jazzy. When I was a little kid, I was cool. They used to say back in the day, 'That little kid is jazzy; he's smooth.' That's how I took the 'Jay' and the 'Z.'"

As much as Jay-Z's initial brush with success in getting signed encouraged Jay to keep at it, the way his deal ended up showed Jay he needed to do things differently if he was to achieve the same success and position in the rap game that he had in the drug trade. As he explained the latter series of events and realizations, "over the next couple of years (in the late 1980s), Jaz and I went back and forth to each other's mothers' apartment in Marcy writing raps."

"Contrary to the claims he's made in recent interviews, when I met him, I already had a notebook full of problems, heat, raps, whatever y'all call it nowadays. Jaz shared his dream of getting a recording deal, and I was like, 'Great, homie, but I need paper now.' I started getting serious about hustling, and Jaz stuck to his music. We had an agreement: He'd holla when something real popped off (a show, a session, a deal), and I'd drop what I was doing and be right there…When Jaz got a deal with EMI (for $400,000 or some outrageous number for a rapper back then), he kept his word and took me with him to London, where the label set him up to record his album."

"When I left the block, everyone was saying I was crazy. I was doing well for myself on the streets, and cats around me were like, 'These rappers are hoes. They just record, tour and get separated from their families, while some white person takes all their money.' I was determined to do it differently. Rap was my way out, the only talent I had, and my shot at making something of myself. And it was legal! I wasn't directly signed directly to EMI, but the plan was for Jaz to blow, and I was to sign and be next."

"But things never go as planned. EMI convinced Jaz to work with Bryan 'Chuck' New, a producer who was riding on the success of D.J. Jazzy Jeff & the Fresh Prince's multi-platinum album. They released Jaz's 'Hawaiian Sophie' as the first single, and when it bombed, they abandoned Jay's album altogether…When I did a verse on this song 'Hawaiian Sophie', that's how I got my start. A friend of mine named Jaz introduces me to the entertainment business, and looking back, I was pretty much grateful for the opportunity to be put on."

"Too bad, things didn't pick up like they should have after that, so I kept hustlin'. But, in every interview I gotta thank Jaz for looking out, because when I didn't know where I might have ended up, and that's when I knew I wanted more of this business in some form or another…(So even though) Jaz got a shitload of money from EMI, like a few thousand dollars…he only saw, like, fifty thousand. That turned me off. I was like , fuck that…I didn't necessarily have a plan B, so it was back to hustling, the only thing I knew. I didn't show it at the time, but I was crazy disappointed and discouraged about the music business."

Returning to the streets, Jay's heart was not broken, but now torn between the fast money of hustling and the long-term potential of the record business as a means out of the streets forever. As such, while Jay took care of business, it was now enough of a routine that he found free time in his mind to work on music, the dawn of his amazing and almost singular ability as an emcee to write entire songs in his head without writing down a word.

Explaining the evolution of this process and his growing interest in hip-hop, Jay explained that "even though I was back on the block, my heart was still in music. I was preoccupied with numbers, weight, and my business, but my mind was flooded with ideas about songs, hooks, and verses. When my thoughts began to crowd each other, I would go to the corner store, get a pen, and empty my head, pouring rhymes onto pieces of paper bags. But how many scraps can you fit in your pocket? I had to start memorizing my ideas until I got home, which was usually in the wee hours of the morning."

"Ironically, using memorization to hold on to my lines is the way I developed the writing style I use today. No pen, paper, or paper bags needed. Just point out the track and I'm all over it...And yet, after witnessing firsthand what happened to Jaz, I became really committed to putting my hustle down. I kept moving further south-from Trenton, N.J., to Maryland, and finally to Virginia. I spent less and less time in New York, but when I did come home, I would go to parties and jump on the mike, freestyling here and there."

"From time to time, I would bump into a DJ name Clark Kent, who would stress to me about returning to New York and taking this rap thing seriously. Clark had started and A&R gig with Atlantic, and he swore he could do this or that for me, and even though he was a cool dude, his words went in one ear and out the other. I didn't want to set myself up to be disappointed again."

Still, Jay knew he couldn't sell drugs as a profession and ever get himself or his family out of the projects, another motivator for him as he quietly honed his skills as an emcee, reasoning that while "that shit just made me shiver...(Big's line about being broke at 30), (it) was my constant struggle. No matter how I was doing, I'd be like, Yeah, I'm alright now, but what am I gonna do when I'm thirty, forty. I can't keep up with this pace...All of a sudden I was trying to get a deal; essentially become a worker...I guess I thought the sacrifice, the cut in money, was worth it for peace of mind."

While Jay stayed mostly quiet about his ambitions to become a full-time emcee with his hustling partners, he did confide to his girlfriend Fannie of his dreams, recalling that "it was in Virginia that I met my second girlfriend, Stephanie (everybody called her Fannie). What people don't know about me is that I've always been in long-term relationships. My first real relationship was with this girl from Long Island, and it lasted five years; I was with Fannie for another five. It was on a long drive from New York to Virginia that I really bonded with Fannie. She told me her dreams of going back to school and making something of herself, and I told her my dreams of being an MC. She was the first person I let know how discouraged I was by the music business."

"When I finally took Clark Kent's advice to commit to making it in music, Fannie followed me to New York. And even though I put her up in a nice apartment in Clinton Hill, Brooklyn, and took care of her material needs, my level of commitment to her couldn't compete with what I was willing to give to make this rap thing work. I didn't record it till years later, but 'Song Cry' had been writing itself in my head ever since Fannie left me to go home to Virginia."

Tightening up his rhyme style and ambition to transition from hustler to emcee, from the crack game to the rap game, Jay explained that his goal as a rapper was "to have a conversation with the world…I'm telling the world my plight. I was speaking about the people and neighborhoods and mentality of someone who comes from nothing…I didn't want to sell drugs. I wanted a better life," he recalls. "I wanted to perform and I didn't know where performing would take me exactly, but I knew it would take me far away from where I'd come from…Not saying that I wanted to leave my peoples, but ain't nothing fun about living in poverty." In 1993, Jay appeared on Original Flavor's single 'Can I Get Open', but the group—and Jay for the moment—were soon forgotten. He cut a demo, but stuck with hustling to keep his pockets tight.

Part II:
Hip Hop Zenith:
The Roc-A-Fella Years

"I guess it's the confidence that you have in yourself. You know, you've got to have confidence to believe that you can do it. I mean, because when those doors were shuts for me as far as, you know, someone signing me to a record label and putting out my material, I could have easily said, that's it, you know, I'm not good enough, this is not for me, you know, but I didn't do that. I did it the other way. I was like, OK, you're a big, multi-million dollar conglomerate, you don't know what you're talking about. That's tough, you know, for someone to say, to look in the face of that huge company and say, you're wrong. And I'm going to prove you wrong... We just—because we just really—we always aspired to have the best, you know what I'm saying? And that name just, it just meant so much to American society, for aspiring to have the finer things, an affluent lifestyle and things like that. We always just aspired to have the best. And that name represents the best for us."

—*Jay-Z*

Chapter 4

The Birth of Roc-A-Fella Records...

Jay-Z and Damon Dash Unite

In 1995, the hip-hop was pregnant with change, though her child—Roc-A-Fella Records—was an industry bastard. Unwanted, and unable to secure a deal with any major label, the fledgling company would set out on its own, and plant the seed for a new breed and generation of rap entrepreneurs who would follow in time. Jay and Damon were moving from the world of tracks on the arm and blacks on the farm, out of the indentured servitude of rap label deals...as they had largely existed up till that point...and into the first truly free era of African-American entrepreneurialism in hip-hop.

Roc-A-Fella was taking over the plantation, moving into the Master's white-columned mansion, and putting the white-run corporate record machine to work making money for someone other than the top one percent for once. The difference between business partners like Jay-Z and Damon Dash and the likes of Enron employee investors, and the reason why Island/Def Jam would never seek to fuck the former parties out of a single dollar—is that Jay-Z made no secret of his background.

After Interscope's success with Death Row Records, and Arista's with Bad Boy, Def Jam Records, deeply in debt at the time they partnered with Dash, Jay and silent partner Biggs, needed an injection of success and renewed credibility on the street level. As such, they had no choice but to deal on the Roc's terms—1/3 ownership only (rather than the standard 50%) of the company's Master Recordings, which basically made the pact a distribution deal.

For Jay, there was something of a personal irony to he and his partners' decision to hook up with Def Jam, as the rapper recalled, "The first time I met Russell Simmons was at a rap talent contest out in Queens. Somebody, it had to have been my cousin B-Hi, entered me and didn't tell me where it was. There's no way they would've gotten me to go to Queens without doing it like that. LL Cool J was one of the judges. I was crazy young, like 15. I remember I had a gun on me, the same one I used to carry around in an empty VHS box. I lost. I got second place, which to me, then and now, was the same as coming in 50th. But Russell came down from the stage and was like, 'Yo, kid, I want you to call me, here's my number.' I tried to call him one day, and they told me he wasn't there. I might've tried calling one other time, but after that I went into asshole mode, like, I ain't calling this nigga again, you crazy! I never told him that story."

Years later, Damon Dash and I had a million-dollar (distribution) deal on the table with Def Jam. I still have that asshole in me, like, If he doesn't remember, I'm not reminding him. Things happen when they're supposed to, what they say about divine time is true."

Years before the founding of Roc-A-Fella Records and the Def Jam hook up, Jay's partner, Damon Dash, had his own legend in the making. Born on May 3rd, 1971 in East Harlem, New York, Dash—like Jay—was raised in a single-parent home by his mother, who worked long hours as a secretary. A bright child with a head for numbers from a young age, Dash won a Scholarship to an elite private prep school in downtown Manhattan—Dwight Preporatory— before being expelled for reasons unknown.

Thereafter, he rebounded to Connecticut, where he was awarded a second scholarship to South Kent Boarding School. On his way toward what would have likely become a scholarship to an ivy-league college, Dash's higher educational pursuits were cut short when, as Damon explains, "my mom died when I was 15 (of an asthma attack). I put myself through school even after that because she gave me the best of everything. I went to school on Park Avenue even though I was from uptown...It was pretty fancy...I was around kids that had country houses and cooks and maids and stuff like that...and I didn't think anyone was that much better than me. I was like, Why shouldn't I have that stuff?...An all-boys school. I did it for a year."

"My homeboys out there are still my friends. But I didn't go back. I was in the 11th grade, I couldn't do 12th...Do you know how hard it was to come back to my neighborhood in penny loafers with khaki pants and a blazer?...When I got back from South Kent, I went to the worst high school in the city, called West Side

High. I was practically teaching the class myself. Then they kicked me out. They thought I was too arrogant…So I ended up getting my G.E.D…"

"I had two lives. My uptown life was in Harlem. My downtown life was P.S. 6 on 81st and Park Avenue. Then I went to Dwight. So I got to see both sides. Taught me a lot." While at boarding school, Dash realized his first entrepreneurial epiphany regarding black culture's potency in white suburban America, explaining that "I was amused to see how rich folks were intrigued by what was going on in the streets…(and decided, in the future, I would do something business-wise) to market the streets (to both)…I needed a business where I could have fun and make money."

Upon receiving his GED in 1988, Dash became "an entrepreneur, hustling to get money in any way. I went to some parties and noticed the easy lifestyle of the MCs, with no repercussions, so I wanted to have fun and enjoy life." Dash's cousin, Darien, hooked him up with his stepfather, who worked for the time at Casablanca Records, and Dame got hooked up with an attorney, and went about founding his first production/management company, Dash Entertainment. As Dash explains, "my cousin put me in the right direction, put me in touch with a lawyer and my cousin got involved, and then things took off. My group, Future Sound got a deal on Atlantis Records."

While Future Sound gave Dash a small taste of success, the deal soon floundered, and Dash was back to the drafting board, revising his blueprint to re-attack the business with a much more potent weapon—one he found in future business partner and at that time, among the hottest underground emcees floating around Brooklyn—Jay-Z. In a similar position as Dash, Jay was also seeking a way to break into the big time, and the two were first brought together with that mutual interest via DJ Clark Kent, a friend of both.

As Dash recalls, "(I first met Jay when I was) 21. I got my first record deal when I was 19...As a manager...two deals. Both of the groups 'caught a brick,' which means they didn't sell. They went cardboard...I was kind of upset about the way we were being carried. And I had to learn the business, I had to learn how to market. When I got with Jay, we just decided to do it ourselves. I couldn't take people telling me what to do and when to do it. This movie is all performance. No effects. All the talent is doing it on the cuff."

As Jay-Z elaborates on the circumstances that brought the two men together, he explains that "when I first met Damon Dash, around the same time, he was doing artist management. All I could think was, dam this Damon guy talks a lot. If he shuts up for two seconds he might give someone a chance to say he's smart. He loves attention-reminds me of an old hustling buddy I used to have."

"Damon is from Harlem, and I'm from Brooklyn. And anyone from New York will tell you how different cats from Uptown and BK are ('Manhattan's always making' it/Brooklyn keeps on takin' it'). But I always had the get-mine mentality Harlem is famous for, and Damon was so hungry for this music paper that he could have been a stick-up kid from Brooklyn."

"What started out as mutual respect and a management agreement between us grew into a fifty-fifty partnership and a lifelong friendship. I'm godfather to his son, Boogie, and Uncle Jay to his beautiful daughter Ava." For his part, Dash recalled that "we started Original Flavor and then Clark Kent introduced me to Jay-Z. Jay was known as a good rapper but did not like the business side. We were from different backgrounds but got along...Clark Kent kept telling me there was this guy I needed to get with named Jay-Z. So I went to Brooklyn to meet Jay at Fresh Gordon's studio, and that was big, because back then cats from Harlem didn't go to Brooklyn. When I met the dude the first thing that I noticed was that he was wearing a pair of Nike Airs and that was something that only cats from Harlem were into, and he was wearing them right—he had them laced right and every-thing. That's when I knew he was a cool dude."

"We became friends from there...people from Harlem and Brooklyn seem to have crazy stereotypes about one another. But we became good friends. I was shopping his demo and I could not believe that some people were not interested...I knew that we could run a street label 'cause people would not tell us what to do." Jay was down with Dame on whatever tip they needed to be to advance both's careers, and while he acknowledges that "me, Dame, and (our other partner) Biggs came from different places— Brooklyn and Uptown—the thing that held everything together was our ambition...After shopping our demo to almost every label and them frontin' on what we had, we founded Roc-A-Fella Records. Later, another friend, Kareem 'Biggs' Burke, joined us as a partner."

"It was on!...We all wanted the same thing, for Roc-A-Fella to win. The record company, the film company-that was all part of the vision. But me and Dame are totally opposite people. He lives for the debate, the negotiation. I love to stay away from that. Even though I'm involved in a bunch of businesses, I'm an artist. I'm more creative. I'm not into all the negotiating, the talking back and forth. Just tell me what happens when it's over, and we'll work from there. I'm the studio guy. Dame did the executive thing, seeing the projects that the three of us conceived all the way through, dealing with the day to day, even protecting me from some bullshit so I could be a total artist when that was necessary."

"So it was great, we complemented each other...We put in so much work over the next couple of years that there was no way we could fail. My first album, Reasonable Doubt, was about what I knew best: hustling. I felt like other rappers had touched on the subject, but I wanted every hustler I ever knew to feel like I had been reading his diary. I wanted to write an album that was honest about the glamour and materialism, because living large was real for us. But I also wanted to talk about the depression, the drama, the sacrifices, and the pain that come with the street life. I made that album like it was my first and last."

We pressed up our own records, shot our own videos, turned our own cars into tour buses, made our own jackets, you name it. I even had my cousin Bryant (who'd always told me I was wasting my talent hustling) make up gift baskets with champagne in them to give to DJs along with copies of my first 12-inch single, 'In My Lifetime.'"

"He didn't come into the game to learn; he came to teach. So fresh, so clean-shaven, and slickly dressed in a dark suit and crisp fedora, a twinkle of bling on his left earlobe and his right wrist, a streetwise Jay-Z knows something you don't: I will not lose. Yes, his pinkie ring and Cuban cigar decorate his confidence. Yes, the card-deck-thick money stacks, all rubber banded up, foreshadow the personal fortune (which now exceeds $50 million) he would amass. But it's the thingysure steel of his almost droopy eyes that speak loudest. He told us in '96 that he came to take this nuts, and he did."

—*Vibe Magazine, 1996*

Chapter 5
Reasonable Doubts Defied:

Jay, Dame and Roc-A-Fella Take Over The New York Underground—1996

Once Jay had made the commitment through his partnership with Dash and Biggs to give up hustling in order to pursue rap full time, he went through a withdrawal process of sorts, explaining that "the funny thing (is): You gotta abide by certain rules when you in the street. It's a certain code you have to operate on to have a good run, where not everybody wants to kill you. And the music business is totally opposite."

"I was operating with that (street) code and that loyalty and that honor and that whole ethic. And they wasn't operating that way. So I had to change my ways…Like, with Priority (which was one company we almost signed with), I had a messed up contract. And everyone knew. But we didn't now. We was like, 'Why were we…'? But they was like, 'Why you so offended? It's just business.' To them it's good business; to us it was deceit…A person wouldn't try you like that. Because either you would have to kill them, or they would kill you. When you make that kinda move, you gotta know that either you prepared to go to war or you prepared to die…Yeah. You can go to war and die…"

"You can always make more money. Once people are gone or locked up, there's no bringing them back or finding lost time. Some cats just think about the money, but it's really about people and relationships." The bottom line, even amid Jay's efforts toward diplomacy, was that he and Dame were taking no shorts in their venture with Def Jam. Moreover, though Jay was committed not to return to hustling, he brought and applied that mentality readily as his label's own in the course of dealing with record executives.

Unapologetically, he explained that while "I don't think any rapper can go back (to hustling once he's out…Still), drug dealing is a part of me. It happened. I don't regret it. It shaped me as a person. It's a thing that, whether I rap about it or not, exists. So I'd rather shed light on the situation-in a indirect way. I don't want to preach. I know it's a lotta people out through the same thing I've been through. 'You're not a Martian, you're not an unusual person. I understand your struggle. I've been through the same thing.' And that's what I think is happening right now. There's a lot of people relating to my story. I don't hide it, I don't avoid it, I don't send my publicists out with 'Don't ask me these questions.' I got nothin' to hide…Hustling got me where I am today."

Throughout 1995, Jay, Dash and Company. worked tirelessly recording tracks for what would become Jay's debut album, 'Reasonable Doubt', releasing singles, and competing on a hype-level as competitively as any major at the time. Prior to signing with Def Jam, Jay and Damon went through several trial and error blueprints of what would eventually become Roc-A-Fella's deal with Island/Def Jam. First, the duo recorded and pressed copies of the single 'In My Lifetime', while independently promoting Jay in his own headlining spots, and selling records out of the trunk of their ride, unable to get any radio play.

Their first break came when local New York indie label Payday Records picked up the single for distribution based on the buzz it was generating. While the experience proved to be commercially anti-climatic, it gave Jay and Damon all the education they needed in the world of indie record labels to know they could do better on their own. As Jay explained, "they (Payday) eventually signed me to a deal, but were acting shady the whole time, like they didn't know how to work a record or something…The things that they were setting up for me I could have done myself. They had me traveling places to do in-stores, and my product wasn't even available in the store. We shot one video, but when the time came for me to do the video for the second single, I had to be cut out. They gave me the money and I started my own company. There was a little arguing back and forth, but our conflict finally got resolved. The bottom line was they wasn't doing their job, so I had to get out of there."

Using the buyout money, Jay and Dame founded what would become Roc-A-Fella Records, renting modest office space on John Street—a low-rent part of Manhattan—that ran adjacent to the Financial District, near the World Trade Centers. They were now officially a small business, starting from the ground floor with the hopes of moving uptown to a spot where they'd be looking down at buildings rather than up at them.

Though they'd eventually arrive there, Jay recalled at the time that "I (didn't) mind being down here in this area, because this is just a starting point for us...I like being away from everybody right now, because I can get all my stuff together, then I can move uptown with all those other niggas when everything's straight. No sense in spending a whole lot of money on office space and moving employees round if your product isn't bringing in any money yet—that's a mistake executives make. I used my money to get this label off the ground and that was the right decision, yaknowhatI'msayin?"

The duo's next step was securing a new distributor for Jay's singles, 'In My Lifetime' and 'Ain't No Nigga', which turned out to be Priority Records, who had often served as an indie conduit between labels in between major label distributors—in the case of Death Row Records, or preferring to go more of an indie route altogether, in the case of Master P's No Limit Records or J. Prince's Rap-A-Lot.

Elaborating on the nature of Roc-A-Fella's deal with Priority in later 1995, Jay explained an arrangement where Roc-A-Fella split cost of business, and did the standard 70/30 split on sales of the label's releases, such that "we didn't need dirty money to start Roc-A-Fella, because we had Payday's money and just so you know, I didn't want to ask Priority for shit. They would have kicked in some money (for overhead expenses), but I wanted to do this on my own so the profit was mine, free and clear. At a certain point, if you ain't livin' right you want to do things legally. You want to leave your past behind and start looking for the future."

For his part, partner Damon Dash explained that "(in the beginning), we put our money together and pressed up some copies and eventually we signed a deal with Priority to press and distribute our cuts...When record companies were first courting us, they came to me with the nigga deal where they make you think you own a label and you really don't...I wanted a joint venture because

I knew I was going to be successful and the equity would be worth something down the line."

While Roc-A-Fella began building credibility on the corporate level, they also focused on keeping a buzz going in the street, employing a street team for promotions was truly a street team, made up of hungry hustlers whose every spoil was an earned one, and who became more competitive with each point scored for their team. Jay and Dame ran their street team like a crew of drug runners, stationing a man on every corner of whatever neighborhood they were canvassing with promotional posters or show flyers, selling singles out of the trunks of cars, counting every dollar, and building a buzz that wouldn't get out of the head of major labels who were starting to take notice.

New York hip-hop is SLAMMING! From the bass in the funk to the woofer in the trunk, windows rattling, crews battling—lyrically, or sometimes harder if required. Hard as the streets they grew up on. There is no fear, only pit bull emcees frothing at the mouth, dying to tear up the mic, and anything else that gets in the way of success. Rap to the inner city is like hockey to rural Canada; its the only way out besides athletics, and the competition inherent in the inner-city hip-hop game makes rap a sport in and of itself.

As a cold, ruthless, cut-throat business, hip-hop entrepreneurs run the record industry the way it was originally designed to be run—with no shorts even though there is no active concept of a bottom-line in the image they portray publicly. A rap star may be iced out, but his handlers know the precise cut of the jewels they're sporting, and the exact ounce to which that gold melts down off the teeth. The streets never change—from the Marcy Projects to Wall St.—perhaps only the suburban neighborhoods they move into out of the hood.

Still, even after the transition is made, most true players in the hip-hop game never forget where they came from. Often times they can't, as the latter is requisite, at its most basic, for continual credibility on the street level. Once a flagship emcee has made it, his next responsibility after taking care of his immediate family, is to bring his crew along, either as part of the entourage, or by putting them on as rap stars in their own right. Artistically, Jay began as the sole focus of Roc-A-Fella's energies, just as Biggie had started out as P. Diddy's.

Completing Jay's debut album, Reasonable Doubt, in mid-1995, Roc-A-Fella had first released the album independently through their distribution pact with Priority, and started building a hype around the project that couldn't help but become contagious throughout the industry. In record time, that buzz reached the A&R executives—including Irv Gotti—at Def Jam Records, specifically Lyor Cohen, who recruited Jay-Z's single, 'Ain't No Nigga', to appear on the Nutty Professor soundtrack.

Jay's appearance on the latter soundtrack launched him into intense negotiations with Def Jam/Island for a full-on record deal. Still, having tasted the freedom following Roc-A-Fella's dissolution from PayDay Records, and seeing the waves Suge Knight and Sean 'P. Diddy' Combs had made with Death Row Records and Bad Boy Entertainment respectively, Jay and Damon Dash decided to go a different route, selling Def Jam a 1/3rd stake in the label for approximately $1.5 million.

As Jay explained the structure of and motivation behind Roc-A-Fella's deal with Def Jam for the rapper's debut album, Reasonable Doubt, "my dream when I did Reasonable Doubt was to do one album. I thought I was being artistic, making a statement. But then we sat down with Russell Simmons and Lyor Cohen to negotiate with Def Jam, I was the only artist on Roc-A-Fella that could close the deal. They were only interested in us because of the heat from Reasonable. So once that contract was signed, I knew I would be in the vocal booth for another five to seven albums...I never waited for anybody to give me anything. If I wanted something I knew that I was gonna have to be the one to go out and get it, because wasn't nothing just coming to the nigga like me. Opportunities didn't come my way. I had to chase them. I finally caught one…In my heart, I always wanted someone else to do it. I wanted to be the businessman."

Being independent during the recording of Reasonable Doubt allowed Jay to make the album he wanted to make, an experience he artistically so relished that, as Jay reasoned, "when I said Reasonable Doubt was going to be my first and only album, I meant it. 'He made one album, then, puff, he's gone with the wind.' I feel like I was saying something that was ahead of its time…The (metaphors) that I hid in there—people still come up to me and say, 'I just realized what you said.'…Coming off the streets, you got Reasonable Doubt. That album was just carefree."

As producer Ski, who produced the tracks 'Politics as Usual', 'Dead Presidents II', 'Feelin' It', and '22 Twos' for Reasonable Doubt recalled the atmosphere as tense with excitement during his work on the making of the record, "Dead Presidents II was the official beginning of recording the album. My beats weren't like DJ Premier's or Clark Kent's, they were a little more melodic. I remember when he was doing 'Brooklyn's Finest', Biggie had to go home and rethink his verse because Jay was putting the pressure on him. Everyone around Jay knew that he was going to be the next dude."

Still, producer DJ Premier, who produced 'D'Evils', 'Friend or Foe', and 'Bring It On', recalled that the atmosphere of the album was consistent with keeping it real edict straight off the block, such that "Reasonable Doubt was strictly street. A lot of artists nowadays sugarcoat their music and go straight for the pop market. Jay is always very descriptive about what he wants before he even lays it. For "D'Evils," he wanted to use the Snoop and Prodigy vocal samples. He described the atmosphere of the song, and I just laid the track down like he wanted."

Looking back retrospectively 10 years later, Reasonable Doubt remains not only Jay-Z's, but also business partner Damon Dash's, with Dash explaining that "Jay-Z's first album, Reasonable Doubt. Jay raps about what's going on in his life and the emotion he feels while it's going on. Whatever he's talking about is exactly what we were doing. That was such a defining time in our lives. It was like our last days outside the music business. It brings back those memories, keeps you grounded and makes you appreciate where you're at." At the time, Jay and Dame couldn't have been in a better position. Def Jam was desperate for its own Death Row or Bad Boy, and all parties knew instinctively that Roc-A-Fella was IT.

"Jay-Z and Biggie Smalls, nigga shit ya drawers
(Where you from?) Brooklyn, goin out for all
Marcy—that's right—you don't stop
Bed-Stuy…you won't stop, nigga!
Uhh, Roc-A-Fella, y'all, Junior M.A.F.I.A.
Superbad click, Brook-lyn's Finest, you re-wind this
Representin BK to the fullest"

— *"Brooklyn's Finest"—Jay-Z and Biggie Smalls, 1996*

Chapter 6
Brooklyn's Finest—Jay-Z and Biggie Smalls

As 1996 unfolded, Jay-Z was rapidly shooting toward rap stardom. While he was garnering a forest worth of print press, Jay and Dame were also quietly developing a roster of artists for Roc-A-Fella under the terms of their new deal with Def Jam. The first Roc-Family included Christion, the Rangers, Sauce Money, Ruffness and Michelle Mitchell, although both female artists were dropped soon enough for the fact that, according to Jay—speaking as an executive—"they were difficult to work with and had no loyalty."

With Jay as the marquee player on team ROC, his label was quickly making its own waves in the ocean of independent hip-hop start-ups operating at the time in the industry. With a well-oiled corporate machinery in place to launch any new rap artist via a series of guest appearances on other rap artists' albums and remixes, freestyle radio appearances, magazine spreads, videos, award show appearances, and any other media medium required to give a new artist spotlight shine. With Jay-Z, there was no star to make, he was ready-made—with a natural charisma the camera couldn't get enough of.

On record, Jay-Z reincarnated the aura of a 1970s pimp's smooth-ness, without wearing that image on his sleeve as thematically as Snoop did in the early 1990s' Doggystyle-era. Both artists shared the same natural suaveness and charismatic confidence, but Jay-Z had a sophistication in his lyrics that was anything but laid back. As the next generation in reality rap, Jay-Z provided the world through Reasonable Doubt an intense pop psycho-analysis of where the ghetto was in the mid-1990s, making a case for why he—on behalf of his hustler generation—was not guilty of doing what they had to do to escape the institutional oppression of the ghetto for a better life in the same way white European minori-ties—like the Irish via Joe Kennedy's bootlegging enterprise—had decades earlier.

Jay had hustled his way into an opportunity for a better life, and he would achieve it not just for himself and his family, but also his race, both in what he proved any stereotypical young, black male was capable of in business to the rest of the world, as well as the way in which the business of hip-hop culture-wide would operate in years to come. Jay-Z was rap's first true capitalist. Still, as much as Jay-Z was celebrating a departure with the album, he was also announcing an arrival of something futuristic in terms of lyrical, instrumental and entrepreneurial sophistication.

In metaphorical context of the earth's solar system, Jay-Z is argu-ably most kindred to Jupiter, traditionally considered one of the more dominant planets within our solar system, with multi-col-ored rings that continuously alter in color and morphology. With an animate rapping style that continually changed moods and energies with each new song and album—while constantly preserving musical consonance and consistency—Jay's importance in terms of maintaining the order and evolution of the various levels of stardom within Hip Hop's larger cosmos cannot be understated. He not only re-set the bar with Reasonable Doubt, he was already sitting above it waiting for the rest of the industry to evolve to his level.

After Biggie and Tupac passed—with the notable possibility of Eminem on some levels stylistically—no emcee would ever surpass Jay-Z after 1996 in artistic or commercial terms. Even before Jay and Biggie's single, 'Who Shot Ya?' was released, which coupled with 'Brooklyn's Finest' put Reasonable Doubt's sales over the top, reaching Gold in just 12 weeks between its release in June and September of 1996, the Source Magazine had already given Jay-Z's debut album 4 out of 5 stars, falling just short of a classic review rating.

Vibe Magazine, meanwhile, has said of the album, that while "Reasonable Doubt, may arguably be the most misunderstood album in hip-hop, its critics cannot deny its classic presence." All Music Guide.com has historically hailed the album as "seamless. Every song belongs here, from timeless hits like 'Can't Knock the Hustle' to personal moments like 'Regrets.' Each song is like a separate chapter, revealing another aspect of Jay-Z's story, which, in 1996, was still untold. Nobody knew who he was when Reasonable Doubt dropped, keep in mind. Jay-Z seemingly came from nowhere...

Beyond Jay-Z's rhetorical wealth of insight and wisdom, Reasonable Doubt also boasts an amazing roster of producers. Granted, most Jay-Z albums do, but this lineup—Ski, Clark Kent, and DJ Premier—is different. They represent the pre-gangsta era, a foregone era when samples fueled the beats and turntablism supplied the hooks. This classic production style...is essentially refined hip-hop in its canonical sense…The lyrics do the same because they're so candidly confessional…Reasonable Doubt is…an anomaly. For most listeners who heard this album in 1996, and perhaps for many who subsequently discovered it after being drawn in by more popular albums like Hard Knock Life, Reasonable Doubt will forever be Jay-Z's one definitive effort."

Jay's public pairing with Biggie only worked to further the aspiring star's credibility among hardcore rap fans—both inside and nationally outside of New York. Not surprisingly, the duet between the two was anything but contrived—arranged not by Def Jam and Bad Boy, but rather by the two rappers personally, based on a friendship that dated back more than 5 years to their upbringing in the same Bedford Stuyvesant neighborhood in Brooklyn when the two attended George Westinghouse Technical High School together.

As Jay recalled, "when I finally released Doubt in 1996, hip-hop was as hot as the streets. I had known Big since high school, and when we reconnected to do 'Brooklyn's Finest' for my album, we became real close…We always said we was going to do something together, and I was doing my first album, so we went into the studio and did 'Brooklyn's Finest'. He was sitting there, trying to memorize his lyrics, and I passed him a pen and paper, like, 'Here.' And he was like, 'No, I'm cool, you can take that.' I was like, 'Nah, I don't need that.' That's so strange, to see two people who don't write down lyrics. At the time, no one else was doing that."

"After that, we spoke every day…He was hilarious, with a big heart, and I never doubted he was keeping it real with me. I thought he was smart to stay quiet when Tupac started his war of words. And on the real, I could tell the whole situation made him depressed. We had worked hard to leave a certain kind of life behind, and from the beginning, that thing felt like more than a rap battle. I didn't take it seriously when Tupac dragged me into it.

I knew he was just trying to get at anybody who was associated with Big. But I never stopped bumping 'Pac. I had been a fan of his since Digital Underground, and when he was killed, I knew we had lost someone irreplaceable."

Though Jay stayed out of the discord in the press going on between Pac and Biggie, the endorsement from King of New York and exposure, the single they recorded together generated—especially amid the height of the East Coast/West Coast beef—couldn't help but work in Jay-Z's favor. He naturally didn't work at the time to correct the impression he was a Shakur rival in the media, as Jay felt he had time on his side in which to make that distinction. Biggie, sadly would not, and without knowing it at the time, the East Coast rap establishment was quietly training Jay to take over Biggie's spot at the top, and continue his reign.

Prior to Biggie's death, Tupac had already raised Jay-Z's profile—acknowledging him on a peer level by calling the rapper out in 'Bomb First', boasting that "I'm a Bad Boy killa, Jay-Z die too!" Still, even as he knew the duet with Biggie would put him permanently over the top with fans, increasing record sales and therein demands for more material, Jay still operated going into the release of Reasonable Doubt on the premise that he may only have one shot to say everything he had to on the record. Explaining the latter rationale, Jay recalled that "there wasn't some big moment when I thought: Okay, this is it. The next album is gonna be the last one."

"Honestly, I've been saying that for a minute. I've been running on fumes for a second. It all gets back to inspiration. I've heard songs I like, but the last time I remember being truly, truly inspired was when I heard 'Who Shot Ya.' Biggs had me drive to Harlem to meet him on a corner in the middle of the night to play me that song. He knows that if I hear something really creative, it's only going to make me want to be more creative with my music." Sadly, 'Who Shot Ya?' would only work to fuel the heat cooking the East Coast/West Coast beef to the extreme of the dangerous and potentially deadly streets Biggie, Tupac, Jay-Z and every other hip-hop recording artist who'd grown up in that kind of environment had seemingly gotten in the game to escape.

In the end, Tupac and Biggie would both be gunned down within six months of each other, leaving Jay-Z as the unintended heir apparent. He would take his time claiming the throne—both because he had that on his side with no truly worthy competitors—and out of respect to his friend Christopher Wallace, a.k.a. Biggie Smalls. As Jay recalled his feelings over the loss shortly after the rapper's killing, "going to Big's funeral was a big deal to me. I don't go to funerals, period. I don't want that to be my last memory of them...

We knew each other since Westinghouse High School. We'd see each other, and we'd nod. Then we both was in the music business, and we always said, 'We gotta hook up and do something together.' Finally we did 'Brooklyn's Finest.' That's when we clicked. I sat there, he sat there. I was like, 'Yo, you need a pen?' No pen. That's how I make my music, too. It was a crazy, it was ill for me...I can't even describe what that loss was like for me. It was worse than someone losing someone in a drug game, because you know that's the risk you take when you get into the streets—death or jail. This was supposed to be music. But I will say that."

"Look, if I shoot you, I'm brainless
But if you shoot me, then you're famous
When the, streets is watching,
blocks keep clocking
Waiting for you to break,
make your first mistake
Can't ignore it, that's the fastest way to get extorted
But my time is money, at twenty-five, I can't afford it
Beef is sorted like Godiva, chocolates
Niggaz you bought it, I pull the slide back and cock it
Plan aborted, you and your mans get a pass
This rhyme, you're operating on fuck time
Y'all niggaz ain't worth my shells,
tryin to do is hurt my sales,
The type to start a beef then, run to the cops
When I see you in the street got, one in the drop
Would I rather be on tour getting a, hundred a pop
Taking pictures with some bitches, in front of the drop"

....The streets is watching...

—Jay-Z

Chapter 7
In My Lifetime
Vol. 1—1997/1998

By the end of 1996, Reasonable Doubt had gone platinum, despite peaking at only #23 on the Billboard Top 200 Album Chart, and one of the album's hit singles, 'Dead Presidents', had gone Gold, and topped the Billboard Dance Music Maxi-Singles

Sales chart for 5 weeks. Ranked the #172 Singles Artist of the Year by Billboard Magazine.

Jay had already gone back into the studio to begin recording his sophomore album, "In My Lifetime Volume 1." The mood of the album was cast in Biggie's passing, a dark but creatively driven climate that Jay depicted as one in which an obligation he felt to his fallen friend was motivating him, such that "I recorded my second album after Big was murdered…I felt Big had elevated rhyming to heights not seen in hip-hop, and that it would be selfish for me to retire. My staying in the game is like a promise I made to Big. He had done so much to represent New York that I didn't want us to return to that time before Ready to Die, when it seemed like New York hip-hop didn't even matter anymore."

With a heavy heart and responsibility upon his back, Jay knocked out what he felt was an album that had "a few mistakes, though, on my second album, In My Lifetime, Vol. 1. I made records I thought radio would want to hear, which is a mistake that a lot of artists are being rewarded for today. Now I know how to bring radio to me. But I'm still proud of that album…I think 85 percent of it is solid…And that 85 percent was better than everybody else's album at the time." Longtime Jay-Z collaborator, producer DJ Premier, who produced the tracks "Intro/A Million and One Questions/Rhymes No More" and "Friend or Foe '98" for In My Lifetime Vol. 1, recalled that "after the first album, Jay started to understand what it took to be a diverse artist.

The record with Babyface, '(Always Be My) Sunshine,' didn't work for him, but he could take chances because he covered the streets first. All the records I do with Jay are never the pop records, they're strictly for the 'hood. We knocked out 'A Million and One Questions' in one night. He's a lightning-fast worker. I guess that's one of the reasons why he can turn out an album so quickly."

Jay-Z's sophomore album represented what All Music Guide.com called "the best rapping heard in the rap game since the deaths of

2Pac and Notorious B.I.G…Though the productions are just a bit flashier and more commercial than on his debut, Jay-Z remained the tough street rapper, and even improved a bit on his flow, already one of the best in the world of hip-hop. Still showing his roots in the Marcy projects (he's surrounded by a group of kids in a picture on the back cover), Jay-Z struts the line between project poet and up-and-coming player, and manages to have it both ways."

Entertainment Weekly, meanwhile, hailed the album's "dense lyrical flow. His phrasing shifts often, and he mixes jokes with visceral descriptions, stealing the spotlight from guests like BLACKstreet, Puff Daddy, Babyface, and Foxy Brown." *Rolling Stone Magazine*, for its part, concluded that "In My Lifetime pumps with more raw practicality, bumping with ominous synths, scratches and sweet '70s samples…Jay-Z telescopes, zooming in on the grainy details of his hustler's world."

Upon completion and release in the fall of 1997, Jay-Z's second album would debut at # 3 on the Billboard Top 200 Album Chart, and quickly go platinum, based in part on its two hit singles, "The City Is Mine", and "Sunshine", featuring Babyface and Foxy Brown. At the time, Babyface commented of the collaboration that it was a mutual artistic respect that drew the two performers together, "I think anything you do with music is terribly creative if you don't practice using a certain formula. Jay-Z is a nice guy and we probably won't hang out or anything like that, but I like what he does musically and he respects me, so we went into the studio and knocked a song out. It was a little hard hooking up at first, because of our schedules, but when we finally did get together, the results were cool." As 1997 wound to a close, Jay-Z was ranked the #141 Singles Artist of the Year by *Billboard Magazine*.

In the winter of 1997 and early spring of 1998, Jay-Z took an opening slot on P. Diddy's "No Way Out" arena tour, which lasted until Jay felt he had to jump ship to pursue more lucrative opportunities, explaining that "to support my Vol. 1, I went on tour with Puff and Bad Boy. I swallowed my pride and opened for him, but by the middle of the tour I felt like I was taking too much of a loss. I went to Puff and told him I respected what he was doing, but I had to leave."

Back in New York, Jay focused on finishing shooting on Roc-A-Fella Films' first release, the straight-to-video Streets is Watching (named after the single from Jay's sophomore album), which Jay-Z and co. shot entirely on his home turf of Marcy Projects, and starring the latest Team-ROC artist roster, including DJ Clue, R&B group Christion, and future rap start Memphis Bleek. Jay recalled the process of making "Streets is Watching" as a dream come true for Jay and Damon Dash, who had a particularly keen interest in film direction, recalling that "Streets Is Watching I'd put up against any rapper's best song. We did a short straight-to-video hood movie, to go with it, and that was the beginning of the Roc's dream to make movies."

Vh1.com, in its review of the "Streets Is Watching" DVD, remarked that "realism pervades within the framework of this music video, or 'videomentary,' about street life…(offering) a realistic view of his neighborhood without the commercial flash of over-the-top rap displays." *Vibe Magazine* proclaimed that "in his Streets is Watching home video, Jay-Z single-handedly revives the movie musical from West Side Story, Oklahoma!, Singin' in the Rain, and a bunch of musty Elvis movies. He does all this on top of flows as curvaceous as Lisa Nicle Carson, lyrics as hard as the J and Z subway tracks that wind through his old 'hood, and with an eye for detail that makes The Starr Report read like a vague summary".

The film helped reinforce the fact that Jay-Z was the real deal, still a soldier on the front lines of a hood as cold as they came in New York, or anywhere else in America's inner cities for that matter. This was an important strategic move for Roc-A-Fella among hard core hip-hop heads as Jay's obvious cross-over charisma began to take root in hip-hop, and beyond as 1998 dawned.

During early 1998, rumors also began to swirl throughout hip-hop about a supposed professional-turned-personal relationship going on between Jay-Z and Foxy Brown, which Brown has confirmed, but Jay denies. Turning into a mini-soap opera by the time it was over, Foxy's side of the story tells of a love-at-first-sight relationship that began when back in 1995 when "Jay used to come around, and every time we saw each other, we caught each other's eye...I had an insecurity about being dark-skinned...And Jay would always say that I was beautiful. He was like, 'I heard you could rap?' I told him to turn around, and I freestyled. He liked what he heard and was like, 'We're gonna be the Bonnie and Clyde of this rap game.' And I'm just like OK.'"

"He picked me up every day after school...Look...We would go to the studio. That was at the time we were doing 'Ain't No Nigga.' At first no one would play that track, but Jay had paper back then, so he took it up to Hot 97. Flex initially said no, but then he broke the record....I had already signed to Def Jam and I told them that whatever happens, Jay has to be involved with it—videos, performances, whatever...it had to be written in the contract that Jay's involved. I'm working on Ill NA NA, and now Jay's starting to book shows. But the promoters wouldn't book him without me. So Jay's like, 'You got to stop what you doing and go on tour with me.' I stopped recording my album and went on tour with him for nothing—meaning peanuts."

Jay reciprocated by ghost-writing five songs on Foxy's debut LP, and their collaboration continued when, according to Foxy, Jay asked her to appear in the video for the "Always Be My Sunshine" single, which featured guest spots by both Foxy and R&B star producer Babyface, "Babyface wouldn't do the video with him, because Jay-Z wasn't who he is now...Jay called me: 'Babyface not gonna do the video. I need you to fly to California.' I left Puffy's tour, missed the tour and flew to California, did the video for Jay and flew back. I felt like it was strictly about Bonnie and Clyde, and I would've done anything for him." After things went south between the pair, Foxy became engaged to Death Row Records rapper Kurupt. Jay, meanwhile, was preparing with his third album to take over.

For Foxy, the fact that her sophomore album, Chyna Doll, under-performed, in 1998, while Jay's Hard Knock Life LP had launched him into the cross-over stratosphere, did not sit well, explaining for her part that "when the Chyna Doll album didn't do so well and Jay was at five million (with Vol 2…. Hard Knock Life) and he didn't look back. I was at my lowest and not once did he say, 'Get on a remix,' or 'Let me get on a remix for you.' I used to do every Jay record for free—never charged him a day in my life. And here I was struggling to get my reputation back, and he had the hottest record of the summer—'Can I Get A….' and instead of going to that lil girl who was with him from day one, he went and got someone from no where (Jay-Z's own Roc artist Amil)…I think Jay felt like he created me, so maybe he could create another Foxy."

"But the industry made a mockery out of it. Jay-Z and Foxy are believable—original. Now you have Amil, and the record is blaz-ing, and I'm gasping for air…I realized (it was over) at Summer Jam. He'd asked me to come to perform 'Ain't No….' I got there and he performed it. But right when my verse was coming on, he cut it off. And I'm backstage. So he comes back, and I say, 'We gon' do the record?' And he was like 'Nah, I don't think I'm gonna do the record.' And I looked at him like, 'How could you not do that record? That record is the record that made you!' I left with a pit in my stomach. I went home and I prayed like, God, anyone but him. This guy is too smart to be loyal…(The final straws for me were) two things…(First), I took the loss on the Chyna Doll album."

"Then we were supposed to do the Bonnie and Clyde album together. So (Def Jam president) Kevin Liles was like, 'You and Jay need to get back together. It can't happen no other way. You guys are the epitome of the male\female thing.' 'Listen, you can't just go to Jay with a business proposition.' Because when it comes to Jay-Z and Foxy, it's Shawn and Inga. We just can't talk like nothing's happened. There's a lot of hurt there. I was hurt that he couldn't come back to say anything to try and help the situation we were going through. Jay-Z is his own man. He doesn't owe me anything. But if you're a nigga from the streets you are suppose to have loyalty…(So) I was at the studio to do the Sisqo 'Thong Song' remix, and Jay comes. He's like, 'I know I fucked up. How do you feel?' Then he said he felt like I wasn't doing everything I should have done, that I wasn't active. And I explained to him that I'm a female—we deal with emotions—and I'm going through a very hard time."

"I had to really break it down for him to understand it. And he's like, 'This is what we going to do. I'm not going to let you fall.' We sat there in my truck and talked all night. It was really emotional. Then we hugged. And I didn't hear from him after that…(Next) Kevin Liles calls me from Cali: 'Foxy before you see the video (Jay's "I Just Want to Love You") let me tell you Kim is in the video.' OK remember Jay's not my man, He's not my blood brother. But he was my Clyde."

"So Kevin says, 'I told him this not going to look good, this is her rival.' He was right, to me this was like…Remember when Pac was airing Jay out on every record? Imagine if you turned around and saw Pac in my video. That would never have happen when he was beefing with my boy. That right there was a direct slap in the face. Not only was she in the video, she was by his side, on his shoulder like, 'It's me and you now.'…I was in shock."

"I didn't want our friendship to end like that. He could've been in the video with MC Lyte, for all I cared…But my direct rivals, my direct rival who didn't make it a secret that she was my rival. Then Kim had a single (Notorious KIM remix). And she was destroying me on the record. Kim never was subliminal about it. She was straight out. She went after me. And Jay was co-signing it. So that's when I said no longer am I fucking with him…(After that, there was) no relationship."

Continuing, Foxy-clearly wounded—explained that the "last time I saw him out was at the Giorgio Armani party about a year ago. Everybody was whispering to him like, 'She's here!' And he walked over to me and said, 'What's up?' I just sat there and barely nodded my head. He looked at me like, 'It's like that?' And I looked at him, and I had nothing to say. And you know who was always right there, not even getting half the credit? Gavin and Anton (her brothers). I know they had to feel weird. Their little sister, attached to this whole other being who doesn't give a shit about her. But they were there at the sidelines, just waiting to catch me when I fall…My crutches were Jay. Those crutches are gone."

For his own part, Jay-Z makes the duo's relationship sound much more a professional than personal affair, explaining years later in 2003 that "I think she got her story mixed up. She wasn't signed to me. If she had to work with the Firm I had to fall back. I told her 'Do your thing baby; the hotter you get the hotter we get.' As far as having Kim in the video, how can I not mess with Kim? She comes from my dude (Biggie). I knew Kim back from the Lafayette Apartments. I knew Kim before I knew Foxy. I tried to still do tours with her, even when I had Amil—but they would be on the road fighting over catty shit. One time they got into a fight in a Virginia Hotel lobby. I had to make a choice. It looked like I was rolling with Foxy hard and it would make Amil feel terrible, so I had to go with my family…"

"(Foxy) is fucking amazing; her timing is great. I would love to have her on the team…(The most we ever had though was a) working relationship. I know at times people hinted at (a romantic relationship)...Even if she wasn't young, we just not there, you know what I mean? And I know people (are) gonna say that, especially if you get the kind of reputation I have. But it just never happened." In the end, Jay would make a business decision to make up with Foxy in 2004 for a farewell concert at Madison Square Garden, eventually signing her as an artist to Def Jam. Foxy commented at the time that "I can't leave him alone. We been in the game together for ten years strong and we gonna keep going!"

Back in 1998, Jay's career was on a fast track that took no shorts, and wasn't looking anywhere but up toward the sky, at the time, seeming like Jay and Roc-A-Fella Records' only ceiling.

"I don't how to sleep, I gotta eat, stay on my toes
Gotta a lot of beef so logically I prey on my foes
Hustlin still inside of me and as far as progress
You be hard pressed to find another rapper hot as me
I gave you prophecy on my first joint, and ya'll lamed out
Didn't really appreciate it till the second one came out
So I stretched the game out, X'ed your name out
Put Jigga on top, and drop albums non-stop for ya nigga"

—Jay-Z—"Hard Knock Life"

Chapter 8
Hard Knock Life

The Year Jay-Z Took Over the World 1999

As 1998 progressed, Jay-Z's star wasn't just on the rise, it was already part of hip-hop's most elite constellation. Though he had sold only 3 million records in 2 years, because of Roc-A-Fella Records' deal structure with Def Jam, Jay-Z and Damon Dash's were already multi-millionaires, with their company generating revenues in the $10 million range between 1996 and 1997.

Reinvesting much of their capital in new ventures, Roc-A-Fella Enterprises was formed, and plans were immediately hatched to branch out into a signature clothing line, a film company, and within the realm of record making, Roc-A-Fella was signing a new generation of stars that would blow up over the remainder of the 1990s—including Memphis Bleek, Beanie Seagal, and Freeway among others.

Throughout the summer of 1998, Jay kept in the limelight by appearing on the Jermaine Dupri hit "Money Ain't A Thing", among others. Above and ahead of all else, Jay and Dame's secret weapon was Jay-Z himself, whose newly completed 3rd album in 3 years—Vol. II—Hard Knock Life, would cement Jay and Dame's status respectively as moguls, and make their label a powerhouse as Bad Boy and No Limit's stars both began to fade. Death Row was already no more. A void had to be filled, and Roc-A-Fella was there to take over the reigns.

Jay's third album was released September 29, 1998, and driven by the lead single, "Hard Knock Life", set aptly in the context of the rapper's rags-to-riches saga to the instrumental theme the Broadway show and movie Annie, the album quickly moved 3 million copies by December of that year. Recalling his creative mood during the making of the album, markedly improved from that of his prior album—recorded amid Biggie's passing, Jay explained that "I was in a zone when I did that album, completely focused, completely creative."

Jay worked with the hottest producers in the game in his third album, matching fire with fire, wherein, according to producer Swizz Beatz—who produced 'If I Should Die', 'Money, Cash, Hoes', and 'Coming of Age'—the chemistry was explosive because "my sound was unorthodox and fresh—no samples. Everybody was sleeping on the track for 'Money, Cash, Hoes.' It was so different, making a beat out of sliding across a keyboard, but Jay's flow matched it. Working with him was serious business. He nails it every time."

DJ Premier, meanwhile, who collaborated with Jay on 'Intro— Hand It Down', recalled that Jay had reached for what was personally for him, a pinnacle, wherein "Jay was there through the whole process. I remember him going through the way he wanted Bleek to deliver it. At that time, Jay already wanted to retire. Bleek was going to be the one to hold it down for the Roc, since they didn't have a lot of other artists." Hard Knock Life...Vol II debuted at # 1 on the Billboard Top 200 Album Chart, staying in that position for 5 straight weeks, and atop the R&B Album Chart for 6 weeks. That winter, Jay's pop stock had risen in value so substantially that he jumped to #44 on Billboard Magazine's Singles Artist of the Year chart. The industry's most prestigious magazine also named Jay Top R&B Album Artist and Top R&B Album Artist—Male. Rolling Stone Magazine also named Jay-Z Best Hip Hop Artist of the Year.

In superstar terms, as an artist Jay had definitely arrived. By the time 1998 had concluded, Roc-A-Fella Records had netted $11 million after cost-of-business and splits with Def Jam/Island.

The spring of 1999 was in full bloom for Team ROC as Jay, in January, was nominated for 3 Grammy Awards, including Best Rap Album for Hard Knock Life Vol. II, Best Rap Solo Performance for the smash single Hard Knock Life, and Best Rap Performance by a Duo or Group for his collaboration with Jermaine Dupri on Money Ain't A Thang. To everyone's surprise, in February, Jay and co. chose to boycott the Grammys, a decision which the rapper rationalized as one in which "I am boycotting the Grammy Awards because too many major rap artists continue to be overlooked... Rappers deserve more attention from the Grammy committee and from the whole world."

"If it's got a gun, everybody knows about it, but if we go on a world tour, no one know...When I stayed home from the Grammy's (and won), the decision not to go wasn't even a question. Them telling the nominees in my rap category we were invited but Hweren't going to be televised-what's that? That's like inviting me over for dinner and asking me to eat in the basement." A Roc-A-Fella publicist elaborated further, explaining that "if they want to give us awards, we'll take them. But we aren't gonna drop everything and run to the show to get a small pat on the head when they don't even air the award he won."

As it turned out, Jay did win—for Best Rap Album—the most prestigious award in the hip-hop category. While he may have been turning his nose up at the elite, the move only worked to strengthen Jay's credibility with hard core hip-hop heads. In March, Jay's second single, "Can I Get A..." hit radio, and quickly soared to number one on the Billboard Top 100 Singles Chart by April of 1999. With a hypnotic beat that was years ahead of its time, the track became the party anthem of the year, featuring Roc-A-Fella R&B artist Amil, and Def Jam up and comer Ja Rule. The single went gold its first month out, and that same month, Hard Knock Life...Vol. II was certified 4 times platinum.

As Jay-Z continued his commercial take-over on the charts, Damon Dash was quietly hatching a plan to pull off what would become the history-making Hard Knock Life tour, featuring Jay-Z and DMX as headliners, set to begin in late April. The first truly hard-core hip-hop concert tour, the stakes were high for all parties involved to prove that not only the rappers headlining the tour, but also fans coming to the shows, could maintain a 'keep it real' atmosphere without involving violence. Promoters were skeptical, to say the least.

As Dash recalled during the planning of the tour, "I researched it, got the booking agency and put the whole thing together. Stakes were high." The 54-City tour would go on to sell out every date, grossing $18 million dollars, and charting as the # 10 most successful tour of the year in Pollstar Magazine. Reflecting on the success of the tour, its success proved truly rewarding for Jay personally, explaining for his part that "When we put together the Hard Knock Life Tour in 1998...we had to really take what we could get (in terms of cities...Still), with Ruff Ryders, I wanted to make history."

"First of all, we brought together artists like X, Red, Ja, Eve, Beans, Bleek, and the whole family. And then, after selling out 52 stadiums across America without one incident of violence, we knew we had reopened the possibility of stadium-sized, hardcore hip-hop tours…(On that tour), every day was tiring. Every day was like 'Groundhog Day,' if anybody's ever seen the movie—you know, every day the same thing over and over again. But once I touched the stage, it was like I was doing it the first night, because the energy was just incredible, and then for it to be sold out all over the place…It was a magical ride…You can never do that again. It's like trying to capture lightning in a bottle. I don't believe it's gonna be like that, but I definitely want to tour again…(Jay-Z and DMX), that combination right there is hot. I like it; it works because we're just so different from each other, but we look at a lot of things the same. But you know, when you've got a chemistry like that, you just don't want to burn it out. You want it to be a special thing."

Showing a layered sense of civility on the tour, Jay-Z, Dame and DMX made the joint decision to donate one night's worth of concert proceeds to the families of the Columbine victims when the tour traveled through Denver, CO. Coming from violence-plagued inner cities, all three men had a uniquely personal appreciation for the tragedies gun violence brought to any community, and in making the donation, were arguably seeking—on some level—to point out that such tragedy isn't unique to the African American inner city, but possible in its affects in any American community.

Publicly, Jay-Z explained the decision more simply as a natural and instinctive act of humanity in which "we decided to donate the proceeds from this show as soon as we saw the date on the schedule." Dash took the tour's wider success as an opportunity to maximize Jay and Roc's exposure by documenting the wildly successful tour in what became the second release for Roc-A-Fella Films, Back Stage. In addition to his fledgling film company, which would take off the next year as the millennium dawned, Dash also was planting the seeds for what would become Roc-A-Fella Enterprises most valuable and profitable asset in the coming years with a signature clothing company.

Following in the footsteps of Sean 'P. Diddy' Combs' wildly successful Sean Jean line, Dash founded Roc-A-Wear, explaining that in founding the company, "I came in with the same concept I had when I did my joint venture. I'm not licensing to you. I want to own half of the company...I may not know how to manufacture and design clothing but I have a brand that I can bring to it." For Roc-A-Wear's partner, New York-based clothing manufacturer Comet, the partnership was a no-brainer, such that they agreed to Dash's requirement that he and Jay put up no initial investment capital on their end, though they retained a 50/50 split on all profits the line generated after production and marketing costs.

As the company's premier model for their male clothing line, co-owner Jay-Z explained that "when you're a kid, you want to wear the clothes all the other kids are wearing. Then you get a little money, you want to show off. So you buy a nice piece of jewelry. I guess needing to show off never fades, because you aren't used to having shit. I guess the style I have now has a lot to do with what's going on out there in the streets. I'll always be in style, casual and neat."

As the summer wore on, Jay and Dame also began introducing a new roster of rappers who would become stars in the millennium, using the Hard Knock Life tour to premier Beanie Sigel, Memphis Bleek, DJ Clue, and Amil among others. Regarding his own status as hip-hop's leading superstar, Jay explained that he was over it personally, as it was never his desire in getting in the game to start with, such that "this whole thing, me reaching the zenith of my fame on my third album, it seems backward to other people, but this is how it's always been...People are looking for the sensational, and I'm just not that nigga..."

"Who doesn't want to be loved? I understand women (and like that attention)...I know they're smarter than me, that's why I can't write for them...plus, I think it's my lips or something...maybe they think I'm gonna eat their coochie, In '99 that's be my thing, I'll just hit broads off....But mostly, I think they're attracted to The Life. If they don't want to be apart of it, they're at least curious." Elaborating further, Jay sought to broaden the credit deserved for hip-hop's expansion as a truly competitive industry genre, in the same time revealing his savvy as an executive in commenting that "Will Smith, (for example), did a great thing for hip-hop...he brought light onto it, exposed people to it who normally wouldn't be listening."

"Some people are gonna love and stick with Will. Some people are gonna say, 'I want to little more edge to my music.' The more educated people are, the more they're gonna look for the cream of the crop...Me and Will make different music. He's a very creative person. I think mine has more edge and is more reality-based than his...People could say that about 'Hard Knock.'...(That its a Puffy-like instrumental.) Puffy could probably use that, but I can't see Puffy rappin' over 'If I Should Die,' or 'Can I Get A...' Nah. No beats that I've ever heard him rap to was similar to 'Can I Get A...' or the Too Short record or the Bleek record or 'Paper Chase.' I can't see him rappin' to none of those tracks."

Still, Jay was making plenty of cross-over appearances, although none were extraordinary to the transition hip-hop was naturally making during this period in its evolution into the most lucrative, and therein, mainstream medium in pop terms. In addition to the hit singles from his own album, which additional to the platinum-selling 'Hard Knock Life' and 'Can I Get A...', also included 'Jigga What, Jigga Who' and 'Money, Cash Hoes', appeared on 'Gangsta Shit' with Roc-A-Fella artist DJ Clue, Timbaland's 'Lobster and Scrimp', and Foxy Brown's 'Bonnie and Clyde Pt. II.' He also contributed to the Martin Lawrence hit-movie soundtrack for Blue Streak on 'Girl's Best Friend.'

Perhaps Jay's most successful collaboration—outside of his own album singles—that year was on 'Heartbreaker', a duet with Mariah Carey, which went on to become a smash that fall, in a move Jay saw as appropriate given that "hip-hop has crossed over...Parents started coming home and their sons and daughters had big posters on the wall of tall black guys with do-rags, and they wanted to know what was going on." Jay's collaboration with Mariah Carey—who suburban America adored—would later splash the rapper all over that demographic and forever change his status as a hip-hop/pop icon, rivaled in popularity only by Eminem in the years to come.

Jay's cross-over with Mariah would hit # 1 on the Billboard Hot 100 and the Billboard Hot 100 Singles Sales chart for 2 weeks apiece respectively, as well as the Billboard R&B/Hip Hop Singles & Tracks chart for 2 weeks, the Billboard R&B/Hip Hop Singles and Tracks chart for 2 weeks, and the Billboard Maxi-Singles Sales chart for 8 weeks. Heading into the fall, the industry accolades continued, as Jay was named Lyricist of the Year—Solo at the Source Magazine Hip Hop Music Awards.

That September, as the Hard Knock Life tour concluded, Jay attended the MTV Video Music Awards, where won the Best Rap Video award for 'Can I Get A...', as well as the coveted Viewer's Choice award for the same song. He rounded out the month by topping the Billboard Rap Singles Chart with his 5th hit single from Hard Knock Life, 'Jigga My Nigga', for 2 weeks. While Damon Dash had his hands full managing Jay's wildly successful career, the rapper himself played an equally as hands-on role in decisions concerning both his own career, as well as those of his label's artists, explaining that "(being a record executive is) a demanding a job."

"People imagine every day is shrimp, lobster, and champagne—but I'm in marketing meetings, we're arguin' constantly, I'm fighting to get records played, videos played, get vinyl in. It's not easy.

Not to knock anyone who works at UPS…(My goal is) to create a comfortable position for me and everybody around me. Like we doin' with Roc-A-Fella. 'Cause, like blacks, when we come up, we don't normally inherit businesses. That's a common thing for us to have old money, like three or four generations, inheriting our parents' businesses. That's what we working on right now. A legacy." Dame and Jay were definitely on the same page with that goal, and in a short time, it was a destination they would arrive at, premature to any expectations the industry had had in mind.

In October in 1999, Jay—amid the recording what would become his fourth album—was also working hard, from the corporate side of the table, prepping debut releases from Roc-A-Fella artists Memphis Bleek and Beanie Segil, both Philadelphia natives, along with Freeway. Jay was proud of the latter emcees because he and Dame had personally discovered, signed, and developed the trio, giving them invaluable experience and exposure as part of the Hard Knock Life tour, featuring all three rappers on countless high-profile album slots, and tutoring each rapper on the value of thinking beyond the first generation of their respective careers as emcees in terms of life after rap.

Elaborating on the latter, Jay-Z explained that "I always wanted Memphis Bleek to be the star of the label. That's why Vol. 2…Hard Knock Life begins with him. Bleek went gold, and that's great for any artist. But I think my presence at the label has been a gift and a curse. There's no way to explain why the public connects with certain artists. But, I know that at another label, Beanie Sigel and Bleek would be bigger stars than they are now…Mark my words, Beanie's gonna be one of the great ones. He's gonna be mentioned in the same vein as Biggie, Pac me, and Nas; he's on that level."

Not surprisingly, Jay was grooming both Memphis Bleek and Beanie to not just become superstar emcees, but also to follow the Roc-formula of becoming moguls in their own rights. Cultivating and encouraging a team atmosphere where everybody cheered the other on, Jay and Damon Dash flooded the market with Roc-A-Fella releases as 1999 came to a close and 2000 began. For Memphis Bleek, whose debut LP was 1999's Coming Of Age—which made a Top 10 debut at # 7 on the Billboard Top 200 Album Chart upon debut in August of that year, he had a sophomore album already in the can, 2000's The Understanding.

In defining his own motivation to be an entrepreneurial-minded emcee in the tradition of the ROC, Bleek credited "the Hard Knock Life tour (with making) me want to get my own business…The main thing I picked up from traveling was owning something. I feel that Jay put me on not to be beneath him, but to do as he did and be successful doing it. This (career as a rapper) is just a step-up stool. He put me in the game, and now it's my job to help other people get in the game and get my own label and do my own tours…Being that me and Jay came from the same projects, he was the 'Big Willie' dude of the projects. I was the small fry. So we can't talk about the same thing, 'cause I don't know what he's done, you know what I'm saying? I only know what I've done. So I talk about the streets…and speak for the unspoken…I want to be the reason for someone else's success…And I want to explore my own creative capabilities."

"You need different music to find out if you can rap that way, rap this way. If you keep getting the same kind of beats from the same producers, you're just going to be one regular MC…I give the credit to Jay and Beanie…They're two talented artists who are getting a lot of respect. I wanted to be up there with them. I couldn't just be the 'all right' guy of the clique. I had no choice but to step it up." Both of Memphis Bleek's albums would go Gold. For his part, Beanie Sigel's debut LP, The Truth—featuring guest appearances by Jay-Z, Eve and Scarface among others, was recorded throughout 1999, and scheduled for release in the first quarter of 2000.

Beanie described his debut LP as "a real album, not a compilation, no skits or nothing between the songs to help sell the album. Ain't nothing funny, just straight hot tracks…Besides the Roc family, Jay, Bleek, and Amil representing, I only did a joint with Scarface, and I got Eve doing a hook. No compilation here, it's all Beanie Sigel." In differentiating himself artistically from his mentor, Beanie continued, explaining that "Jay-Z is responsible for (influencing other MCs) to change their styles and talk about jewelry and shit…but that's not me…I'm Beans. I'm doing me. I mean, I got jewelry and Bentley's, but I don't talk about it in my rhymes. That's just something I got."

"Some people need to talk about that stuff, but I got my own flavor. I don't really talk about me, like what I got or what my life-style is now. I talk about how I was and what made me where I am right now. It ain't about where you at, it's about how you got there-that's what counts. What happens in between the start and the finish is what the people wanna know, so that's what I talk about…You know how it's you and your right-hand man?" he responds. "I'm what you would want your right-hand man-to-be. All the way around the board, that's me," says the lyricist, who has blessed many mixtapes and other rappers' albums and created a name for himself during his short stint in da game…I always knew I could rhyme…But I was just playing with it most of the time—'til now, until it was like I was gonna be signed and had to make an album. That's when I started takin' it seriously."

Rolling Stone Magazine's review of The Truth raved that "Beanie Sigel may be a Jay-Z protégé, but as he proved on his powerful, plain-spoken 1999 debut, The Truth, he's no B-team megastar stepchild. On such tracks as The Truth's 'What Your Life Like,' the Philly MC showed the grim consequences of the criminal life, a rarity in the increasingly conscience-free world of mainstream hip-hop." Sigel's debut album would go Gold by the end of the 2000, adding more revenue to Roc-A-Fella Records' rapidly swelling coffers, and specifically those of Jay-Z.

Amid his new found wealth, Jay was taking no shorts—from the corporate suits at Def Jam to the hustlers on the streets, specifically the bootleggers, Jay's newest sworn enemy. As the rapper reasoned, "its really up to the fans. We work hard to put out quality products for people who love the music and the videos. If every Jay-Z fan decides not to buy bootleg videos and tapes—not just mine, but every artist's—these bootleggers will have fewer people to sell these inferior products to." Despite the civil appeal of his press statement, Jay-Z was quietly PISSED about the amount of money he stood to lose—and in some cases had already lost—at the hands of New York's considerable illegal bootlegging trade. The latter made no mention of the coupling of Napster's new file-sharing boon at the end of the 1990s, and the revenues it was robbing artists genre-wide of potential and owed royalties.

The tensions underlying this issue boiled over on December 2, 1999, when Jay-Z displayed to the world just how serious about his money he was. The occasion was a routine social outing for any rapper, a release party at the Kit Kat Club on West 43rd Street in Manhattan, for Q-Tip's (of A Tribe Called Quest) new solo album, *Amplified*. After performing earlier that evening at an event in promotion of his own forthcoming fourth album, Jay-Z showed up around at the club, and was informed by several fellow party-goers that rival, Lance 'Un' Rivera was present. Jay calmly approached Rivera—rumored to be behind a wide-spread bootlegging operation of Jay-Z's releases in an effort to undermine his competitor (a charge Rivera has denied to date)—and according to reports, in front of several hundred witnesses, motioned at first as if to say hello, instead plunging a knife into Rivera's stomach, whispering into his ear, 'You broke my heart.'

In the aftermath, according to MTV.com News, "Jay-Z turned himself in to police (that) Thursday evening as authorities sought the rapper for questioning after a stabbing at a New York nightclub. However, Jay-Z (maintained) he had nothing to do with the attack...During a party celebrating the release of Q-Tip's new album at Manhattan's Kit Kat Club Wednesday night, music industry executive Lance Rivera (better known as 'Un') was stabbed once in the abdomen and once in the shoulder just before midnight and was taken to New York's St. Vincent Hospital. He was released in stable condition under a doctor's supervision early Thursday afternoon..."

"Jay-Z (real name Shawn Carter) turned himself in to authorities at Manhattan's Midtown South precinct Thursday night after police named the rapper as one of the many people they wanted to question about the stabbing...Def Jam Records stated that 'Jay-Z absolutely denies any allegations that he was involved in the incident.'...The incident took place onstage in the V.I.P. area of the club, and authorities say no weapon has been recovered. A spokesperson for Q-Tip told MTV News that the former A Tribe Called Quest rapper was being interviewed in the balcony during the fracas and was unaware of what transpired."

"Party guests Puff Daddy, Lil' Kim, and Lil' Cease had left the club 20 minutes before the incident. Earlier Wednesday evening, prior to the Q-Tip party, Jay-Z himself held a music industry listening party at New York's Irving Plaza for his upcoming album 'Vol. 3...Life And Times Of S. Carter' which doesn't come out until December 28. Jay-Z was joined by Roc-A-Fella cohorts such as Beanie Seigel, Amil, and Memphis Bleek at the party and performed several tracks from the record. 'Life And Times' has made its way to bootleggers and street vendors, and it has been alleged that the dispute at the Kit Kat Club was over the rampant bootlegging of the album."

"Just before Jay-Z hit the stage at Irving Plaza, manager Damon Dash even went as far as to declare to the crowd over a microphone, 'Fuck the bootleggers!'...On December 3, Rapper Jay-Z (was) arrested and formally charged with felony assault in the second degree for allegedly stabbing a record executive at a New York City nightclub on Wednesday night...Jay-Z (had) voluntarily turned himself to authorities at the Midtown South Precinct in Manhattan last night, and was subsequently arrested and taken to Central Booking for processing and arraignment..."

"The rapper's attorney, Harvey Slovis—who also represents Sean 'Puffy' Combs—told MTV News on Friday morning that Jay-Z was released at approximately 2:15 a.m. ET on $50,000 bail. A court date has been set for January 31 for the case. Despite the arraignment, Slovis maintained to MTV News that his client was innocent of the charges. 'To think that this guy, who is as gentle as can be, has anything to do with this is crazy,' Slovis said...As the rapper was being held by police, Jay-Z's legal team addressed the press gathered outside of Midtown South and reiterated its stand that Jay had nothing to do with the stabbing."

"At that time, Slovis also stated that the rapper had not been evading the police on Thursday, as other media outlets had speculated. 'We Came in', Slovis said, 'we're cooperating with police. (Jay-Z) didn't do anything, and I'm sure this will all be resolved shortly.'... (Sadly, Jay's attorney was wrong, and on January 31st,) Jay-Z's trip to Manhattan Criminal Court on Monday ended in bad news for the rapper, as a Grand Jury indicted the performer on two counts of attempted assault stemming from the alleged stabbing of hip-hop impresario Lance 'Un' Rivera."

Commenting on the incident in hindsight, Jay admitted that "a fight got out of hand...It had nothing to do with bootlegging... There's alot of stories being told wrong. I can't correct every story. Me and Un, we talk—we're not cool, but we're not mad...I don't want to talk about the knives...One time, I heard Russell Simmons say 'I don't even want to see a gun. I don't want no friends with guns.' I was like 'He's crazy!' But now I feel the same way. What's wrong with me...I'm a mirror...If you cool with me, and we talking socially, I'm cool with you. But if you threaten me or attack me, I have no choice but to go back at you..."

"Where I grew up, I seen a lot of people get wronged…No matter how much you believe in the truth, that's always in the back of your mind…(so I took the guilty plea…The Un situation) was the dumbest thing I ever did…That was the turning point for me…It was like, O.K., this can all go away fast. You work hard for years, and it can all go away in a night. Slow down, big boy. Think…I think that was a wake-up call and a calling card for me that that—to let me know, like, it could just all go down the drain. Like, it can all be taken away from you…I felt I was untouchable, but that let me see that it could all go away in an instant, it made me more careful."

Jay eventually settled the case with Rivera out of court for between $500,000 and $1,000,000, according to the Associated Press. As 1999 wound down, outside of Jay's arrest, December proved to be the Season of Jolly for Team ROC, as Jay-Z was named by Billboard Magazine as # 26 Singles Artist of the Year, steadily climbing toward the number one slot that he would top in years the years to come. That same month, Jay released his 4th album in 3 years, "Volume III…The Life & Times of Shawn Carter" on Dec. 28th, which shipped platinum, and sold 3 million copies in just two months. As expected, the album debuted at # 1 on the Billboard Top 200 Album Chart, moving 426,000 copies its first week.

In explaining the reasoning behind his proficiency in delivering so many new albums to fans, Jay explained the motivation behind his fourth album (besides the obvious dollars he was clocking) as one in which "in hip-hop, we have 'the haters'. You know, when people say 'haters', that's a very, very big term. But last year, after my success, so many people were really, really genuinely happy for me, I didn't experience the hatin' and all that, so I really want to give it back to the. That's why I'm doing so many songs, to make sure I pick the best ones…I'm not trying to make 'Thriller'. I'm not trying to make 'Beat It.' I'm not trying to moonwalk. I might get a bubble, but that's about it. No monkeys, nothing. I'm just…as far as the songs, it was nine songs. Nine hot songs, you know what I'm saying. Nine singles."

Timbaland recalled working with Jay on his fourth LP, particularly on the production of what would become the album's signature hit, Big Pimpin', as an collaboration where "when I did Big Pimpin', I knew it would get Jay in a place where he would be accepted in a lot of different ways. You have to give him a beat that's going to challenge him, something that will make him think about it for a little bit. He's up for anything."

In addition to writing hits for his own albums, Jay had quietly been writing for other top industry stars, including the lyrics to Dr. Dre's comeback smash, 'Still Dre', the lead single off The Chronic 2001. Before the millennium had dawned, Jay would collect the Billboard Music Award for Rap Artist of the Year, and top the Magazine's Year-End chart as the Top Hot Rap Artist. Jay's lead single off his fourth album, Big Pimpin', would become his biggest hit to date, and the title couldn't have been more apt in characterizing Jay's position as hip-hop's greatest living legend going into the millennium.

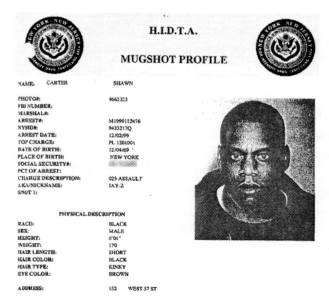

CRIMINAL COURT OF THE CITY OF NEW YORK
COUNTY OF NEW YORK

THE PEOPLE OF THE STATE OF NEW YORK

-against-

1. Shawn Carter (M 29)

                      Defendant.

FELONY

ADA CONROY

STATE OF NEW YORK)
) ss.:
COUNTY OF NEW YORK)

Page 1 of 2

DET. Brian Senft, shield #160 of the MTS, being duly sworn, deposes and says as follows:

On December 2, 1999, at about 0030 hours at 124 W. 43 STREET - KIT KAT CLUB in the County and State of New York, the defendant committed the offenses of:

1. PL 120.10(1)   Assault 1st Degree
2. PL 120.10(2)   Assault 1st Degree
3. PL 120.05(2)   Assault 2nd Degree
                (defendant #1: 02 counts)

in that the defendant, with intent to cause serious physical injury to another person, caused such injury to another person by means of a dangerous instrument; the defendant, with intent to disfigure another person seriously and permanently, caused such injury to another person; and the defendant, with intent to cause physical injury to another person, caused such injury to another person by means of a dangerous instrument.

The offenses were committed under the following circumstances:

Deponent states that he is informed by Lance Rivera, of an address known to the District Attorney's Office, (i) that informant observed defendant slash informant in the stomach and stab informant more then once in the back with a knife; and (ii) that informant was taken to a hospital for medical attention.

Deponent further states that he is informed by an individual known to the District Attorney's Office, that on 11/26/99, at the above

CRIMINAL COURT OF THE CITY OF NEW YORK
COUNTY OF NEW YORK

THE PEOPLE OF THE STATE OF NEW YORK

-against-

1. Shawn Carter (M 29)

                        Defendant.

FELONY

ADA CONROY
    (212) 335-3743

STATE OF NEW YORK }
                  } ss.:
COUNTY OF NEW YORK}

location, informant observed defendant hit informant in the head with
a bottle, causing informant to sustain a gash to informant's head
which required treatment at a hospital.

Deponent further states that he is informed by Marcus Delgado, of
an address known to the District Attorney's Office, that on 4/12/98,
at the Carbon Club in N.Y. County, informant Delgado observed
defendant hit informant in the head with a bottle, causing informant
Delgado to sustain a gash to informant's head which required treatment
at a hospital including staples to the head.

False statements made herein are punishable as a class A misdemeanor pursuant to section 210.45 of the penal law.

Sworn to before me on _____, 1999.

Cmplnt: 991203000823

Date and Time:

Part III

The Blueprint—
Dame and Jay Take Over Hip
Hop in the Millennium

"I'ma break bread
so you can be livin it up? Shit I….
parts with nothin, y'all be frontin
Me give my heart to a woman?
Not for nothin, never happen
I'll be forever mackin
Heart cold as assassins, I got no passion
I got no patience
And I hate waitin…
Hoe get yo' ass in
And let's RI-I-I-I-IDE…
We doin…big pimpin, we spendin G's
We doin…big pimpin up in N.Y.C."

—Big Pimpin'—Jay-Z

Chapter 9

Vol. III—The Life and Times of Shawn Carter

Making of a Dynasty—2000

The millennium…The sails of our times blowing into the 21st century were full with both expectation and anticipation…would clocks work once the countdown to New Years was over? Would illegal file swapping bankrupt the record industry? Some even theorized that a Terminator-esque Judgment Day would befall the world, and in the context of the domination Jay-Z would reign down upon all competitors in his iconic weight class—and there were few—as well as all up-and-comers, he did.

Jay settled all family business on January 1, 2000, and started out the Millennium holding all his own strings. His album sat atop the charts, his legend sat atop all existing understanding among musicologists, because it had not been witnessed in any of hip-hop's years prior. Jay-Z reset his own bar as he continued to climb wildly higher than even he or partner Damon Dash had ever dreamed possible.

In explaining how he kept interested in topping his own records— both in terms of sales and accomplishments, Jay boiled it down to a matter of having "something to talk about. People want to hear the struggle, the story. They want to hear something they can relate to. Back in the day, of course, the audience for hip-hop was young black dudes, and they wanted to hear something that they can relate to. They could go home, and they're standing in front of the mirror, and they're singing, and it's close to their own story. So that's what hip-hop was built on, right there; you've got to have a story."

"You know, I have a struggle right now: my struggle to maintain my own identity in the midst of all this…Somebody told me the other day that no matter where you are, there you are. You put me in a big car, you put a couple of chains on me, and you put me in a room with Mariah, I'm still the same person. If you took a person who wasn't that dude and you put him in there and you just dress him up, it's going to show. You know, with me it's solid, no cracks. I'm not falling apart…I don't believe that (a backlash against my success will) happen, because what I make is true. It's a real struggle. These are real situations that people can relate to. So even above and beyond it being good music, there's something else there, some substance. You know, not to take anything away from Puff, but that's how it is."

In commenting on the latter, Jay was drawing a chief distinction between himself and all predecessors who had begun as emcees and become entrepreneurs (or the reverse)—with P. Diddy and Master P as just a couple examples—who outgrew their moment in time with overexposure. Jay's secret to avoiding the latter pitfall—for one—was the fact that he was an artist first, which implied that his fan base wasn't a second-generation by-product of another rapper's coattails, as P. Diddy's had been with Biggie.

By continuing to rap, Jay was keeping a social contract of sorts with his fans, as he continued to hold down Brooklyn and the East Coast in the absence and spirit of Biggie, reasoning that "first and foremost, I'm an artist. I like to be creative. I like to make music and I like to get the reaction from people after they have heard the music. This (promotional appearances and interviews) is not something that I want to do. I want to make music. I want people to get into my music. I want people to relate to my story, and I like it when people find things that I hide in my songs…"

"I have this one song that people could really understand. It's called 'Come And Get Me.' I was driving around one day, leaving the projects, and everybody was like, 'Yo, you know, be careful, blah blah blah.' This is a place where I grew up, I've been going through this place since I was a kid. What makes you think that because I sold five million records that you could do something to me? That song was really true. I started thinking of the verses right there in the car, right after the conversation. I was a little frustrated about the whole thing…"

"It's not as bad as I think it could be; a lot of people still view me as a regular dude. I still pretty much move around the same way I've been moving around. But people, they change around you. I guess it's because they expect you to change, or they don't know what to expect from you. You know, I was just in an elevator with some girls coming up here, and they were like, 'Look at Jay in the elevator!' Like I wasn't even there! So they come at you, you know.

However they imagine you to be, they come at you that way, and then they're like, 'Oh, he's acting funny,' or He's changed.'"

Secondly, because Jay had such a personal financial stake in his own success as an owner in Roc-A-Fella Records, he was incentivized beyond the average emcee given the payout he saw at the end of each tax year to keep releasing records. Moreover, by continuing to act as his label's sure-thing, he could take even greater chances on pushing new acts toward the level of success and status he'd already achieved, and was in a comfortable enough place in his own legacy that the pressure wasn't as great on Jay where his own sales were concerned.

In elaborating on his plan with album number 5, which was already in the works for 2000 even as Jay was still promoting album number four, the rapper explained that he and Dame were in the midst of building hip-hop's first true dynasty, "y'all take my words too lightly. That's the problem. I keep telling y'all that: Don't take my words lightly. I'm dead serious, man. I know what I'm doing here. I got an agenda…(My next album is) a Jay-Z album."

"The family, they're on a lot of tracks, and they're dominating the tracks, and they're showcasing their talent. But that was my whole plan. We got plenty of time to do that when we retire. I'm here to work. I have so many different ideas and I want to go on and challenge myself musically. I can't stop. I'm almost obsessed with this music. I had alot to talk about, also. I had all these things on my mind and no outlet for 'em, and I don't write lyrics (down); they just come to me. I can't just hold it for another year, just holding 16 songs in my mind. Anything can happen. I trip and hit my head, its over. Its all gone."

"(On this coming album), I talked about my life within the year, all the things that happened. All the things that happened to me and the way people reacted to me, just off a hearsay and off assumption. I talked all about that: the way people reacted, the way the press did…(I keep getting bigger and bigger, so) before I get annoyed, I really think about where it's coming from. A lot of the time, people see you, they see you every day, and they have a certain type of love for you, and they don't know how to profess that love. So they come at you in different kinds of ways. I take the extra second and I think about it: 'Where is this coming from? Why is this person coming at me like that?'"

"The more success that you have, you've got to have a lot of patience. A lot of people are looking at you, and a lot of people want to deal with you on a one-to-one, but you're only one person. There's not enough hours in a day for me to deal with everybody the same way I would love to…I didn't know a thing about the music business five years ago; I didn't care, sort of like how (Memphis) Bleek is now. He's the young guy coming into the game; he don't really know all the politics. He's not concerned, he don't care. He just raps. That's all he knows. 'I pulled the rap, and y'all supposed to pay me', and that's it. That's all he knows: rap, pay me. He don't know about the politics, (like) if you offend this person at radio, the ramifications; or you defend this person at MTV, the ramifications…"

"It's really good (between me and my artists), because I (can) share my experiences and the things that I know—the things that I had to learn on my own—I (can) share with them. Its really good for me. Its another outlet; its another way to show them how to make music and how to make songs from your heart and your soul and not just make it for whatever other reason. I'm ready for them to just take it over; that's what I'm preparing for. That's what The Dynasty is about."

As the spring of 2000 unfolded, while Jay was already discussing his fifth album in interviews to promote his just-released fourth album, *Volume III…The Life and Times of Shawn Carter* was already on its way to double-platinum certification—a status it reached in February of 2000. In the meanwhile, Jay tided himself over with a nomination for Favorite Rap/Hip Hop Artist by the American Music Awards. In February, Volume II…*Hard Knock Life* was certified 5 times platinum, and the critical acclaim continued.

A review by the *Daily* pointed out correctly that "few hip-hop artists can balance staying true to the streets and go platinum at the same time; Jay-Z happens to be one of them. His latest chapter, Vol. 3…Life and Times of S. Carter, closely walks that fine line, but never disrupts the equilibrium…He maintains his rhymability and smooth narrative flow. Jigga also satisfies both his street and suburb audiences. Jay-Z sells records, not his soul."

NME.com, meanwhile, proclaimed that Jay's fourth album "inevitably…will triumph at the global musical box office…(Jay) treats the listener…(to) a series of uptempo party tunes much leavened by threats to the masculinity of competitors, as Carter uses his pen to cast himself as 'Dope Man' (in which he's on trial for selling albums), hustler, pimp and teacher. An intelligent man, with a gifted turn of slang, Jay-Z spits venom one minute and cools out the next. But he always has the jealous, the weak, and those who have crossed him in his sights."

Rolling Stone Magazine concluded that "this is his strongest album to date, with music that's filled with catchy hooks, rump-shaking beats and lyrics fueled by Jay's hustler's vigilance…Jay has become a better architect of songs."

As the spring bloomed outward, Vol. III…The Life and Times of Shawn Carter passed the 2 million mark, and in April, Jay won an Online Hip Hop Award for Album of the Year. Big Pimpin', featuring UKG was also burning up the airwaves as summer approached. To keep himself visible throughout the summer, Jay contributed the track 'Hey Papi' to the Nutty Professor II: The Klumps soundtrack, and dropped in on Busta Rhymes new LP Anarchy on the track 'Why We Die.' Big Pimpin' cracked the Top

40 of the Billboard Top 100 Singles Chart in July of 2000, and became one of the summer's top party anthems.

As the summer of 2000 rolled on, Jay and Dame released their second Roc-A-Fella Films release, Backstage, which documented the 1999 Hard Knock Life Tour, the first under their distribution deal with Dimension Films. The company's venture into a clothing line and filmmaking cast a new media spotlight on Roc-A-Fella co-CEO Damon Dash, the brains behind much of Roc-A-Fella's corporate success thus far.

USA Today commented positively that the film "moves at a fast clip and is surprisingly slick", while *The San Francisco Chronicle*, in its review of the film, pointed to Dash as "among the film's more charismatic characters...(Dash,) the CEO of Roc-a-fella Records, (is) a micromanager who tears into an employee in one scene for not including the name Roc-a-fella on the tour jackets. When criticized for being a prep school graduate, an accusation tantamount to being called suburban, Dash counters that he put himself through prep school, worked hard and is proud of it."

Meanwhile, Pop Matters.com's review of the film called "the documentary's look approximates a raw and honest insider's view of life on the road, powered by handheld video footage, fast-cuts, and commotion in the frames...(Roc-A-Fella C.E.O. and film co-producer Damon) Dash resembles one of those movie mafia dons who get manicures while planning their insidious business. Looked... from that angle...Dash is transformed...from behind the scenes wheeler-dealer to movie star...The film addresses racism in the business by underlining the tour's lack of "incidents." This stands as proof to the rest of the planet that it's possible to mount an expensive, large-venue hip-hop show...(One Roc-A-Fella rapper points out that) at white rock shows, mosh-pits are 'normal' and 'bloody,' but if a similar violence were to happen at a hip-hop show, 'they'd shut it down.'"

"The point is well taken and far too familiar to anyone who pays attention to such things, and it's sad testament to current media culture that it has to be made at all...The most insistent note struck by Backstage—in interviews and performances—is that everyone is glad to be there. They have flashes of homesickness and boredom, silliness and tension, but according to the film, these were more than made up for by the sense of camaraderie, mutual respect, and the genuine thrill they all developed during their months on the tour."

Roc-A-Fella's hometown paper, *The New York Times*, concluded that *Backstage* "takes a close look at the music Jay-Z and his friends created onstage, as well as their adventures—both positive and negative—as they take one of rap's biggest shows on the road... (Backstage) Casts a keen, observant eye on (the rap) world."

Roc-A-Fella Films second release would go onto perform respectably at the Box Office, while the company's clothing line, which featured adult men and women's—as well as shorties' lines, was BLOWING UP, grossing $8 million in 1999, and had grossed a reported $150 million by the time 2001 had arrived. For Jay's part, he explained that "Roc-A-Wear is really keeping us busy. We grossed maybe $80 million in 18 months, so it's obvious that we're doing something right."

Elaborating on the philosophy behind the brand Jay and Dame were quickly developing into a household name, the rapper explained that "when I do something, I want to do it well. I know there's alot of people out there that are going to support it and pick it up. Whatever they buy from Roc-A-Fella, Roc-A-Wear, Roc-A-Fella Films, whatever—when they pick it up, that is serious. They're gonna expect good product."

Damon Dash had also begun generating his own tabloid press for his budding relationship with R&B star Aaliyah, attending the MTV Music Awards together in September. Reflecting later in hindsight on their relationship as it bloomed, Damon Dash recalled that though "we weren't engaged, like she was real busy and I was real busy, so it's like anytime we were separated she'd be like 'We should slow down and spend some time with just each other, we'll probably end up getting married', so it was like we would speak on it but it wasn't anything real official. We were just very in love with each other."

As the fall of 2000 rolled around, Jay's fourth album was certified triple platinum, and the video for Big Pimpin' was nominated for Best Rap Video at the MTV Video Music Awards. At the same time, Jay was hard at work on his fifth album, the aspiration of which he described as "The Dynasty: Roc La Familia was a way for me to open things up for my family, for people like Bleek, who is one of those MCs who will never lose his hunger or his heart; I'm proud of him."

"Beans is our diamond in the rough, truly one of the great ones… I'm just sitting back and letting Bleek and Bennie Siegel take over…For me, it would give me more ambition. I'm seeing the way they're working. Beanie Sigel, he's worked on The Dynasty; he's got another album completed, in the can, with his guys from Philly; and he shot a movie, all in three months. All it's doing is making 'em step up to the plate. They're seeing how far they've got to go. You can shy away from it, you can run away from it, or you could just zip up your jacket, buckle up, and get ready. That's what they're doing right now…"

"People want to see some type of struggle," Jay-Z will say later. "Nobody cares about people who wake up to money their pops left them, someone who's just gonna wild out and blow it all. They want to see a person come from nothing and work his way up so they can be like, 'Yeah, he deserved that.'…They're stepping up to the plate and starting to work hard…(When I talk about Dynasty), I'm not the TV show. Like the Ming Dynasty. The real dynasty, like the Chicago Bulls, San Francisco 49ers, you know what I'm saying? Like a dynasty, not like a television show. Not like Blake Carrington."

Regarding his ability to produce massive material output, Jay-Z explained that his fifth album-like all of his efforts—were never a matter of quantity over quality, reasoning that fans shouldn't "let the speed fool you. We put out albums in seven months, eight months, whatever—we're definitely puttin our heart and soul into it. This album right here is so strong and so powerful, I might have to put out 10 singles for y'all." Commenting on Jay's artistic genius, producer Pharrell of the Neptunes, who produced 'I Just Wanna Love U (Give It 2 Me)' described their collaboration as one in which "I called him one night, and I sung him the hook over the phone. He didn't even hear the beat, and he was like, 'I'll be over there.' He's like Rain Man when he's working. He just stands there and mumbles to himself. Next thing you know, he's going into the booth and laying down 16 bars.

Jay-Z's a chess player. You can tell the guys who play chess, because they know how they're gonna move four moves away from now." Meanwhile, producer Just Blaze, who produced four cuts off the album, including 'Intro', 'Streets is Talking', 'Stick 2 the Script', and 'The R.O.C.', explained that "the Dynasty, from a production standpoint, was almost a demo for The Blueprint. You could see us gravitating toward what The Blueprint would eventually be."

On October 31, 2000, Jay released the much-hyped *Dynasty: Roc la Familia*, which debuted at No. 1 on both the Billboard Top 200 Album Chart and the R&B/Hip Hop Album Chart, and was certified gold in its first week of release. NME.com's review of the album acknowledged that, by this point in his career, "you can't knock Jay-Z's hustle…(as) far as being consistently good and prolific…Now on his fifth album, Jigga gives you more of the same: a bi-coastal production effort aimed to satisfy all the different markets, complete with a plethora of collaborations and Jigga doing what he does best, namely talking about his own riches, the drug game and past hustles. Of course, what allows Jigga to keep getting away with this, where others fail, is that he is a supreme writer, hence his verses are always engaging…Jay-Z is at the top of his game, and while he, perhaps, has yet to push his talents as a songwriter to its full potential to produce his opus, his albums continue to be tight and shift millions of copies. Now how many rappers can claim that after five albums?"

Amusingly enough, a review in the *Yale Daily News*—reflective of the broadness of Jay-Z's fan appeal—proclaims that "thankfully, there's much more than hustler rap on '*The Dynasty: Roc La Familia 2000.*' Jay dwells on serious themes such as the experience of growing up without a father, which helps explain his self-proclaimed paternal role in the Roc-A-Fella Familia, described as a somewhat Yale-relevant 'secret society / all we ask is trust.'" *Rolling Stone Magazine* concluded that "in the pantheon of street-cultural gods, the hustler is the bejeweled strategist, a ghetto politician who moves with the money and mommies—the cat who can hang with the thugs, high rollers, Los Angeles Bloods and Brooklyn gods with equal grace. And Jay-Z is his pop personification."

"Outside of Iceberg Slim, no one has offered a more detailed portrait of the hustler as a young man. Over the last four albums of his reign, Jay-Z has offered crime-born insights edged with a razor awareness of not only the dangers and angles of the streets but also the consequences of his actions—on himself, his family and his community. For every glamorous 'Big Pimpin,' there is a document of his fear and loathing like 'Streets Is Watching.' In return for his crimes, he gave us a window into the process of his evolution from hustler to pop phenom—all the while keeping count of his progress in diamonds, cars and bottles of Cristal."

"In his latest offering, the strangely titled The *Dynasty Roc La Familia (2000—),* Jay settles into a more natural role: that of the hustler-teacher. Sensing correctly that bling fatigue has set in, Jay steps away from the flash and floss of Volume 1, 2 and 3 and focuses on more weighty subject matter. La Familia is not without its pimping and posturing ('Get Your Mind Right Mami,' 'Parking Lot Pimpin'), but it is much more about family. On track after track, Jay confronts the new, unfamiliar demands of being a father figure with the same determined egoism and intelligence that he used while hustling in the streets of Brooklyn. There are unanswered questions and unresolved emotions. And throughout, Jay returns to a core theme."

"In an offhand moment, Jay calls to the father he hardly knew: "But I ain't mad at you, Dad/Holla at your lad.'…The production is as reflective as his lyrics: pulled back, less frenetic and more full-bodied than on his previous album…La Familia is closer, in many ways, to his seminal 1996 debut album, Reasonable Doubt…Dynasty is Jay-Z working back toward his roots musically, all the while creating a solid foundation for the next generation…Jay's tendency to associate with Southern and West Coast cats reveals not only his market savvy but also his recognition of where the current heat in hip-hop resides…"

"As he continues to develop, Jay's turn to family-building adds another dimension to an already intriguing figure. The hustler now seeks to become the father he never had. He articulates new struggles with love, and defines his next levels of success in familial rather than financial terms. Perhaps this change in emphasis by hip-hop's most credible voice suggests a new reorientation in the culture's priorities as well. We can only hope." In November of that year, Jay-Z won Artist of the Year: Hip Hop/Rhythmic at the Radio Music Awards, and hit # 1 for the second time on the Billboard R&B/Hip Singles & Tracks Chart with 'I Just Wanna Love U (Give It To Me)', which stayed at the top of the chart for 3 weeks.

At the end of November, Jay-Z's fifth album, released just a month earlier, was certified double platinum, topping 2 million copies sold. In December of 2000, Jay-Z was ranked by Billboard

Magazine as the # 29 Singles Artist of the Year. As Jay and Dame prepared to conclude the first year of the Millennium, they were sitting atop a hip-hop kingdom, with a view both back down upon all they had accomplished in 5 short years, as well as ahead to all they still planned to accomplish in the year to come.

2001 would take Jay-Z and Damon Dash from "Rich" status to that of "Wealthy", and Jay-Z would release his most popular and influential album since Reasonable Doubt among both fans and critics. In laying out the Blueprint for how to create the Dynasty he had with partner Dash, Roc-A-Fella Enterprises' various businesses would be booming as loud as the woofers bumping their records all around a ROC-crazy nation.

*Above: Jay-Z and Beyoncé
perform together*

*Right: Jay-Z and Beyoncé attend an
awards show*

Above: Jay-Z backstage at Sprite Liquid Mix Tour w[ith] members of the Island Rec[ord]ing artist Hoobastank (photo by Walik Goshorn)

Left: Jay-Z and P Diddy (photo by Walik Goshorn)

"Excuse me, What's your name?" Jay-Z on the set of the "Excuse Me Miss" video shoot (photo by Olu)

"I don't land at the airport, I call the clearport"
(photo by Olu)

Jay-Z pictured here with Cam'ron and AJ and Free from 106th and Park, presents Quinton Little with a check for a college scholarship worth $50,000.

Jay-Z greets a fan onstage at the Sprite Liquid Mix Tour (photo by Walik Goshorn)

*Above: Memphis Bleek,
Jay-Z and Lil' Mo
(photo by Walik Goshorn)*

*Right: Jay-Z with Faith
Evans
(photo by Walik Goshorn)*

106

Jigga gets his exercise on   (photo by Walik Goshorn)

Jay-Z gives a lucky fan an autograph
(photo by Walik Goshorn)

Jay-Z and Naomi Campbell on the set of Jay's "Change
Clothes" video   (photo by Walik Goshorn)

Chris Rock, Jay-Z, and Al Sharpton
(photo by Walik Goshorn)

Jay-Z at his 40/40 club
(photo by Walik Goshorn)

Above: Jay-Z and Russell
Simmons
(photo by Walik Goshorn)

Right: Jay-Z in the booth
on the set of the "La La
La (Excuse Me Miss
Again)" video shoot
(photo by Olu)

"I do this for my culture,
To let 'em know what a nigga look like...
when a nigga in a roaster,
Show 'em how to move in a room full 'o vultures,
Industry shady it need to be taken over,
Label owners hate me I'm raisin' the status quo up,
I'm overchargin' niggaz for what they did to the Cold Crush,

Pay us like you owe us,
for all the years that you hoe'd us,
We can talk, but money talks so talk mo' bucks..."
"H-to-the-I-Z-Z-O"

—Jay-Z, 2001

Chapter 10
The Blueprint—2001

To write a blueprint, you must first be an architect—and by 2001, Jay-Z and Damon Dash had become just that, rewriting and designing the rules for the rap game that they now ruled with an iron grip. With perhaps Dr. Dre's Aftermath Entertainment as their only real competition—and this time, that rivalry was good natured (as Jay-Z had ghost-written Dre's comeback hit)—ROC was truly hip-hop's heavy-weight champion.

Unifying all the title belts—those of record sales, fashion, film and collective earnings—Roc-A-Fella Enterprises was undeniably making the greatest overall impact on the industry. Roc-A-Wear, since its launch in 1999, had grossed around $150 million in just over 2 years by the end of 2001, and Damon Dash's expansion into film-making was paying off with a new feature in the works under a distribution pact with Lion's Gate Films—State Property, starring Roc-A-Fella rapper Beanie Sigel, as well as featuring cameos by Dash and Jay-Z, due in September, 2001.

As MTV.com news reported, "after bringing the highs and lows of cross-country touring to the big screen with last year's documentary 'Backstage,' Roc-A-Fella Films is set for a second round of Hollywood swinging. The movie company headed by Roc-A-Fella Records co-CEO Damon Dash hopes to release 'Paid in Full' based on the lives of infamous '80s Harlem drug kingpins Rich Porter, Alberto 'Alpo' Martinez and AZ by early fall. 'The movie is about something I personally saw from a distance... These guys were real ghetto celebs. As I look at what's going on today, I don't think some people understand how influential Harlem was in the '80s. How it's still influential.' Many current rappers can be heard referencing Porter, Alpo and AZ on their records, including Shyne, who often refers to himself as 'Shyne-Po.' Filmed on location in Harlem and Toronto, the movie, which stars Mekhi Phifer, Wood Harris and rapper Cam'ron, started production late last summer and is on its last three days of re-shoots...In addition, Roc-A-Fella is gearing up to start production on the Lion's Gate drama 'The Criminals,' which stars Beanie Sigel and will feature his Dynasty family members Jay-Z and Memphis Bleek."

"Beans also appears a movie titled 'Get Down or Lay Down,' which is scheduled to come out this year. Dash has a film in development with Universal pictures called 'Paper Soldiers.'" Incidentally, Beanie's third Roc-A-Fella Records release—State Property, due in the first quarter of 2002, bore the same title as his first starring film role. In the meanwhile, Beanie had wrapped his second album, The Reason, which Roc-A-Fella was preparing to drop in June of 2001.

For Jay-Z as an artist, the year began like any other, with another # 1 hit on the Billboard R&B/Hip Hop Singles Chart for "I Just

Wanna Love U (Give It To Me)" in January. In February, the accolade and acclaim continued when Jay was nominated for and WON 2 Grammy Awards for Best Rap Performance by a Duo or Group for Big Pimpin', and Best Rap Album for Volume III… The Life and Times of Shawn Carter.

That same month, the aforementioned album was certified triple platinum, and Jay received another nomination for Best R&B/ Soul or Rap Album for The Dynasty: Roc La Familia 2000, as well as winning the Sammy Davis Jr. Entertainer Of The Year Award. Topping the latest round of awards off, in April, Jay was nominated for a Blockbuster Entertainment Award for Favorite Artist-Rap, and he scored yet another Top 40 Hit record with R. Kelly on 'Fiesta.'

Amid all his professional highlights, April of 2001 proved to be a trying one personally for Jay and his fellow East Coast rap community as the NYPD began staking it out on the presumption that art was imitating life, such that, as MTV.com News reported, "the New York City Police Department has a message for the city's hip-hop community: we're watching you…Based on what it claims is a 'culture of violence' in the hip-hop world, the police's gang intelligence unit has begun watching nightclubs frequented by celebrity musicians. Police are also compiling a dossier on rappers and others in the music industry with criminal histories."

"'It would be ignorant for us to ignore the fact that there have been violent incidents where the only common denominator is the music industry,' police spokesperson Sgt. Brian Burke said… April 20. 'In an effort to ensure the safety of individuals in the music industry as well as other additional victims, we've initiated this effort.' The effort…began this year, according to Burke…A police source said the 1997 murder of the Notorious B.I.G., in Los Angeles, and more recent incidents allegedly involving Shyne, Jay-Z, Lil' Kim and Lil' Cease led authorities to launch the campaign…Burke said the effort is meant to protect rappers from becoming victims of crime as much as it is intended to prevent what police see as music industry-related violence. 'We monitor clubs and nightlife to prevent future acts of violence and to prevent persons from the music industry from becoming targets or victims,' he said. 'It's not just hip-hop; it's the entire music industry.'"

"Murray Richman, the Bronx defense lawyer who has represented Jay-Z, DMX and Jamal 'Shyne' Barrow (commented) 'I think it is racial profiling at its worst…What they're saying is that they've designated a group who are performing a legitimate function in life—to wit, entertainers—as a group they're watching for criminal activities. It is absolutely fascistic in its nature and orientation. It is a violation of every constitutional right I can think of.'"

"Peter Frankel, a defense lawyer who has represented Ol' Dirty Bastard and other members of the Wu-Tang Clan, as well as members of the Fugees, Mobb Deep and Run-DMC, called the police initiative 'unbelievable…Since when are rappers organized crime? What they're saying is that even though there are a thousand different artists, all of whom perform rap music, they're pulling them all together and saying they're the same…What they're really thinking is all rappers are thugs and criminals and as a result they're going to start profiling them.'"

Sadly for Jay-Z, he would be an unwilling poster child for the NYPD's logic behind the surveillance program when, that same month, he was picked up in an arrest for gun possession when he didn't even have a gun on him. According to MTV.com, "three days before Jay-Z was due in court to face charges that he stabbed a record executive, the rapper and a man who's been identified in the past as his bodyguard were arrested early Friday morning when police allegedly found a loaded gun in the bodyguard's waistband…"

"Members of the New York City police department's street crime unit saw bodyguard Hamza Hewitt retrieve a gun from the front passenger seat of a car parked in front of Manhattan's Club Exit, according to police spokesperson Detective Carolyn Chew. Hewitt then entered the car, which drove off with Jay-Z and two other men inside. Police pulled it over moments after it left the club, Chew said...Police found a loaded Glock .40-caliber gun in Hewitt's waistband, and arrested Hewitt, Jay-Z, and the other two occupants of the car, Romero Chambers and Tyran Smith, according to Chew...Hewitt was arrested last November for allegedly carrying another .40-caliber gun—a Ruger—backstage at a radio concert in Boston that featured Jay-Z, the Boston Herald reported at the time, identifying Hewitt as a bodyguard for the rapper."

"Smith, a longtime friend of Jay-Z, is the co-founder of the hip-hop label Carter Faculty. Chambers' name and age, meanwhile, match that of the owner of R&K Limousines, a Brooklyn, New York, company that boasts on its Web site of driving rap celebrities. A company employee would not comment on whether its owner was the man arrested Friday morning...Jay-Z's lawyer, Robert Kalina, released a statement Friday afternoon saying, 'We believe that the evidence in this case will show Jay-Z to be not guilty. We expect a quick resolution...I would like to point out that numerous other celebrities have often used armed security guards.'....New York state law dictates that if police find a gun in a car, everyone in the car can be charged with possessing that gun. An exception to that rule, however, occurs when the gun is found on the body of an occupant; usually, in that case, only that person would be charged."

"It's unclear how officers' claims to have seen Hewitt remove the gun from the car would affect charges against the other passengers, but for now, all four men are charged with criminal possession of a weapon in the third degree...A person can also be charged with possessing a gun carried by someone else if prosecutors argue that they exercised 'dominion or control' over the person with the gun..."

"The same laws were at the heart of the recent trial of Sean 'P. Diddy' Combs...(Upon arraignment on Friday, April 13), Jay-Z declared himself '100 percent innocent' of gun possession charges Friday night as he was released on bail in a case that began 18 hours earlier, when police allegedly found a loaded gun in his bodyguard's waistband. A group of fans who had gathered outside the courthouse cheered and broke into a chant of 'not guilty, not guilty' as Jay-Z hurriedly made his way to a waiting Mercedes a few minutes before 10 p.m. 'That's my mother,' the rapper said before he left, pointing to a woman in the crowd. 'She can go anywhere that she wants and hold her head up because her son is 100 percent innocent.'"

"After Jay-Z's arraignment on a charge of criminal possession of a weapon in the third degree, Judge Laura Ward released him on $10,000 bail—less than the $30,000 demanded by the prosecutor...The judge was clearly not a hip-hop fan, however. She appeared baffled when Jay-Z's lawyer, Stacey Richman, declared him a 'musical genius' in asking for reduced bail. Richman then explained that her client, whose real name is Shawn Carter, is known by the name Jay-Z. 'I still don't know who he is,' Ward said...Richman went on to argue that the gun possession case against the rapper is 'very slim.'"

"Just before his arrest, Jay-Z was in the back of a car, behind a partition, and was unaware that his bodyguard had a gun in the front of the car, Richman claimed...The bodyguard, Hamza Hewitt, was also arraigned and released on gun possession charges, as were the other two people in the car, record executive Tyran Smith and limo company owner Romero Chambers...Hewitt's lawyer, Robert Kalina—who represents Jay-Z in other matters—said Hewitt is licensed to carry a firearm in Georgia. The judge told him, however, that it would still be illegal for Hewitt to have a gun in New York."

"Members of the New York City Police Department's street crime unit claim to have seen Hewitt retrieve a gun from a compartment in the front passenger door of a Chevy Suburban parked in front of Club Exit...Hewitt then allegedly placed the gun in his waistband and entered the car, which drove off with Jay-Z and two other men inside, according to police. Officers pulled the car over moments after it left the club, and they arrested all four men."

The trial for the gun possession charge was postponed till October 16th of 2001, and eventually dropped altogether. Still, looking back in hindsight on the incident, Jay-Z seems to feel that prejudice on the part of the NYPD against the hip-hop community definitely played a role in the arrest to begin with, explaining that "I'm seldom with a bodyguard. I like to go and come as I please. I go to games by myself all the time. But if I'm going to be in a party-like atmosphere, where there's a bunch of people? Yeah, definitely, 100 percent. Like Michael Jackson or Britney Spears would... I didn't have a gun. I was in a limousine with a partition. The partition was up. I don't know what's going on in the front. But I'm thinking, All right, he's going to straighten it out."

"I was joking around with the cop. I was laughing. Then the cop was like, 'Turn around, put your hands behind your back.' I wasn't laughing no more. They said they charged me because it was my car. Took my fingerprints and a picture. I understood it later. It was just for the media. The DA has a publicist who came down to the station house. That was all about imaging."

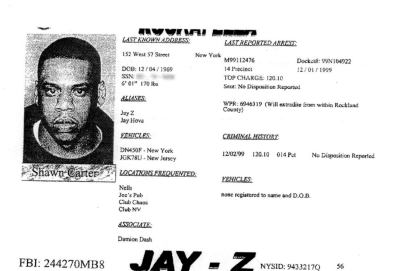

As the summer rolled around, things only got hotter for Jay and company, as the rapper's scored his umpteenth # 1 hit with 'Fiesta' on the Billboard R&B/Hip Hop Singles Chart, and won the BET Award for Best Male hip-hop Artist. Jay-Z protégé Beanie Sigel's sophomore album, The Reason, dropped in June, scoring a # 5 debut on the Billboard Top 200 Album Chart, quickly going Gold, and as a sample of the caliber product Roc-A-Fella was moving on the streets among fans, Segil's album again they had the best shit on the market. *Rolling Stone Magazine's* review of Segil's new album hailed it as "a relentless…breakdown of the G-Code…"

"The album's opener, 'Nothing Like It', where Sigel admits he fears the kind of world his son will inherit, has the humanity and the up-from-the-streets passion of his debut." Phillyhiphop.com, the hottest hip-hop site local to Beanie's native Philadelphia, for its part, concluded that "the Reason to be excited about Beanie's sophomore effort is the obvious strides that he's taken as an artist…It seems apparent that being surrounded by some of Hip Hop's biggest players has rubbed off on the South Side Assassin. Everything from the beats to the production to the comfort and command of Bean's delivery are light years ahead." Sigel seemed to agree with his critics' glowing assessments of his latest effort, commenting that "if The Truth was a classic, then I'm gonna have two classics on my hands. Pretty much. Cause on this album I really just gave 'em me…"

"On this album, that's what you get. Beanie Sigel. I took it back to what got me signed, what made people want to listen to me. From the mix tape stuff. The best of Beanie before The Truth, before the album. And I just gave 'em raw beats and rhymes, man. I didn't really try to go in any direction with the album. I just followed up The Truth. There's always a Reason behind The Truth. If you play The Truth, then play The Reason back to back, it's like one album just going all the way through…I just kept the rawness of my style on the first album…Rap is too happy right now."

"Besides the Roc, it's weak…The first album went gold—that's great for me…I would've love to come out and go double-platinum. But say you come out and just go platinum on your second album—that's failure to me. I got room for improvement…We got the titles right now…People want the belts. Step in the ring, we don't turn down no fights." In classic Roc-fashion, the Jay-Z protégé was also being groomed for his own empire, explaining that his entrepreneurial pursuits reflected an attitude wherein "I can't predict the future. As of right now, the present right now has Beanie Sigel, young entrepreneur, black man that made a 180-degree turn in my life as far as my lifestyle and how I was living and maintaining."

"Right now, I'm no longer indulged in the worldly things out there. I'm a businessman right now. I got a clothing line I'm working on called Versatile Clothing. I just opened a clothing store in Philly. I'm working on a restaurant right now that I'm opening up in Philly. My record label, we're getting the paperwork done with Roc-A-Fella called Criminal Records…I feel no pressure cause if I felt the pressure I wouldn't do what I do. It's like when before The Truth came out, I was hearing that I was supposedly the next 'this one' the next 'that one' and being compared to the illest rappers out there. To be compared to people like Nas, 2Pac, Biggie Smalls, that's crazy. And Jay even. There's really no pressure cause I'm gonna do me. I'll leave it up to the people to decide."

While Team ROC's lieutenants were in the field scoring strategic victories on the charts for Roc-A-Fella, their General was quietly back in the studio at work on what would become the masterpiece of his career—The Blueprint. As Jay explained, "I got 15 (tracks) now; I'm ready for them…I usually make an album a year. Since *Reasonable Doubt* in '96, if you listen to any one of my albums it's just the emotion and what I felt at the time. I had a lot going on at the time, so I had a lot to write about. Anything that (went) on in the past year is definitely gonna be included on this album."

"I went in the studio one day, I made seven songs. From there it just was spilling. Now we up to 15. I don't know, I might make 30…When you on top of the game, or on top of your game, everyone is frustrated, everyone wants to be in your position…It's ambition. That's what rap is built on. What (diss records do) to me, it makes the competitive spirit come out. Like, 'Yeah, lets do it.' It just gives me fire."

Superstar producer and Roc-A-Fella Records multi-platinum recording artist Kanye West, who produced many of the album's best tracks, including 'Take Over', 'Izzo (H.O.V.A.)', 'Heart of the City (Ain't No Love)', and 'Never Change', recalled that "(by working on that record), I'm part of history…Diamond D, Pete Rock, RZA, and Primo were doing [soul samples] since a long time ago. We just helped bring that style back. The beat CD I gave Jay for The Blueprint had 'Never Change'; [State Property's] 'Got Nowhere,' which would've had Sade singing on it; the joint that is now Alicia Keys's 'You Don't Know My Name'; and 'Heart of the City,' which R. Kelly initially sang on.

For 'Heart of the City,' Jay came up with what he wanted to say in his head, as usual. In the studio, the 'Fiesta (Remix)' video came on TV, and Jay walked into the booth, started recording, finished the entire song all the way to the outro, and came back in the studio. The video was still on. Those Blueprint records are all classics." *Rolling Stone Magazine's* review of the Blueprint in late August of 2001 best summed up Jay's mastery at performing and producing hits under pressure, such that, as Neil Strauss summarized the commercial result, "this is how the rap game works: when someone is pushed, they push back harder."

"That's why the more someone like Eminem is criticized, the more unapologetic and extreme his lyrics become. There's something about being persecuted, or at least believing oneself to be persecuted, that makes people embrace and reaffirm their own identity—witness Jay-Z's sixth album, The Blueprint. At the time of its recording,

Jay-Z was feeling less Rockefeller and more Michael Milken—nine songs on The Blueprint were reportedly cut in two days."

"Jay-Z was awaiting two criminal trials, one for gun possession, another for assault. In addition, he had become one of hip-hop's most dissed artists—with Nas, Prodigy of Mobb Deep, Jadakiss and others attacking him in song. Not unlike Tupac and his Makaveli persona, personal and legal problems have provoked Jay-Z to write what may be his most personal, straightforward album but also his most self-aggrandizing work. Though Jay-Z came on the scene like he'd stepped out of the pages of The Robb Report, obsessed with the make of his watch and the president in his billfold, he has almost outgrown his materialistic obsession."

"It's no longer enough to be the godfather he portrayed on Reasonable Doubt; he must now be God himself. Jay-Z makes earlier rap megalomaniacs pale in comparison as he identifies with Jehovah (nicknaming himself J-Hova, H.O.V.A. and, on this album's hits, Hovito and H-to-the-izzoh V-to-the-izzay). Elsewhere, he's the 'God MC,' 'the eighth wonder of the world,'…Half of The Blueprint becomes, then, a battle album, in which Hova, from on high, attacks Nas, Prodigy, and all manner of prosecutors and persecutors. For much of the rest, Jay-Z gets real…"

"In many ways, The Blueprint is a new-school old-school album, full of playground boasts, harmless battling and simple odes to the good life. Delving further into his roots, Jay-Z deepens his sound on The Blueprint. Here, Jay-Z and his producers (especially Kanye West) turn to vintage soul, fueling almost every song with a stirring vocal sample: Al Green, Bobby 'Blue' Bland, David Ruffin and the Jackson Five, for starters. In addition, instead of rallying the Roc-A-Fella family around his songs (as on his eleven-month-old Roc La Familia album), Jay-Z takes on most of the tracks single-handedly, without guest rappers. These tactics are…the album's strength…He's a sharp, detailed writer, a meticulous craftsman and an influential stylist—as well as lifestylist."

Released on September 11, America's most embattled day in modern history, Jay's sales figures proved how loyal they were to Jigga, and how restorative Jay's music truly was for fans who needed an escape in the wake of the horrid terror attack. Driven by the smash single 'Izzo (H.O.V.A.)', Jay-Z's sixth album was a bible on how to attain everything that he had in the past 6 years, and not surprisingly, its disciples were many as Jay scored his sixth number one album, moving 426,000 copies in its first week.

Retaining the top spot on Billboard's Top 200 Album Chart for 3 weeks, Jay also topped the MTV Top 20 Video Countdown that month with 'Izzy (H.O.V.A.)', and performed at the network's Video Music Awards, where his hit single 'I Just Wanna Love U (Give It To Me)' was also nominated for Best Rap Video. Perhaps Jay's biggest personal victory of the massive acclaim that *The Blueprint* was generating was the 5 Mic rating *The Source* finally gave him, a nod he'd been waiting 5 years for, and given the status of the magazine at the time within hard core hip-hop, it was a coveted and rare achievement for any street rap artist.

Elaborating on the design behind *The Blueprint*, Jay explained, "my plan was just to do one album in the beginning. But, I really started getting into a groove as far as recording. The more I do, the more I just want to do better albums. That's what I do. Every year since 1996, I've dropped an album...It would be fast for a lot of artists, but it's really on schedule for me...(This album is) definitely up there (as far as being one of my best), but I feel that all the time, so it ain't for me to say. It's for the people to say...I'm a person that believes everything that happens to you in life shapes you as a person. Every struggle, every challenge, everything that is placed in front of you is to see how much stronger a person you're gonna become. Any problem that you've had in your life, you look back (at problems) and remember saying 'I'm never ever gonna get over this. This is the worst thing ever. How am I gonna go on from here?' But you look back and they're all behind you..."

"In rap, everything moves so fast. You can be on top of your game and next year you're not. I just want to let them know I'm still right there. I'm right here on top...*The Blueprint* is two different things. It's the blueprint of my life, the things that made me the way I am, that shaped me—all my beliefs and ideas to date. There's also a blueprint for rappers in this business. The songs are like a person in that situation. How would they deal?...(All of my albums are) personal and had something to do with my life. That's the inspiration for my music...Growing up, my mom and pops played a lot of soul music. If I was gonna do—'*The Blueprint*'—it had to be (the right) music in the background. So I used a lot of soul samples, because that's what I grew up on. I used a lot of that to give it that feel from back then, so those emotions and all those thoughts can come up easier...It made me vibe; it brought back memories. I felt comfortable recording...The songs just started happenin', comin' out of nowhere...I was in a zone..."

"For me, *The Blueprint* takes up where *Reasonable Doubt* left off. In general, I'm a private person-years on the street taught me the importance of keeping secrets-but sons like 'Song Cry' and 'Blueprint (Momma Loves Me)' represent those times I really try to forget there's a mike in the room and can just be really honest. I feel like I can create a summer anthem in my sleep, but songs like those are a real challenge for me...It's really a weird thing to talk about. it's weird, but I wouldn't be honest if I told you anything else."

"On Sept. 11 when the (Blueprint) CD came out and it still moved like half a million units, I was like, 'Wow, that's huge.'... I'm conflicted through all this...I feel sorry for everybody (who died on 9/11). I got empathy, compassion, I'm really sick. Same time, this is still a land that's not really for my people, and I can't just forget that. I wanna say that during this so no one else forgets."

Quickly selling 2 million copies between September and early October, Jay entered the latter month professionally triumphant, and looking to put his criminal past behind him for good, pleading guilty to Misdemeanor Assault for stabbing Lance 'Un' Rivera almost two years earlier in December, 1999, and receiving 3 years probation. Though not required by the court, Jay also performed a public service by participating in The Concert for New York City, which raised money for various 9/11 charities, and both he and Damon Dash, personally and through Roc-A-Fella Records, made additional financial contributions to aid the victims of their hometown's worst tragedy in its 200+ year history.

Later in the month, Jay released his second single, 'Girls, Girls, Girls', which quickly became a Top 10 smash on both the Billboard Top 200 Singles Charts and MTV's Top 20 Video Chart.

As November dawned, amid the hype surrounding Jay's wildly successful 6th album, a beef was intensifying with Nas, who Jay had first called out the previous summer during the Hot 97 Summer Jam, and then in the course of a track off of *The Blueprint* called 'The Takeover', a response to Nas's diss of Jay's boy Beanie Sigel. In the rap, Jay boasted "No, you're not on my level get your brakes tweaked, I sold what ya whole album sold in my first week, You guys don't want it with Hov', Ask Nas, he don't want it with Hov', nooooo!, I know you missin all the—FAAAAAAAME! But along with celebrity comes bout seventy shots to your brain, Nigga; you a—LAAAAAAAME! Youse the fag model for Karl Kani/ Esco ads, Went from, Nasty Nas to Esco's trash, Had a spark when you started but now you're just garbage, Fell from top ten to not mentioned at all to your bodyguard's "Oochie Wally" verse better than yours, Matter fact you had the worst flow on the whole fuckin song, but I know—the sun don't shine, then son don't shine, That's why your—LAAAAAAAME!—career come to a end, There's only so long fake thugs can pretend, Nigga; you ain't live it you witnessed it from your folks pad, You scribbled in your note-pad and created your life, I showed you your first tec on tour with Large Professor, (Me, that's who!) Then I heard your album bout your tec on your dresser, So yeah I sampled your voice, you was usin it wrong, You made it a hot line, I made it a hot song, And you ain't get a corn nigga you was gettin fucked and I know who I paid God, Serchlite Publishing, Use your—BRAAAAAAAIN! You said you been in this ten, I've been in it five—smarten up Nas, Four albums in ten years nigga? I could divide, That's one every... let's say two...two of them shits was due, One was—NAHHH, the other was "Illmatic", That's a one hot album every ten year average, And that's so—LAAAAAAAME! Nigga switch up your flow, Your shit is garbage, but you try and kick knowledge?"

"(Get the fuck outta here) You niggaz gon' learn to respect the king, Don't be the next contestant on that Summer Jam screen, Because you know who (who) did you know what (what), with you know who (yeah) but just keep that between me and you."

Explaining his rationale for the beef, Jay explained that "for me it was like a sport. 'Takeover' was like a sport...I respected the dude lyrically. I feel like I'm on top of my game. I don't feel you can compare his career to my career, but that's just my opinion. It just pushes everybody to sharpen their skills. That's what rap is about. It's a competitive sport...Rappers don't really like each other, they never did. It's just so competitive. You have to be a really strong person and be secure about yourself not to feel envy. Rap is a competitive sport. That's how it was built ...When you add money to the equation, a lot of feelings come up. I've watched the game. Every person that was on top went through it. I don't know if they ever went through it to this degree...(The hatin') don't bother me. I accept the challenge. I think I can hold my own as far as challenging rappers...If these guys really had a problem with me— outside of me as a hot rapper—I'm sure they wouldn't put it on records. That wouldn't make sense to me. That's how I know it's just music. Once it comes out on a CD or a mixed tape for the whole world to hear it that you have a problem with this person, then I know there's nothing there..."

"Freestyles usually go away in two weeks...I didn't know it was gonna be the official battle of the beats, seven-hour marathon. It was an answer to disrespect. I didn't go in the studio to make a song. I made a two-minute freestyle…Nas is definitely going to bring out the best of me. He's gonna put me at the top of my game. I hope I do the same for him. It's like playing basketball with a guy. It's just verbal sparring—no one's fighting, it's just records."

On the defensive, Nas replied, "Big was the king of New York, and now Jay-Z wants that title, I don't want that title…Any nigga can shine. That's the last thing I'm worrying about. I shine without jewelry. If I'm gonna use this time, I'm gonna use it for something real."

Ironically, the attention Jay drew to Nas would reignite the latter rapper's extremely stalled career, a testament to Jay's stature at the time of the beef. Nas responded with 'Ether', off of a quickly assembled album called 'Stillmatic', to which Jay came back with perhaps the most vicious battle record since Tupac's 'Hit Em Up' 6 years earlier, rapping in one bar that he'd left 'condoms on your baby's momma's car seat.'

In the end, only a chiding from Jay's mother caused the rapper to apologize for taking the beef as far as he had, explaining that the beef made "(me) get angry, but at the end of the day, I'm not going to do nothing. It just pushes you to make better records. I got mad and went into the studio…(When he called me ugly), a guy's not supposed to judge another guy. So that didn't bother me. But there's an imaginary line in the sand, and most people cross it when they are off balance. You don't say things about another guy's genitalia…You can't say that to a man. It's like when you have nothing else to grab on to and you say, 'Fuck you! Your mother!' I take comfort from that."

"I dropped some heavy records, and he was a little off balance…(Boxing with him, I had) too much to lose. Especially in rap. People get knocked out, they lose that image. When you're listening to a record, 'I'm the illest!' I don't know, man, I just saw you get knocked out [laughs]. I hear what you're saying, but my eyes are seeing something different. I would have boxed him…(Had we, I would have won on) my will. My will alone. I'm too strong, man…(In the end, my) mom put in a call and said, 'That went too far.' And she's never, ever called me about music. So I was like 'Okay, okay, okay. I'll go shut it down'…I apologize. I felt like I didn't think about women's feelings or (Nas' former girlfriend's) feelings, or even my mom…I said some real mean things about Nas and his family and I felt I was a man about that by pulling the record publicly, although that wasn't 'gangster' thing to do…It was really like, 'Let me meet your level of disrespect with this level of disrespect.'"

On a more positive note, as the Thanksgiving Holiday approached, Jay, as reported by MTV.com news, announced that "for 10 days this month, Jay-Z will act as principal of different schools across the country, addressing students, holding open forums and tending to other daily duties…Jay-Z will also perform at intimate venues for contest winners in each city on what is certainly one of the more unique promotional outings ever…Dubbed the Principal for the Day Tour, the trek kicks off in Philadelphia on Wednesday and wraps up November 26 in San Francisco…"

"The schools will be determined by spirit contests hosted by radio stations in each of the cities, and announced the day Jay-Z arrives. DJs will also announce local retailers in each city that will hand out approximately 300 tickets to the rapper's performances." Jay explained that "I figured I was into the marketplace, so I'd just stop with the kids and share my stories. Maybe I could help them out…They go crazy. They're very excited. I walk through the school, I go to every classroom and meet the teachers. Then we do an assembly where I talk to the kids. I tell them my story about where I'm from and how I came to owning my own company."

Heading into December, most artists were preparing to shut down for a few weeks, to take a rest—especially those who'd just released a wildly successful album three months earlier. Not Jay-Z. Rather than slowing down, he was revving up for the release of...you guessed it, ANOTHER ALBUM! Number SEVEN, and while it was a live album, the pace was still staggering for the watching industry. Backed up by the Roots, *Rolling Stone Magazine*, in its review of the album, commented that "Jay-Z gives himself an unexpected artistic makeover on the loose *Unplugged*...Abandoning his usual sample-based production to mix it up with the fiery Roots rhythm section and a string quartet that provides more than just window dressing, he expands his familiar anthems with extemporaneous freestyle forays and smart instrumental interludes. If *The Blueprint* and previous studio recordings are carefully scripted affairs built on pop song forms, *Unplugged* celebrates the possibilities of off-the-cuff interplay: The Roots sound like they've been backing Jay-Z for years—they push him to new heights just by working that minimal, relentlessly funky backbeat, supplying sparky little counterlines in the margins. The rapper responds by syncopating and scatting, launching slightly rejiggered choruses...Everything clicks."

Jay's seventh album in 5 years was released late in the month, moving 143,000 copies in its first week on the Billboard Top 200 Album Chart, the top soundscan debut for any hip-hop live album in history. Roc-A-Fella Records, in addition to Jay's fourth quarter Christmas bonus, had signed rapper Cam'ron, who commented that "I bring a different essence (to Roc-A-Fella)...You got Philly (MCs), Brooklyn (MCs), they got some R&B, but they ain't got no Harlem flavor...It's time to blow (up)...I've been sitting around with two gold albums. It's time to hit that next level. My album's been done. That's why I signed to Roc-A-Fella; they hurried and bought my album from Sony."

"I'm doing some new songs, but if I didn't touch a song, it would still be hot." Jay-Z would end 2001 as Billboard's # 29 Singles Artist of the Year, and he showed no signs of slowing his rise to the top of that chart, as Jay also announced in December, 2001 that he would release his EIGHTH album in the first quarter of 2002, a collaboration with R. Kelly entitled 'Best of Both Worlds', which the R&B superstar described as "a duet album...We're trying to put it down in a different way and give people something...Me and Jay-Z are in the studio...together...We're, like, nine songs deep...We've been talking about it, bragging to each other. If I see him in New York or he's in Chicago, he'll come by the studio. We've been talking about it for such a long time, bragging about 'who's this in R&B' and 'who's this in hip-hop,' so we decided to put it together."

2002 would prove to be as successful a year for Jay-Z as 2001 had been, and Roc-A-Fella continued to dominate the industry, they would reach yet another new plateau, as the industry watched in awe, seeking to follow the Blueprint Team-ROC had laid into a second generation, and Jay-Z would give them that opportunity with The Blueprint II: The Gift & The Curse, a double-album, his ninth in 6 years.

"I'm now more focused than ever on my music. I love rap because you have to prove yourself every time out. It doesn't matter that my sixth album is a classic when the average rapper's career is 2.5 years or less. It's all about what's next, and that's what drives me after all this time. I love that people are still passionate about me, whether its love or not. Here I am, a guy from Marcy projects making people react to the music I create in my head...Most of the time, I walk around feeling real blessed. If God had shown me this life beforehand, complete with all the drama, I'd say-without pause-I'll take it."

—Jay-Z

Chapter 11
The Blueprint II—2002

Its one thing to catch lightning in a bottle, i.e. create a flawless album, which most agree Jay-Z had done in 2001 with his sixth, The Blueprint. To do it twice is a feat most would consider impossible, especially in the sense that most sequels are usually only half the classic of the original, and there is usually only a 50/50 chance that a sequel will perform as well as its predecessor.

Perhaps needing a new challenge, as 2002 began, Jay-Z had plans to not only release the first sequel in hip-hop history, but also only the sixth or seventh double album in rap's memory, following behind 2Pac with All Eyes On Me and Biggie Smalls' Life After Death among an elite few other hip-hop superstars with enough commercial moxy to pull off such a feat.

Certainly, Jay was the only other rap star who equaled Tupac's proficiency in terms of the sheer amount of material he had recorded and released over the course of his career. Jay-Z was also the only other living legend currently active in hip-hop, if critics were measuring in terms of icon status, album sales, cultural and commercial impact, and relevance.

Commenting on the latter question of his icon status, Jay felt "there was one person: Big. If I heard Who Shot Ya? in a club, I would leave and go make some music. That's not to take anything away from Eminem or Nas, I just don't look at them as that...I heard Jordan say, when Magic had AIDS, he felt like he was cheating him."

"'You leaving now? Yo, I need you. You're going to define my greatness.' It was selfish...I can't get into that argument...because the people at the top of the game are no longer here with us. Big and 'Pac didn't really get a chance to grow as artists. We never got to see where it woulda went. But I always felt that's what I was comin' to do, to be the best. I wasn't comin' in the game to be nothin' less."

Certainly, Jay had his contemporaries generationally speaking, such as Dr. Dre, Snoop Dogg, or Eminem, but none had maintained such a consistent track record, both in terms of output and longevity. Because Dre acted as a producer the majority of the time, and had only released 2 solo albums in 10 years, while Jay-Z had released 8 albums in 7 years, and because Snoop's album sales never came within striking distance, as well as due to the fact that Eminem was still so new to the game—although well on his way to attaining Jay's status in time—Jay-Z had already reached the pinnacle, and was now defining new heights for the industry's bar of what was success's ceiling.

For Jay-Z it appeared the sky was the only true limit, and since he was already a mega-star, perhaps he was sitting even above that boundary. He never sat around long enough to ponder the latter, and while Jay was a number of months off from his double-CD, *The Blueprint II's* November release date, he prepared to tide fans over with album number 8 since 1996, a collaboration with R. Kelly entitled "Best of Both Worlds."

Recalling the circumstances under which the collaboration was inspired, Jay-Z explained that "we had the 'Fiesta' remix and 'Guilty Until Proven Innocent.'…Hearing how those are, we would always talk back and forth: 'We should do a whole album together.' We're creative people—creative people create. Just the idea of having a whole album with myself and R. Kelly is such an amazing prospect…I can't really say when it started…We did 'Fiesta,' and 'Guilty Until Proven Innocent,' and it was like, 'Man, those records came out crazy, holmes.'"

"We threw the idea of doing an album together back and forth, and before I knew it (it happened)…(Our songs are) about just real-life situations…(since) we both came from the dirt…It started out back-and-forth because we wanted to know how serious it was…'Let's see what you can do with this one right here.' He'd send it back in one day. 'All right, send him two.' We got together at the end, the championship round, and put it together…(We hope this is) a trend for more unity for black people on a whole… You've got a cab company, I've got a cab company, we're fighting for the same money? Maybe we can join forces."

For Kelly's part, he explained that "It only takes but a few seconds to establish a relationship with somebody real. So they knew I was real with mine, and they were real with theirs, so we bonded right there. 'Cause we all come from the same 'hood, just not the same city, and we go through the same things, so we kind of felt each other…I've worked with Jay-Z in the past so I know him. I know a lot of these rap guys because in the industry you run into each other. But we didn't only run into each other, we had relationships and conversations…"

"(When we finally did hook up, we) were like mad scientists…You want to get together and mix potions…We're not afraid to talk about the things we go through in our music…We're gonna continue to do that…On the last four songs we plan to come together and do them…because the ideas we wanna put together, we have to be together to do them. Other than that, I do tracks in the studio and write the hook and do some lyrics and send it to him. He puts his thing down. Then he'll send it back and send me something…Tone from Trackmasters, him and [his partner] Poke have been like the referees, making sure we get the tracks back to each other. Tone flies to Chicago and goes back to New York. It's been working out."

Jay and Kelly's initial plans surrounding support for the forthcoming album, at least as they stood in early January of 2001, as Jay-Z explained them, called for a "Best of Both Worlds tour coming soon to a theater near you…We're gonna put the show together. Just one set, one long set. He's doing the songs people love him for. I'm doing songs from my album, and we're doing songs from the Best of Both Worlds album." Sadly, before a tour could get off the ground, and just prior to the album's March release, R. Kelly would be indicted on multiple counts of child pornography.

Meanwhile, as January came to a close, a Roc-A-Fella lieutenant, Beanie Sigel, launched his own record label, Criminal Records, distributed through his parent labels, Roc-A-Fella and Def Jam. Sigel, a mini-mogul in the making, explained the creative dichotomy of his artists as one in which they "(are) spitting fire…I believe their story. It ain't like I just met (fellow State Property member) Freeway. I heard him and was listening, like, 'Yo, Freeway spitting.' He was around for a year before he even signed. Go to his 'hood—what he's rapping about is real. Oschino, he just came home. He beat two murder raps. I don't know nobody that beat two murder raps. Sparks, he hangs out with the winos. That's why I got them, whether people think they hot or not. Once you be around them, you feel them."

In February, Jay-Z went through the usual round of yearly Grammy nominations, numbering three this time, including Best Rap Solo Performance for 'Izzo (H.O.V.A.)', Best Rap Performance by a Duo or Group for 'Change the Game' featuring Beanie Sigel and Memphis Bleek, and Best Rap Album for *The Blueprint*. Not Surprisingly, Jay-Z boycotted the 2002 Grammy Awards Show, explaining that "I didn't think they gave the rightful respect to hip-hop...It started that they didn't nominate DMX that year...DMX had an incredible album. He didn't get a nomination. I was like, 'Nah, that's crazy.'...I really wanna see how they do as far as televising the (hip-hop) awards."

In early March, Jay-Z won a Soul Train Award for R&B/Soul or Rap Album of the Year for *The Blueprint*, just as Jay-Z was making plans to issue his eighth album with R. Kelly, the highly anticipated 'Best of Both Worlds.' R. Kelly pronounced prior to the album's release that "R. Kelly—the expectations of what this album will be are so fucking high we'll probably never meet them...We started bragging, the best of R&B, the best of rap. Let's put it together and see what happens...I've had niggas come up to me talking about, 'That's seven million off the top.'"

Def Jam Records president Lyor Cohen chalked the excitement up to something resembling a fixed horse race where all bets on the record were a sure thing, "People are going fucking bananas for this shit!...This is like throwing a cow into the piranha-filled Amazon! This is full-fledged pandemonium!...Jay told me to fasten my seat belt and watch this shit go down!" *Vibe Magazine* echoed the latter predictions, proclaiming in a feature on the forthcoming release that "it's safe to say that (Best of Both Worlds)—produced by Kelly and Tone of Track Masters and featuring Lil' Kim, Beanie Sigel, Boo & Gotti—will be one of 2002's most sought-after albums."

So confident were the executives at Jay's Roc-A-Fella Records and Def Jam, and Kelly's label, Jive Records, that preceding the album's release, MTV.com news reported that "the streets still can't wait— the bootleg bandits have struck Jay-Z again. His tag team effort with R. Kelly, *The Best of Both Worlds*, isn't due until March 26, but already a version of the LP has been leaked…

In the past, Jay and Roc-A-Fella Records have gone to great lengths to counteract pirating, adding and subtracting songs at the 11th hour and even pushing up *The Blueprint's* release by two weeks when the album found its way onto the black market. However, Roc-A-Fella said it has no plans to push forward the release of *The Best of Both Worlds*… The bootleg includes such cuts as 'Take You Home With Me a.k.a. Body,' 'Get This Money' and 'Honey,' which also have all been released to radio and are scheduled to appear on the official LP… The rest of the bootlegged disc features 11 songs produced by Kelly, the Trackmasters and Megahertz, ranging from firsthand street narratives like 'It Ain't Personal' to boastful game spitting on 'Somebody's Girl.'"

Both camps knew trouble was brewing when one of their competitors on the bootleg circuit was R. Kelly's sex tape, newly discovered and released, which ultimately resulted in his arrest in the late spring and early summer of 2002 on various charges. The media hype surrounding the arrest ironically worked to fuel the sales of both the sex tape and the 'Best of Both Worlds' bootleg releases, but negatively affected the commercial release.

Unfortunately, as word of the tape broke fast across the nation's airwaves, news papers, and on-line gossip columns, it was immediately clear that the greater world was taking the contents of the tape a lot more seriously than R. Kelly would have preferred. Though Def Jam Records moved forward in releasing the long-awaited and much-hyped album on March 19 as scheduled, the impact of Kelly's breaking scandal was instantaneously evident in the record's poor first-week showing at retail, scanning a disappointing 230,000 copies (in light of the million-plus predictions of many industry insiders) and debuting at # 2 on the Billboard

Top 200 Album Chart, when Jay-Z, and for the most part, Kelly had never been denied the coveted # 1 slot for the majority of their respective releases prior.

Even though it did score the top slot on the Billboard Hot R&B/Hip Hop Album chart and eventually went Gold, then Platinum, the lackluster sales were considered a massive black mark for Jay personally on his overall A+ sales record. Worse yet, Def Jam cancelled all touring, video and print promotion for the album that had not already occurred, and Jay-Z began to rapidly distance himself from any potentially negative exposure or fall out within his own core fan base as Kelly's sex scandal began to captivate a gossip-hungry nation.

While the rapper tried to be publicly polite and supportive of Kelly's unfolding drama, he was careful not to be overly diplomatic in his pledge, telling MTV that "I wished him luck and said 'Take care of yourself.'" Privately, most believed Jay-Z was taking more aggressive and elaborate measures to insulate himself from Kelly's mess, including one example in which, according to *Time Magazine's* online website, "Jay-Z, through an intermediary, thanked the editor of Vibe magazine for removing him from current cover with (R.) Kelly."

The singer made matters worse when he attempted to cry conspiracy, claiming at first that the tape was a fake, commenting that "I'm not a professional in that area but I do know this: It's not me, and if it's gotten me to this point sitting in this chair talking to you about this, then it's obvious someone who is real good at doctoring or whatever did this. The world is getting ready to watch me sing…and you've got a tape out there trying to ruin my career… It's crap, and that's how we're going to treat it."

Kelly's attorney, John M. Touhy, reiterated this position, stating unequivocally that "any tape (the media) have is a fake." Sadly, the tape would turn out to be authentic enough to convince a judge to order Kelly to trial on the charges, which are still pending to date thanks to crafty legal maneuvering that has gotten over 2/3 of the total charges against the singer dismissed on technicalities. R. Kelly would go on recover commercially in 2003 with several solo releases, but the 'Best of Both Worlds' album became the sacrificial lamb at the time.

In hindsight, Jay-Z has reflected that his album with Kelly and its commercial failure marks his biggest disappointment to date in his extraordinarily glorious career, admitting that "I would say (it was). I had such high expectations for it. I made the album with somebody I think is the greatest writer of our time. And we didn't finish the story, with the videos and performing…People were talking about it before the album. Damn, why didn't nobody tell me? It seems like this was a known fact for a while, and people just started telling me a week before the album dropped. 'You didn't know?' Then it finally hit the news…I have no idea (how it will affect him in the long run professionally). It's going to be really tough…I don't want to speculate, man. I don't know what half of America is doing behind closed doors. When it's an entertainer, it's headline news. It ain't the first time it happened. Look at fucking Elvis, man. How old was Priscilla when he married her? Eleven?"

"People even ask me why I distanced myself from R. Kelly when the allegations about him came out. I spoke to Rob and told him to speak to the people 'cause the media was killing him and everything was looking one-sided. Am I supposed to answer all the questions they had for him? How do you fight for someone who won't fight for himself? I never said one bad thing about the dude, and I'll never judge him. I'm not God, a judge, or a jury. That's the last time I'm going to talk about it."

At the time, Jay's only recourse was to wish Kelly well and focus on distancing himself from the whole affair by focusing on the future, chalking the whole affair up to the fact that "we're entertainers, man…(My) new album coming out in November is (*The Blueprint II:*) The Gift and the Curse. We accept the good with the bad. It is what it is…He's cool, it's the gift and the curse."

Jay wasn't totally out of the wilderness of negative press yet, as in April of 2002, his former ghetto-mentor Jaz O released a new album. Though Jay made a guest appearance on one track, Jaz apparently felt he was owed more from his former protégé, commenting that "everything that I did for him as far as his career was concerned, I did all of those things to be an agreeable person... The feeling just wasn't reciprocated in the way that I understood it. I feel that there is a code to friendship, and I never thought that we would do things together in the business as business. I thought it was all personal, that we were on the same page. Obviously we weren't. I really found that out when I tried to get back in the game."

For Jay, he rebutted that "no success story comes without its drama. Jaz, whom I offered a deal for $150,000 when the Roc was a pebble, didn't see our vision and turned me down. Now he feels like I owe him something. This guy! I made the hook, found the sample, and wrote the lyrics to 'Ain't No Nigga,' then let Jaz arrange the song, gave him the production credit, and now he's screaming he made my first hit. Haaaaaa! Okay, homie, make your first hit now!"

Things were going much better for Jay-Z's company, Roc-A-Fella Enterprises, who, proving that the strategy of diversification works well as insulation and insurance against putting all your bets on one horse, i.e. the record label, Team-ROC was about to put the unfortunate press that had arisen out of the R. Kelly sex scandal behind them permanently with the onslaught of ROC-brand name product that was hitting the market throughout the summer.

Beginning with Roc-A-Fella Films, as MTV.com News reported that "after a healthy serving of hype and a side order of flop, Jay-Z and Dame Dash's Roc-A-Fella Films division is set to release a new full-length movie as well as move into production on another.... More than a year after its completion, 'Paid in Full' will finally hit theaters on September 6. The film, which stars Mekhi Phifer,

Wood Harris (currently starring in HBO's new crime drama 'The Wire'), and Roc-A-Fella's own Cam'ron, is based on the lives of legendary Harlem druglords Rich Porter, AZ and Alpo..."

"For many theatergoers, the big-screen version of 'Paid in Full' will be something of a rerun, as rampant bootlegging contributed to the delay of its original release...In the meantime, Roc-A-Fella Films released...'State Property' as well as wrapped production on its first comedy, 'Paper Soldiers'...According to Roc-A-Fella co-CEO Damon Dash, the company's next film project, tentatively titled 'Death of a Dynasty,' will be another comic effort—this time a parody of the hip-hop industry in general, and of Dash and his franchise player, Jay-Z, in particular."

On May 22, Cam'ron's debut album, *Come Home With Me*, fueled by the hit 'Oh Boy', debuted at # 2 on the Billboard Top 200 Album Chart, moving 225,000 copies in its first week at retail—the album would go platinum by summer's end. Meanwhile, as the summer unfolded, Jay expanded his company's target audience even wider by hitting the road as headliner for the Sprite Liquid Mix Tour, alongside such rocks as 311 and Hoobastank. Additionally, given the massive success of his overall catalog, which had logged upward of 15 million albums to date, Island paid Jay-Z and his partners $22 million to extend their partnership with Def Jam as a partner label until 2004.

Dash wasn't doing too bad for himself or his partners either, overseeing his company's expansion into every conceivable area of the hip-hop cultural marketplace, beginning with his acquisition of the U.S. rights to distribute the distilled Scottish vodka Armandale, commenting that "I just got the business and I'll learn it...Every business we get into, I kind of hands-on have to learn the shit because I think someone's always trying to jerk me...We're not saying kids should drink it...We're saying, 'Hey, kids, you can start a business.' Is it a negative thing when someone else starts a vodka company? As soon as hip-hop does it, there's criticism. It's really funny to me."

The venture would produce a $700,000 profit by the end of 2003. Moreover, the Dash-helmed Roc-A-Wear clothing line was projecting $250 million in sales over 2002, half of which Dame and his partners pocketed directly. Dash confirmed the latter, commenting that "We have a team, but I approve every sample, every skew…Last year, we did 80. This year, we'll do a buck-160. The year after, we're gonna do about 300, because we added our juniors line, girls…"

"The thing about the clothing business is like you build equity but you still get profit. In the music business, you have to build equity and be consistent then you sell but there's not too much profit because it costs so much money marketing." Jay, for his part, gets a kick out of walking "into a meeting with my jeans hanging off while everyone's all stuffy. I want to go in there with my sully pulled down and my boots on and they gotta accept it. It's the thumb-in-the-eye theory."

Given his many successful extensions of the ROC-brand name beyond merely running Roc-A-Fella Records, Dash commented that, inevitably, because "I'm knee-deep into fashion, I'm knee-deep into movies…I produced *Backstage*. Before that *Street Smarts* went straight to video but it went platinum. I produced this movie *Paid in Full* with *the Weinsteins*. It opens in September. I directed and produced *Paper Soldiers*, a comedy, it might come out in January. *State Property* I produced for Lion's Gate. That was supposed to be a straight to video, 600 grand, but we put it out in 50, 60 theaters and it averaged like 9,000 per screen. Made a lot of money on that one. I didn't use any actors. Just people from the office and artists…"

"(Basically as a producer, people give me scripts and) I develop them. They're mostly personal experiences, things that I've witnessed, or knew about. Ghetto legends and shit…(While all that going on, with Roc-A-Fella Records) there's only so much I can do. (Beanie Sigel) has his own crew, Cam'ron has his own crew, (Memphis) Bleek has his own crew. Now it's time for them to step up and be executives and take responsibility for the people that they're stepping up for, and I think they can do it. I think they're just as good at being executives as they are at being artists...I've got a lot of things to do...If I can't do things to the fullest, I don't want to do it. So I'm gonna fall back."

"It's not like a semi-retirement. It's kind of like me passing the torch, because I think we all have the capability to be business-men...Beans and Cams run the State Property part and the Dip-lomat part (of Roc-A-Fella) together...They make sure the albums get done, they A&R their projects and they do the mar-keting as well. I'm just there to advise them. They take care of their cliques."

Dash was also facing personal battles during this period, including his personal mourning of the loss of girlfriend, Aaliyah, to a tragic plane crash in August of the previous year, recalling wistfully that "She was the best person I ever knew...I never met a person like her in my life...Every day that we were together, we cherished. Every memory—every day was a special event, whether it was going to a store or going to a movie or just sitting in a house. Wherever we were was like our own little party, in our own little world...She was the only girl that got to hang out with my homeboys on the level of a homeboy...It was like being able to be with your homeboy and your girl at the same time...We just gen-erally had a lot of fun together...She would just carry herself like such a normal individual. We just would pop into McDonald's or Wendy's or something, and people just wouldn't believe (it)...We were definitely gonna be married. As soon as she had time, we were getting married—like after 'The Matrix,'...She was the one—she was definitely the one for me. It wasn't an official pro-posal, we had just talked about it, you know?...Once I realized how many people depend on me at Roc-A-Fella, I knew I had to recover."

Additionally, Dash was involved in a custody battle over his 10 year old son, such that, as he detailed it, "there's been a battle for the last year. The court gave me custody even though I have to be running, and the nature of, my business. So we had an official trial and the mother talked bad about me on the stand. Everyone in her family talked bad about me. Things that didn't happen. My witnesses were experts. I would never say anything bad to the kid about his mother. That's unacceptable...She plays mind games with everyone. She's a genius. But now she has to have supervised visitation...I picked someone who taught me a lot. I was 19 or 20 when I had the child. But it's cool. I like being a daddy...(I also have) a daughter, she's two. Her name's Ava. The cutest thing I've ever seen. She can spell her name." Still, Dash was definitely tasting the fruits of his success, revealing that "I have a place in Tribeca (6,500 square feet), a place in Jersey, and I do East Hampton on the weekend...When I'm not working, I hang out every night, everywhere. I like to dance."

Jay-Z, for his part as an equal and substantial financial partner in all of the aforementioned ventures, and who had quietly been contemplating retirement, commented that "my retirement is not based on Roc-A-Fella as a company...I don't put out an album every year to meet a quota, I put out an album every year because I love to make music and that's what I was feeling at the time. But it's definitely nice to know that you have young artists, so if I decided I wanted to come to the South of France for two years I can do that."

With *Rolling Stone Magazine* calculating Jay-Z's personal net worth at $22 million by 2002, most felt it was much higher, but all could see why Jay was beginning to feel more relaxed about his album release schedule. Def Jam Records president Lyor Cohen put it "north of $50 million...He has nearly the same lifestyle as a billionaire…except he doesn't have a wing of a museum named after him." *Rolling Stone Magazine*, in an article profiling Jay-Z late in 2001, described his house in "East Hampton, Long Island. Every forty-five minutes, his chef, Cynthia, emerged from the kitchen with something new—French waffles with blueberries, jumbo fried shrimp, barbecue wings, banana daiquiris, home-made thick-crust pizza, candy salad, figs, mojitos, lobster with special sauce. 'You gotta hide from her,' Jay says. 'She'll feed you nonstop.' Manicurists and masseuses dropped by. Supermodels Carmen Kass, Leilani and Naomi are regular guests."

Reflecting for his part on the success the duo had attained at that point in their partnership, Jay's partner Damon Dash commented that "you know, we've been doing this for like seven years, so if you can't get it right by now…not to say that he was doing anything wrong. You've got to understand, all this stuff is new to us. Like being famous, and rich, things like that—so half of the struggle is how it may be perceived. Like a lot of what they say (Jay) does, he's not really doing. But it seems like it because he takes it so power-ful. If he walks in a room and he's with five people, he's held accountable for everything those five people did…The blame, the charge, the suit."

"There was a period of time the police were riding around with a little black book, and people who were in hip-hop—they'd just pull us over and fuck with us. It was almost like being a crime family, because there is so much prejudice and misconception. Why would we jeopardize what we have now—we're not that stupid. I came from Harlem, you know what I mean? I didn't have a million dollars. We had to make it. If we're smart enough to get here, we should be smart enough to stay here. So I'd rather be sit-ting in the back of the Star Room than eating in Rikers Island… So now it's time to do other things, like the movies. And we bought a vodka company…I'm going to take over the world…My company will be worth billions of dollars—maybe worth a quar-ter of a trillion."

The industry hadn't just taken notice, they'd been put on it, as Jameel Spencer, President of P. Diddy's Blue Flame Marketing and Advertising, acknowledged, pointing out that "Damon isn't just marketing the culture, he's creating the culture…He's the new America."

Jay wasn't doing too bad in the acknowledgement department either, catching the attention of Michael Jordan, who sat down with Jay to discuss the parallels between the two men's careers, a meeting Jay recalled in which "We just really sat down and kicked it like gentlemen…I was like, 'Dawg, I'm-a ask you everythin'. I'm comin' right at you.' He was like, 'Man, you could ask me anything.' …I was talkin to him on the phone, and he was talkin' about 'Hard Knock Life,' and he was like, 'You was just so in pocket on that record, landin' right on the beat. Incredible.' I'm like, 'Thanks.' But I'm lookin' at the phone like, 'What? Stop playin', man!…'"

"Mike was a superhero when I was a kid. Him wantin' to work with me, period, was bananas!…I'm making progress in this game…I'm able to buy a Bentley now. Could you believe that? I came from the gutter. I only had three pairs of pants growing up." Jay topped off his summer with a two-month European vacation—his first ever—wherein MTV.com detailed Jay's activities to include "mingling with music A-listers (he had drinks with Quincy Jones, recorded with Mariah Carey and went to Bono's house for lunch). He rubbed shoulders with sports royalty (he just had to go to Wimbledon to see his buddies, the Williams sisters. play in the finals) and politicked with official bluebloods in St. Tropez, the kind of people who have no problem going to the club and buying a $20,000 bottle of Magnum Cristal that's as tall as a five-year-old child. Jay-Z just chilled."

Personally, at some point in early 2002, Jay had also secretly begun a romance with Destiny's Child lead singer Beyoncé, which—outside of rumor and tabloid photos capturing the two together on vacations and at industry events—would remain a mystery until late in the year. Whether it was because they feared the sort of tabloid-career threatening backlash that Ben Affleck and Jennifer Lopez had experienced from their very public romance, or just because they preferred to keep their love life quiet, Jay and Beyoncé, though spotted in public together all over the world (literally), kept largely mum on their romance at first.

At the time, Jay-Z—consistent with the aforementioned—said the following about the status of the duo's relationship, "we're not engaged or anything…We're just cool. We're just friends. We don't really, ah, know each other like that yet…Beyoncé's a woman. A very attractive woman. But we're friends for now…She's beautiful. Who wouldn't wish she was their girlfriend? Maybe one day." Yeah, right!

Later, looking back, Jay would acknowledge that much of his vagueness on the topic of he and Beyoncé's romantic status was by design because "we don't play with our relationship…In celebrity relationships, the only time it's news is when people get together and when they break up…We try not to do anything to heighten anybody's interest…If you are from the 'hood and you got 1,000 people living in the projects, you got 1,000 people in your business…It's going to put a strain on your relationship that you would never, ever believe. So, I wouldn't put 80 million people in (our relationship.) So I'm not saying yes, I'm not saying no. Listen to the record, maybe its entertainment, maybe its not."

Beyoncé, for her part, has shyness in common with Jay, to the point that, as she explained, "even in school I was private. I kept my name out of people's mouths. Not because I was ashamed of anything or because I wasn't passionate about whatever it was, like who I was dating, but because it seemed more pure when I treated it like it was sacred. I don't mind being vulnerable, but people scrutinize celebrities and make up stories. Then when everyone in the world is talking about you, it makes things really hard—not normal. That doesn't work for me because I'm a regular woman… I like to wear no shoes in the house, watch TV, and eat donuts… I'm very grateful…"

"(Jay's) helped me a lot on my album. He helped me write some of the songs." In the liner notes to her 2003 debut solo album, "To my baby, I'm your No. 1 fan. U R so smart and talented it scares me sometimes. U inspire me to be better. U challenge me for the better. U R my muse. I'm so in love."

By October of 2002, Jay and Beyoncé had made their romance public, in a song, when the two dueted on the appropriately titled '03 Bonnie & Clyde', which paid homage to late hip-hop legend Tupac by sampling 'Me and My Girlfriend'. Producer Kanye West recalled that "I remember (Jay) called (and) said, 'We got this joint, it has to be the best beat you ever made.'…Just picture if you got my first single—Hov and Beyoncé—how big you would be then.'"

Jay knew the song would cause controversy, recalling that "I knew that record was going to cause a stir…Suge was real cool…He was like, 'We are above that bull or whatever, I'm cool with it.' Tupac's mom and Ms. Wallace gave me an award one time on MTV, (and Afeni Shakur) said to me, 'When I hugged you onstage, whatever my son had (with you) was over.' I was like, 'It was over for me before that.'"

"Every show I did there was a moment I took to say, 'Put your two up for Tupac, put your lighter up for Big.' She asked me to be on (Tupac's) next album and this is probably an album that has more stuff on there about me and I was like, 'Cool.' Like I said, he's not here to repair our relationship." Appearing in a video together, which became an instant smash on MTV, the two also attended the MTV Video Music Awards together in September of 2002.

Whether Jay was just press-shy where it concerned his personal life, or because he was hard to get at personally because of his street upbringing, even the rap star admitted that, in the context of relationships in general, "I'm not the most I-love-you guy. That's one of my problems. 'What, you want me to tell you? Those are just words—everyone is going to tell you. Look at what I do.' I have to change that…That's half the battle…But half! Shit. It was zero before—be happy." Beyoncé was helping him overcome that shyness, and Jay clearly seemed to be falling in love as he approached the release of his ninth album in October of 2002.

Preceding the release of The *Blueprint II: The Gift and the Curse*, which Jay was awaiting as eagerly as the rest of the world given the negative performance of 'Best of Both Worlds.' Jay explained his desire to move past it as simply a situation where "I wasn't there, I know that I had nothing to do with (Kelly's) alleged incident. When I think about the opportunity, (I see it) as a blown opportunity. We were in the process of touring, we were putting together like a two-hour show. It would have been something so creative. The whole reason the album came together was we said 'Let's do something creative that nobody's really done before. Let's bring these two genres of music together and make something really crazy and let's go on tour and make history.' We'd probably be in Europe right now. It would have probably had four tour legs together, it would have been a beast…"

"He's getting calls from everywhere and everybody. Some people are concerned and some people just want to be nosy they want to know what's going on in the guy's life and I don't want to be a person like that. I got love for the dude. If he's guilty, I hope and I pray that he gets help. If he's not, I hope that everybody embraces him…I did not want to be influenced by the outside (on) *The Blueprint II*. I want it to be about my thoughts and where I am in my life, what's going on, what I see in the future…I have a gift and with that gift certain things come with it…With this album, I want to go different places and use different types of songs and music."

"You go from Lenny Kravitz to Dr. Dre to Young Chris...I just believe everything happens for a reason. I don't sit and say 'Why did this happen?' My energy and focus is to make sure it don't happen again, (what happened with the R. Kelly project.) My saying is 'It is what it is.'"

Jay appeared on the wildly successful Eminem motion picture soundtrack to the movie '8 Mile' on the track '8 Miles and Runnin', and that same month, his disastrous collaboration with R. Kelly was finally certified platinum. Concerning the collaboration with Eminem, Jay, in commenting generally on his process for deciding whose records to guest on, explained that "I rap with people for different reasons. Sometimes I like them, sometimes I respect them. I was on a Juvenile remix because I liked this record he had, called Ha. He did something new. So I called him and said that I would love to do the remix..."

"I respect Puff on a creative level. As a rapper, you ain't got to respect him. As a producer, he gave Juicy to Biggie. Biggie didn't want to do it. (The song made Biggie a star.) 'That beat is soft. I ain't doing that.' As a rapper, I can't say I want to hear him. He's not a rapper." At the time, any guest appearances Jay was making that became hits, or even scored him additional visibility couldn't hurt in his effort to turning the controversy Kelly's scandal had caused him into a distant memory. As such, with '03 Bonnie & Clyde' burning up the airwaves, Jay starting doing press on the making of his latest opus, discussing its evolution as one in which "I started (before I went on vacation)...I did seven joints when I started this one. I got some new producers, I always gotta bring out the new talent as far as production."

"The new guys hit the drum machine, I think they hit it hard...I didn't want to do it...I knew it was going to be difficult to follow *The Blueprint*. (Then) I started recording a lot of songs, and the songs were coming out so good...(The tracks on The) *Blueprint* were all familiar. This one, I wanted to take it everywhere...Some next level shit...I recorded all the songs for a double album in a little over a month." Recruiting the likes of Timbaland, the Neptunes, Kanye West, Dr. Dre, and Just Blaze among others to produce tracks for his new double-LP, Jay also recruited Faith Evans, Scarface, Latoiya Williams, Sadat X, and of course Beyoncé, to contribute to tracks.

Underground rap legend Scarface recalls that "Our studio session was more or less like a big joke...You go in there and see Jay shooting pool. You see Beans on the sofa asleep. Jay always plays shit for me, torturing me, playing the new *Blueprint*. I think he does that to fire me up. Then he'll play the song he wants me to get on. I'm like, 'How can you do this to me, man? You play all this heat and you want me to compete with the heat?'" As producer Just Blaze, who produced 'Hovi Baby', 'U Don't Know (Remix)', 'Meet the Parents', 'Show You How', and 'Bitches and Sisters' recalls, the atmosphere surrounding the recording of the album was one in which "after, a lot of people started getting back to the samples and having singing in their beats."

"Even though there is some of that on, we couldn't really take it there again. If you listen to the joints I did, none of them sound the same. Jay is always trying to be a step ahead, creating what the new, hot sound will be. With Jay, I can get a little more creative." *Rolling Stone Magazine's* review of Jay's ninth album in 7 years, raved that "on Vol. 2 Jay-Hova ups the ante, producing something of a hip-hop "White Album": two discs worth of party anthems and serious songwriting, with a small army of guest rhymers and producers in tow. With his dexterous, rhythmically devastating flow in full effect...The gift-versus-curse concept helps hold things together, as Jay wows you with his jet-setting lifestyle one minute, then contemplates the darker side of fame and his ghetto upbringing the next. Mo' money, mo' problems, to be sure. And one more strong record from hip-hop's most dependable voice."

Heading into the album's November release, Jay performed on *Saturday Night Live*, and when *The Blueprint II: The Gift and the Curse* dropped on November 12, Jay was righteous again, entering the Billboard Top 200 Album Chart and the R&B/Hip Hop Album Chart at # 1, moving 545,000 copies in the first week of release. By the beginning of December, Jay's new double-album had already been certified triple platinum.

With the negative press from both Jay's assault case and related arrest, as well as the R. Kelly scandal, firmly behind him heading into 2003, Jay-Z had reached a mecca professionally that began to privately feel even he could surpass as an artist. Rumors, by this point, had begun to swirl wildly around the industry rumor mill that Jay would retire after 2003, which called everything into question where it related to Roc-A-Fella Records, since Jay-Z was the label's flagship artist.

With the sheer volume of material Jay had produced in his glorious 7-year career, no one would have blamed him if he'd claimed writer's block, but for hip-hop's most prolific emcee next to Tupac Shakur, it was something else entirely motivating his desire to retire as an artist. Jay explained that in coming from nothing, in "the beginning, we were entrepreneurs, roc-a-fellas…It was a bet that paid off…(Last summer, we) went to the south of France, Sardinia, Corsica, Monte Carlo."

"For a month I didn't do anything…We saw some things. We lived life. And that pretty much sealed the retirement…I've been poor and I've gotten money…After you've had money, you start thinking about how to change things, (about leaving a) legacy…I give so much of my life in music…As an artist you have to have something private for yourself or you just go crazy. You'd be on '10' every second. The only person I know who can do that is (P. Diddy)…You start thinking past just having money, but when you first start getting paid, it's natural—you're supposed to act a fool!...I'm just cleaning out my desk...I just wanted to make sure I ended everything the way I came in—strong."

Professionally, Jay had defied the boundaries of even his wildest dreams, and that success had allowed him to find both peace and love in his personal life. Admitting that "it's getting tired now, but in the beginning, yeah, it fuels you. As far as being creative, definitely...It's basically a done deal...(Personally, in my relationship with B), she's wonderful. I give a lot of my life on music. I talk through the things I go through, and this is my therapy. Also, you have to keep some things private or you go insane...A lot of people get addicted to fame...I've never been that person that really wanted to be in the spotlight...I'd rather be able to eat my spaghetti without a camera (in my face)...(More importantly), the business of business has always been something I focused on, and rightly so..."

"Rap is a young man's game, and I thought about that even when I was young—it has to come to an end. Whatever job you have, be it hustling on the street or working at the mall, you gotta have a plan for when it's over." So, as 2003 began, the question Jay would be asking everyone else in the industry was 'What more can I say?' Jay would do his best to sum it all up in one final album—his tenth—which he called 'The Black Album' for obvious reasons as he sought to phase out one phase of his extraordinary career and fade into the next. It wasn't a question of whether Jay was ready to let go of his title as the Heavyweight Champ of emcees, but whether the fans would let him retire.

"When Alexander saw the breadth of his domain he wept, for there were no more worlds to conquer."

—Plutarch's (AD 46-126) Life of Alexander.

Chapter 12
What More Can I Say?—2003

If Biggie was the King of New York at the time of his demise in 1997, by 2004, Jay-Z was definitely hip-hop's emperor—both in terms of his status as an emcee, and for the fact that he sat atop a literal empire. But unlike the movie *Alexander*, Jay wasn't crying—his most recent album had been a huge success; in Beyoncé he had a woman as fine as Angelina Jolie; and his company's film division was having a far better year than Oliver Stone's last few. Nor were there any conspiracies behind why Jay was leaving hip-hop as an artist—his legacy had been realized ahead of schedule, and as the rapper reasoned "as you grow as a person you start to view life differently—not just rap—and that's what happened to me..."

"If you're not challenging yourself, you might as well be dead... I've had it with the rap game. Time to focus on other things. That's why I'm retiring...Right now, I don't really have any goals. I've reached all the goals I set for myself. I feel like I'm in bonus coverage...There is a glass ceiling for blacks in the record business...I know I'm in the position now where I could break that glass ceiling and open doors for everybody else...The business of business has always been something I focused on, and rightly so...Rap is a young man's game, and I thought about that even when I was young—it has to come to an end."

"Whatever job you have, be it hustling on the street or working at the mall, you gotta have a plan for when it's over...I've talked about wanting to have enough to get out since my first album. I was always more interested in the business side of things...I've taken the whole ride...I didn't skip any floors. I started at the lower lobby. Went all the way up to the penthouse."

As fellow hip-hop legend and pioneer of the concept of Hip Hop Mogul commented around this time on Roc-A-Fella's position in the game, the Def Jam Records founder praised Jay's business partner Damon Dash, commenting that "people shouldn't be asking me about what I've taught Damon Dash. They should be asking me about what I've learned from him."

Reserving perhaps his greatest praise for Jay directly, Simmons commented that "he's not following in my footsteps...He's leading me." If Simmons was passing the torch, and Jay felt compelled to in turn pass the mic, then the rapper must have felt a pretty prodigious responsibility to his race and culture in feeling he needed to focus exclusively on the business of rap, such that "there is something I'm proud of that never gets written about: my company provides a lot of job opportunities."

"I employ so many people at Roc-A-Fella Records, Rocawear, Roc-A-Films, and Armadale Vodka—young black women and men with little to no experience in the music business. I donated money to the Columbine effort, World Trade Center relief, Thanksgiving drives, the Jay-Z Santa Claus Toy Drive, Team Roc, and the Shawn Carter Scholarship Fund. I never give to get props. I give because I can, because it's from my heart, and because I was raised right...I believe that every black person has a responsibility. When you do good, everyone is looking at you—every black person. So you're the same person as Rosa Parks and Martin Luther King and Malcolm X."

"I'm not just representing the hood and Roc-A-Fella Records, I'm representing for the whole culture. A lot of people look at me like they looked at Martin Luther King...I'm not like a politician who says he never did nothing wrong. I'm not a saint—I did bad things. I fucked up. But I'm a very legit person. I try not to do bad things anymore. I try to be a decent citizen...We're the first generation of hip-hop guys to really make the big money...The generation before us never made this type of cash, so it's on us to keep it going and give it back...Five guys in one room control everything...I have to get into that room. Then I can really effect change...I don't know what's going to happen...I'm looking for a situation where I have a real meaningful role and break the glass ceiling for black executives."

Before Jay could effect his retirement, he had enough unfinished business already lined up that it would take a pair of extremely successful additional years before the limelight would even think of letting him out of its shine. For starters, Jay was still in the midst of promoting his ninth album, *The Blueprint II: The Gift and the Curse*, which by the early spring of 2003, was already pushing its second hit single, 'Excuse Me Miss' featuring The Neptunes' Pharrell. As usual, when February rolled around, Jay was inundated with Award Nominations, ranging from a Soul Train nod for R&B/Soul Album Group or Duo for 'Best of Both Worlds' with R. Kelly, and a Grammy Award for Best Male Rap Solo Performance for 'Song Cry.'

Over the course of March and April, Jay's second single continued to climb the Billboard Singles Charts for both Pop and R&B, and in late March, Jay topped the Billboard R&B/Hip Hop Singles and Tracks Chart, and the R&B/Hip Hop Airplay Chart, for a week with 'Excuse Me Miss', and Roc-A-Fella released an abbreviated version of his double album, entitled "*The Blueprint 2.1: Gift*

& Curse" which included two unreleased bonus tracks, and debuted in the Top 20 of the Billboard Top 200 Album Chart.

As April began, VH1 ranked Jay at # 10 among the 50 Greatest Hip Hop Artists, Jay also popped up on another hit single as a part of Panjabi MC remix for 'Beware of the Boys (Mundian to Bach Ke)', an anti-war song which topped the Billboard R&B/Hip Hop Singles Sales Chart. Proving the of his appeal culture-wide as a result of the success of Roc-A-Wear, Jay partnered that same month with Reebok—as part of the company's 'Sounds & Rhythm of Sport' marketing program—in announcing that they were introducing an exclusive Jay-Z Signature athletic tennis show—The S. Carter Collection—which became the fastest selling in the company's history at $150 a pair, beating out lines by including Allen Iverson, Venus Williams, Steve Francis, Shakira, Jadakiss and Scarface.

Preceding the release of Jay's shoe line on April 18th, the rapper commented at the time that "as a hip-hop artist, my job is to take things to a whole new level. So when Reebok expressed an interest and wanted to start this relationship, I jumped at the opportunity. This is an event in itself because it is to announce that for the first time a music artist has a signature athletic shoe collection." So successful was the collaboration that Reebok signed on to co-sponsor Jay-Z's 'Roc The Mic' summer amphitheater tour, with 50 Cent in the second headlining slot. In an article written by journalist Peter Kafka entitled 'The Road to Riches' reporting on the climate of the industry in the 2003, Jay-Z's viability was reinforced, wherein Kafka reported that with "CD sales (sagging) under Napster-style piracy…Jay-Z and other hot acts—especially craggy veterans— have turned to concert tours…

The 33-city Rock the Mic tour (Jay-Z is) headlining with 50 Cent, the muscled, glowering rapper du jour. Touring with them are the hyperactive Busta Rhymes, the playful Missy Elliott and several other acts. Playing to crowds of 20,000, Jay-Z should net around $100,000 per performance, or more than $1,000 per minute onstage...That's $3.3 million or more for a summer of work, good pay even for Jay-Z, who has sold 30 million records... hip-hop performers like Jay-Z used to miss out on touring's big upside. Promoters and venues balked at hosting rap gigs, citing increased insurance costs and worries that violence would erupt.

When Jay-Z organized his first big tour, in 1999, available dates were so hard to come by that the tour hopscotched back and forth across the country...Three years later, booking Jay-Z's tour is a snap. Clear Channel has guaranteed most of the 33 dates, and Reebok and Footlocker will kick in a combined $5 million to defray costs...Jay-Z's crammed lineup requires all the acts to give up some dollars to make the tour work. His guarantee, an esti- mated $100,000, is perhaps half of what he might command if he weren't splitting ticket fees with a bevy of other acts. The acts will also save money by sharing the same stage and lighting, and they will travel by bus rather than chartered plane. There's no free backstage liquor...Also, Jay-Z will squeeze more value from his shows, using them as a cross-marketing opportunity for his new line of Reebok shoes and his Rocawear clothing business."

As the Roc-The-Mic tour kicked off in June, 2003, Jay and girl- friend Beyoncé hit the top 10 of the Billboard Top 100 Album Chart, guesting on Beyoncé's 'Crazy in Love' from the aptly titled 'Dangerously in Love' LP. Jay and 50 kicked off their tour in Con- necticut, the atmosphere within the wider hip-hop culture and community nationally was celebratory to say the least. Most hard core Jay-Z fans knew this might very well be his final live tour, and 50 Cent's popularity and phenomenon spoke for itself, such that, as Entertainment Weekly put the pairing, "it's like Frank Sinatra hitting the road with Elvis Presley."

50 Cent, for his part, had no problem deferring to his elder in the game, remarking that "(Jay's the better emcee), by far. I've been listening to him for a long time. I'm the new kid...I know, because

I'm confident. I've always been competitive. But when you've got eight (years) under your belt and a kid only has one summer." Jay elaborated on the tour's hierarchy, clearly identifying himself as the headliner—and no doubt he could pack amphitheatres all summer long—but still sought to give 50 his due props for being the next in line.

Seniority rules...but all records are made to be broken. You've got Dr. J and then you have Michael Jordan and then you've got Kobe, you know what I'm saying? The game just keeps surviving. That's what it's about. If (50) continues on this path, he could be the greatest. Who knows? It's hard to judge...A lot of the time in hip-hop, things that could be big never get to happen. You used to have the Fresh Fest (in 1984). You had Run-DMC, Whodini, the whole lineup on one tour. You seldom get that now. I believe in putting out the hottest thing. We could have toured separately, but we figured if we bring it together it would be unstoppable."

According to most reviews of the wildly successful tour, such as SOHH.com's review of the duo's New York date, hailing the date as "a homecoming of sorts...for two of hip-hop's finest at the Tommy Hilfiger Jones Beach Theater in Long Island. Despite the rain, the Jay-Z/50 Cent Roc the Mic Tour finally made its debut in New York and the headliners each gave the sold-out crowd their money's worth with pulsating performances...There was only healthy competition between the two rap heavyweights, with 50 Cent acknowledging Jay-Z's throne as rap's reigning king by reserving the coveted finale spot on the tour for him. And...Jay-Z confirmed his crown—and crowd control—as the rap maestro directed the 14,000 fans together in a harmonic symphony orchestra."

Jay-Z's mother realized the actual status her son had attained in the game upon watching one of his shows on the tour, remarking that "little girls were fainting at Jay-Z and they were screaming and I—and I just stood there and I was like, 'He's really a star,' and, of course, some of my friends were there also and they were like, 'Duh. Hello.'"

USA Today, meanwhile, gave the tour a 3 1/2 out of 4 stars review, commenting that "Jay-Z was a commanding presence and 50 Cent gave fans more than their money's worth during the Rock the Mic Tour concert at Nissan Pavilion (in Stone Ridge, Va.)... For more than an hour, Jay-Z riveted the audience—which often finished lines and sang the hooks—with his hits...Jay-Z had no choice but to up the ante with his performance, because charismatic upstart 50 Cent gave an electrifying show of his own."

As the summer wound down, the Roc-The-Mic tour had grossed approximately $25 million, and while Jay and 50 were one of the hottest concert draws around, Jay continued to burn up the charts with Beyoncé on 'Crazy In Love', topping the Billboard Hot 100 Singles Chart for 8 weeks; the Hot 100 Airplay Chart for 8 weeks; the Top 40 Tracks Chart and Hot R&B/Hip Hop Singles & Tracks Chart for 3 weeks respectively; the Hot R&B/Hip Hop Airplay chart for 4 weeks; the Hot Digital Tracks Chart for 6 weeks; and the UK Singles Chart for 3 weeks. Additionally, he appeared on the Bad Boys 2 Motion Picture Soundtrack, P. Diddy's comeback vehicle for Bad Boy Entertainment, on the track 'La, La, La.'

As the fall began for Roc-A-Fella, to no one's surprise, just coming off tour, Jay was already hunkered down in the studio, recording what he had plugged all year long as his 10th and final album. Simply entitled 'The Black Album', Jay kept the project tightly under wraps from the public, tiding them over with plenty of guest appearances, all of which expectedly became hits.

Between September and October, Jay stayed atop the Billboard Rhythmic Top 40 Chart and Mainstream Top 40 Chart alongside girlfriend Beyoncé on 'Crazy in Love', while his smash video for '03' Bonnie & Clyde', also featuring Beyoncé, was nominated for Best Hip Hop Video at the MTV Video Music Awards. At the show, Beyoncé's 'Crazy in Love' won Best Female Video, Best Choreography, and Best R&B Video.

In October, Jay hit # 1 on the Billboard Hot R&B/Hip-Hop Singles and Tracks Chart for 6 weeks, and the Hot R&B/Hip-Hop Airplay Chart for 5 weeks with Pharrell on 'Frontin', and Jay also hit the airwaves with Mary J. Blige on 'Love & Life.' Meanwhile, Jay's company, Roc-A-Fella Enterprises, would wind up the year grossing $350 million between its music, film, fashion and Armadale Vodka divisions.

Ebony's 'The 58 most intriguing Blacks of 2003', which ran in November of 2003, estimated Jay's personal fortune at $50 million, although that projection was WAY off base with what he was truly worth, as *Fortune Magazine* would report a net worth of almost 5 times that a year later. The truth was—all of Jay's peers, business interests, accountants, and business partners were trying to keep up with him, and it was taking them a lot longer to count the millions of dollars he was generating than it was taking Jay to earn them.

In their piece on Jay, *Ebony* provided some brief but fascinating perspective on how Jay had evolved in image between 1996 and 2003, such that, in the highly respected magazine's estimation, "from man of the house to street hustler to hip-hop superstar, Jay-Z has tried to maintain some sense of privacy during his meteoric rise to fame—at least where his love life is concerned. The rapper/producer has kept his long-rumored relationship with Beyonce under wraps for the most part, and neither has discussed the romance publicly. But the unlikely pair (the R&B diva credited him with giving her some street cred in the hip-hop nation) have been spotted everywhere together—including a sizzling performance at this year's MTV Video Music Awards, where Jay-Z seemed to claim Beyonce as his own by a simple grab of her leg. Beyonce was even photographed with Jay-Z's family at the launch of his latest business endeavor, the New York sports bar 40/40."

Joking, at the time about his growing net worth as one of America's richest African Americans—and Americans in general—under 40, Jay joked that "I always have to blame it on the accountants. They have to be tough, they have to be willing to quit if a guy calls up and says, 'I want to buy a new car.' I fire my accountant every year. Every time I pay taxes, he's fired. Uncle Sam did not go in that recording booth with me. He didn't bang his head against the wall until he came up with the hook for Hovi Baby. It's crazy, the checks that I send to the government, for nothing."

"And then my accountant says, 'Be happy that you're fortunate enough to cut this check.' Oh yeah? Fuck you! You're fucking fired! That's my response. Then I hire him back, because he's right." Commenting further on his massive success as it continued to motivate him—not just to make money—but to reshape America's perception of the black male, Jay made the point that "here's something to think about. I enter a building in lower Manhattan last spring to look at a 10,000 square-foot apartment. I'm still in shock that I can even look at an apartment that's selling for $7.5 million. I go by myself, no entourage, no security, no bullshit."

"The next day, it's all over New York daily papers: Thug rapper is not wanted by the neighbors, he came with 30 armed black militants with guns-blah, blah, blah. Can you believe people still have a problem with successful black folks? Granted, I got in trouble once, but so have Winona Ryder and Martha Stewart. It's funny, like 'Pac and Big, I didn't have major legal problems until I got in the music business. What's frustrating is how the media can affect my real (estate) life choices. No one on the board at that building had ever even met me." From a financial view, it would be their loss.

When Jay wasn't out shopping for multi-million dollar penthouse apartments, he spent most of his time locked away in a studio finishing up work on his swan song, *The Black Album*, which Jay was incidentally filming alongside a concert at Madison Square Garden for a documentary he was planning for release in the latter part of 2004. At the same time, he was working on his autobiography, entitled 'The Black Book', and for Jay, the album, book and documentary were a trio that would tie together beautifully at retail.

Unique to most rap albums in the history of hip-hop, Jay had his mother Gloria open the album, explaining that maternal decision, as one in which "I tricked her (into)…talking on the album. It was her birthday and she came by, I told her to meet me there, we'd go to my club, I got a club in Chelsea called the 4040 Club, and we was going to go there to celebrate her birthday. But when she got there, the music was playing and I was like, you should just put something right over here, like talk over this part. Because if I had told her, she would have been nervous to do it. She would have been thinking about it the whole time. So she's on a CD. She's on that CD." Concerning the nature of Jay's tenth studio album in 7 years, the rapper explained that "it's my last album. I want it to be the prequel to *Reasonable Doubt*. I want my mother to open it, then I go through my life and end saying how I want to do *Ain't No Nigga*, which is my first hit, and trying to find a beat for it. 'I keep it fresher than the next bitch' (the first line of *Ain't No Nigga*). Then it ends."

"I want it to come out on November 28—Black Friday. Then, no more albums…I'm in the comfort zone as far as making the music. I know how to structure a song. I know how to construct a verse. I know all the little tricks. I know when people are going to sing along. I've been doing that 10 albums straight. I'm a young guy, but I still have to challenge myself in life. I have to step outside my comfort zone. That's just part of being alive…In a way (this album turned out as I originally envisioned it.)…I mean, just as far as the attack of it, what I'm saying. The approach of it is introspective—this is probably my most introspective album— but it has a lot of current things in it. A lot of things that I wanted to happen really didn't happen with the album, but then again, it's music. I didn't want to overthink it and make it boxy. I didn't want to make it programmed—it should just flow the way it flows. I just got to go with what feels good…(Michael Jordan's) still the greatest basketball player ever, but he could have left it on such a perfect note…He could have left it with 'Six (championships). My second time I three-peated."

"It's done.' I'm not here to judge him, I guess he wasn't fulfilled within himself. Mike didn't have a prototype (before him to show) how bad it could be. I do, I have him. So it's going to take that much more for me to come back now. I already know how that movie ends. I don't know if I want to do that…I wanted my last 12 songs to be my most personal album so far."

"Writing *The Black Book* got me focused on recording my last volume, *The Black Album*. Having to remember stories from my childhood, my days hustling, and my early days in the music business made me ready. Interviewing my mother, I learned things about my parents and their marriage I would have never found out had I not been writing this book. I think one of the things my friends appreciate most about me is my love of privacy. For fans, I know this can be frustrating. So the challenge for me in writing (and recording) this autobiography was to balance that out…(Me and Pharrell, in our work together), we got our Snoop and Dre on right now…We both really love the music. When we do get in the studio, it ain't about nothing else but what feels good. We're not scared to try nothing."

"This ('Change Clothes') sounds like an '80s Cameo record or something…(On 'What More Can I Say?'), I just wanted to capture that emotion, I been doing this hard…Ten albums, outside guest appearances, soundtracks—I don't ever get to a point when I'm just making music to make money. I love it too much for that. I love when other people make hot albums. I love listening to hot stuff outside of my own stuff, just as a fan. I just wanted to vent. What more can I say to you? I've done it all." Producer Just Blaze, who produced 'December 4', recalled the extra-personal nature of the recording of the rapper's last album as a process wherein "Jay was picky like he never was before. He didn't just go for stuff he can rhyme to but stuff where he can tell stories and construct songs with concepts."

Producer 9th Wonder, who produced 'Threat', recalled for his part that "Jay-Z had the R. Kelly joint 'A Woman's Threat.' He said, 'Can you do something with this?' I put it on my laptop and chopped it up, and put the drum track behind it. Jay said my name on the track. All the work I've done, making beats all the time, it all boiled down to that moment when he said my name. Jay-Z told MTV that in two years everybody's gonna know my name. He just has a knack for breaking producers."

A conflicted affair, *The Black Album*, was a celebration of Jay-Z's legacy, but in the same time a wake of sorts in that it was his last album. *Vibe Magazine's* review of the album, preceding its release, commented that "they say they never really miss you 'til you dead or you gone,' Jay-Z raps on the visceral 'December 4th' (named for his birth date). And with that, the first lyrics on his final album are earborne. When the rumors of this LP, *The Black Album*, reached the hip-hop world last year, the imagination of Jigga loyalists ran wild. A black album? Hov's final bow? The notion conjured up the dark and the grimy."

"Finally, the deepest corners of the sharpest mind in rap would be swept clean. Several months, a concept change (originally, there were 12 songs by 12 producers), and a major Internet leak later, said album sets the streets afire…From beginning to end, *The Black Album* documents a marvelous career. It's monumental because it's a culmination of Jigga's natural thoughtfulness delivered with transcendent skill…If the most definitive part of his legacy will be the end, then *The Black Album* gives you Jay-Z at all his stages. The masterful, lyrical content leaves no question as to how Jay feels he should be remembered."

Eonline.com called the album "a streamlined effort that's stylish, cool and has a sense of finality," while *Rolling Stone Magazine*, in a 4 Star review, hailed Jay-Z as "a rare rapper. The dominant figure of the post-Biggie and Tupac era, he spit cool and witty with devastating flows, dropped classic albums, influenced MCs, changed pop culture and built a tall stack of dollars in the process...Given one last chance to make an impact, Jay-Z has come up with one of the better albums of his career, though perhaps a shade lesser than his very best, Reasonable Doubt and The Blueprint. Still, we've witnessed not merely a Hall of Fame career but one of the top-shelf greatest of all time, up there with Rakim, Big, Pac and Nas. And like every great rapper, Jay-Z has never been afraid to tell us he's Number One."

In November, preceding the album's release, Jay-Z held a historic sold-out concert at Madison Square Garden, which featured a host of guest performers, including R. Kelly, Beyonce, Mary J. Blige, Missy Elliott, Ghostface Killah, the entire Roc-A-Fella family of artists, and other hip-hop superstars. The audience was filled with an equal number of peers. Explaining the tie-in with the filming of both the album's recording and the live concert, Jay explained that "the recording of the CD was supposed to be for an extra bonus on the album. And then we shot the Garden. We thought something special would happen to put out a DVD. Then we got the first 15 minutes and it was like hold on...this is a journey. This is a kid from Brooklyn, New York to play the biggest stage in the world... This is much bigger than that, and the inspiration also came cause of the fact of where I come from and the fact that I couldn't get a deal in the beginning."

To no one's surprise, *The Black Album*, released in December, 2003—just in time for the Christmas rush—debuted atop the Billboard Top 200 Album Chart, where it remained for 2 weeks, while the album occupied the top of the R&B/Hip Hop Album Chart for 3 weeks. Released in typical bootleg-battle style on a Friday rather than the traditional Tuesday, *The Black Album* moved 463,000 copies in its first shortened week of sales, and was certified platinum by the end of its second week of release.

Clearly, fans weren't protesting Jay's retirement, rather they were running out to grab up what had been pitched as Jay's final studio album. Jay also oversaw his annual 'Jay-Z Santa Claus Toy Drive', through which the rapper gives away thousands of dollars in toys to children from Jay's Marcy Projects. As the year came to a close, Jay was honored at the Vibe Awards with the TuBig Award, and took home the Coolest Collabo Award with Beyoncé for *Crazy in Love*. Jay also showed up on Missy Elliot's This is Not A Test LP, on the track 'Wake Up', and hit the Top 20 with his own first single from *The Black Album—Change Clothes*—featuring The Neptunes' Pharrell.

The accolade continued when Jay and Beyoncé topped the ARC Top Songs of 2003 ranking for *Crazy in Love*, and his albums *Reasonable Doubt* and *The Blueprint* were rated among *Rolling Stone Magazine's* list for the Greatest 500 Albums of All Time, at numbers' 248 and 464 respectively. While Jay-Z had planned to retire from recording studio albums following the release of *The Black Album*, he was forced to leave the exact definition of retirement vague for the majority of 2004, as Jay prepared to embark on one final and stellar commercial year as an artist.

Not surprisingly, TWO more official albums would come out with Jay-Z's name on the cover, and his status as a mogul would become secure as Jay pondered the dissolution of some of his business interests, and made non-Roc-A-Fella related investments in others, including a Basketball Team! Those within the hierarchy of hip-hop's business ranks reasoned that Jay's decision and desire to retire was entirely consistent with the level of success he had attained, such that a natural shift in his focus was inevitable, with Russell Simmons asking "why should he make records?…Records are a distraction. He could be missing an opportunity to get really rich. I haven't produced a record for 15 years…Making records is over."

That certainly seemed high up on Jay-Z's New Years Resolutions going into 2004. As his relationship with Beyoncé continued to become more serious, speculation would also swirl wildly about his plans for starting a family of his own as a possible part of his motivation in retiring. Moreover, Jay-Z and longtime partner Damon Dash would face the possibility of divesting their entrepreneurial alliance for the first time in a decade as they sought to become masters of their own destiny...

"I don't mean to boast
But damn if I don't brag
Them crackers gonna act like I ain't on they ads
The Martha Stewart
That's far from Jewish
Far from a Harvard student
Just had the balls to do it...
Pound for pound I'm the best to ever come around here
Excluding nobody
Look what I embody
The soul of a hustler I really ran the street
I CEO's mine, That marketing plan was me
And no I ain't get shot up a whole bunch of times
Or make up shit in a whole bunch of lines
And I ain't animated, like say a Busta Rhymes
But the real shit you get when you bust down my lines
Add that to the fact I went plat a bunch of times
Times that by my influence
On pop culture
I supposed to be number one on everybody's list
We'll see what happens when I no longer exist"

—Jay-Z, "What More Can I Say?"

Chapter 13
Fade to Black—2004

While 2004 would prove Jay-Z's most successful one, it would equally prove Damon Dash's most trying. Starting out the year, Dash remained confident that Roc-A-Fella Records would survive without Jay's presence as an artist, although he acknowledged that "we'll miss that 4th quarter sales boost...People are contemplating our demise."

Dash, over the course of his 9 year partnership with Jay, had intelligently—both for his partners and himself—diversified his business interests and investments to the point where his pockets were not only padded with cash, but insulated as a result from the fall-out that would inevitably come with Jay-Z's departure. Jay's uncertain plans for the future also played heavily into the fog of uncertainty hanging over Dash own, as he acknowledged that "with Jay done, we have to take some chances, try new things."

An article in *Time Magazine*, focused on Dash, made it sound as Dash was starting over again from scratch, commenting that "Roc-A-Fella sails through the rough weather that inevitably lies ahead for any young and growing business...'Damon's done a great job, but he's clearly been in the right place at the right time in his partnership with Jay-Z,' says Ryan Berger of advertising agency Euro RSCG Worldwide. 'I'm not sure he can reach that next level without him.'..."

"Dash's new business plan fits him like a Roc-A-Fella hoodie. This fall he started Roc Music, the first hip-hop company to produce rock, alternative and R. and B. He's flipping the turntables: over the past decade, pundits have lauded rap for 'going mainstream' and finding suburban skater punks far from the smoked-out city neighborhoods where the music was founded. With Roc Music, Damon Dash is formally inviting rock into the hip-hop world. 'I've had 20 albums go gold or platinum...Why can't I have that in rock, soul and R. and B.? You can't just sit around and do the same thing for 10 years.'"

"Dash's challenge is one he shares with many other CEOs: Where is the next phase of growth coming from?...Dash wants his people to know that although Roc-A-Fella will move beyond hip-hop, the company won't lose any edge. 'This pop-music thing, it's starting to bother me...Everything that's hot, it's going pop. What sells now is this bullshit.'..."

"These days Dash spends most of his hours building up his less controversial film business. *Death of a Dynasty*, a hip-hop-industry spoof that Dash financed, produced and directed, will be released soon. Dash Films will shoot *State Property 2*, a revenge drama, in February...'With Jay retiring, now more than ever we are going to be critiqued on every level.'...The pressure sometimes is evident." If *Time Magazine* had their finger on the pulse of the climate in and around the Roc-A-Fella camp, the rest of the industry was certainly taking notice as well. Still, because Damon Dash felt pressure didn't mean he wanted out of the kitchen."

"Quite to the contrary, Dash's confidence in his own ability as a business man was based, in part at least, on what he had built under Jay's commercial flag. Now that he had operating capital to branch out into virtually any venture he pleased independent of Jay-Z, Dash was going crazy with his green, declaring at one point to a journalist in mid-2004 that "I'm going to take over the world...My company will be worth billions of dollars—maybe worth a quarter of a trillion."

Still, some industry insiders, in addition to *Time Magazine*, had their own doubts, including Morris Reid, president of powerful urban marketing firm Westin Rinehart, who commented that "we wouldn't know about Roc-A-Wear clothing without Jay-Z...If Jay-Z isn't making any more albums, then the whole company loses its platform."

Jay was definitely retiring, and Dash seemed to be operating without any illusions about the aforementioned. One credit Dame always did get was never stepping out of Jay-Z's shadow musically as "artists" like Sean 'P. Diddy' Combs, Percy 'Master P' Miller, and Lorenzo 'Irv' Gotti had all attempted to, with mixed results at best. While Dash had admitted that "if I could rap to sell my shit,

I would…We'd be way ahead, and I wouldn't have to work as hard," he knew better.

The dynamic between Jay and Dash had worked as well as it had because Dame had been able to paint himself as a less-intimidating Suge Knight of sorts, while Jay was allowed to play the Dr. Dre-like position of artist/co-C.E.O. That formula had paid off handsomely too, as by 2004, Roc-A-Fella Enterprises was reporting annual revenues of $450 million, and employing around 500 people. The key to the company's success had been cross branding, which pioneers like Russell Simmons and Sean 'P. Diddy' Combs had invented, but Roc-A-Fella had innovated to a whole new level.

Dash, even after 50 million records worldwide under the Roc-A-Fella Records umbrella, was still lamenting in 2004 the fact that "we're doing well, but it's hard for anybody to make money in the music business…I think it's time our company showed the world we can be professional, dress in suits, and change the perception of a hip-hop company…Tommy Hilfiger isn't urban, but he sells urban clothes. Why can't I do the opposite." It was hard to argue with Dash's logic, who reasoned that "we shouldn't let other people make money off us, and we shouldn't give free advertising with our lifestyle…I can sell anything I understand."

To hedge his bets, with Jay-Z's impending retirement, Dame was branching out into just about every conceivable market he could, his rationale being that "with my work ethic, I can have a company in every part of fashion and entertainment…Just because I am an urban individual, I don't have to do just urban things."

Among the licenses Dame had secured by 2004 or subsidiaries he had founded from the ground-up, Dash's widely varied interests included *American Magazine,* which Dash co-founded with *Source* Editor Smokey Fontaine, with Dame explaining that "I was looking to get into the magazine business. At first I went to my man Carlito (of The Source) and told him come get with me.

He was like, nah. I ain't trying to do that, but Smokey is and it was cool cause I knew Smokey. Smokey presented the whole thing to me. We wanted to make sure it was being objective and not mess with the integrity of the magazine. You know me putting all my Roc-A-Fella shit in there."

For his part, Fontaine may have been charged with running the company's day-to-day operations, but Dash kept a tight editorial reign, with Smokey explaining their arrangement as one in which "the first cost of entry for me doing business with Dame…(was) that he had to sign away all creative and editorial control…And he was with that from the gate. It wasn't even a concern. This is not going to be a *Notorious* or a *One World* where it's branded with the name of the financier. He's like my wizard of Oz behind the scenes and is very eager to allow me to execute my vision the way I see it…It's a totally different ball game…like in some ways I don't even like comparing it. This is going to be the magazine for the time that marries the [fashion and hip-hop] worlds and it's sophisticated enough to create the best images possible, but at the same come from a very authentic music place and Hip Hop place without apology…"

"Hip Hop is as broad as Pharrell Williams. It's as broad as Andre at the same time it's as credible as Jay and Missy and whoever else is out there like Lil Jon and The Eastsideboyz. To me Hip Hop is a very broad term and that's what we're representing, just everything that Hip Hop can be…Everything in 'America' is going to be grand. It's going to have a lot of scale to it so expect lots of in-your-face, full blown, almost full body images. And it's not going to be alternative. It's going to be the major artists covered in the best way possible."

Another of Dash's new ventures was the C. Ronson clothing label—producing trendy tank-tops and skirts, which he'd licensed from socialite Charlotte Ronson, grossing around $2 million by 2004, a move which Dash defended by pointing out that "in the same breath that I'm putting out C. Ronson (clothing), I'm putting out Team Roc and State Property. You can't get no harder than that"; a Tiret Watch line Dash had launched, which priced out at between $17,000 and $130,000 retail; a cigar line; a lucrative license on PRO-Keds, which one media outlet reported as a partnership in which "the Stride Rite Corporation has signed a licensing agreement with hip-hop mogul Damon Dash. The agreement will give Dash, CEO of Rocawear clothing and Roc-A-fella records, the rights to distribute footwear under the PRO-Keds brand. The line will be on sale under Dash's management from January 2005."

Additionally, Dash had invested in a European cable television channel, and a sports and boxing promotion company that he co-founded with Lou DiBella, which had already signed Olympic boxing star Andre Berto and undefeated New York City prospects, Jaidon Codrington and Curtis Stevens. Then there was the RocBox Digital Music Player, released by Dash's Roc Digital company in two versions of the portable audio player—20GB and 256MB, with Dash explaining that "we wanted to take a bite out of Apple, so to speak...I'm an entrepreneur by nature...I saw the opportunity and thought it would be a fun and innovative way to sell music...We wanted to get some of that iPod money. We have to capitalize off of every opportunity...There will be special editions customized for Roc-A-Fella artists—and any other artists that are interested, for that matter."

The company's day-to-day president Shae Hong, commented additionally that "we saw a real opportunity to take our urban strategy into the electronics market...The digital music market has taken such a major role in pop culture in the last few years, but there was no one speaking to the urban consumer. We are doing that." Additionally, Dash got into the Ice Cream business, launching ROC Ice Cream trucks, themed around various Roc-A-Fella products, be they recording artists or fashion lines, for example, Beanie Sigel's signature ROC Ice Cream Truck, which rolls through Philadelphia's inner-city hood where Beanie grew up, or Samantha Ronson's fashion line through the Hamptons, where the socialite resides and is well known among locals.

Dash even got into the children's toys business, creating the Debonair Dash teddy bear, which his partner introduced as "1-800-Flowers.com Presents Debonair Dash Bear by Damon Dash! Damon Dash, Urban music and style entrepreneur, and CEO of Rocawear, has taken his street smarts and turned it into a multi-billion dollar urban fashion, music and film empire in collaboration with recording artist and entrepreneur Jay-Z. Damon's Debonair Dash Bear is wearing a tee shirt designed by Rocawear in support of Save the Children, which will make its debut in children and adult sizes in January at Hecht's, Strawbridge's, Macy's, Famous Barr and Robinson's May. The winning bidder will also receive the original sketch signed by Damon Dash."

Dash also found time to give back, founding Team Roc (partnered with SCAN, Supportive Children Advocacy Network, and an outgrowth of Dame's longtime work with the Mission Society, who promotes and supports community organizations that aide 'high risk' youth by offering after school programs, summer programs, and additional education opportunities and classes.) Dash launched the non-for-profit in 2004, which he described as "a dream come true for me...It's been in the works for a long time. Every great company, every empire, should have its philanthropic goals. The idea is simple: to put something back into the community that has given us so much. Team Roc started with the Mission Society up in Harlem, where I'm from. Now we have the opportunity to turn it into something really big on a national level. My love for sport really equipped me with the tools I needed to succeed in business and in life; competitiveness, will, teamwork. That's what Team Roc is all about."

Using his vast success in the clothing business, Team Roc, among its other activities, teamed with the New York Knicks to design an exclusive, co-branded line of athletic clothing sold exclusively at Madison Square Garden Pro Shops. Further described in a press release, "…these special lines in the future, as well as endorsing all-star professional athletes in its advertising campaigns and promotions."

"With each season, Team Roc draws inspiration from sports franchises across all disciplines for its cutting-edge colorways and designs; Fall 2004 will be geared toward football. Holiday '04 will be inspired by boxing. Spring '05 will draw on Dash's love for rugby. Of course, the "Boys Of Summer" will be represented by a baseball theme for summer '05. And hockey, rarely associated with urbanwear, will follow in Fall '05."

Then there was Dash and Jay's true cash cow—Roc-A-Wear, which they agreed to continue co-operating despite Jay's retirement from the record business. So keen on defining his own mainstream with Roc-A-Wear was Dash that he secured supermodel Naomi Campbell as a spokeswoman for the company's women's line, and pursued Kate Moss with equal vigor. Among others he did succeed in hiring, according to a press release by the Business PR Newswire, were "Ron Artest, (who) has found a new place to hold court in his time away from the game of basketball, taking on a role in 'The Roc's' advertising campaign that launches this month. Artest was offered a spot in the ad by long-time friend and co-star of the campaign, Damon Dash."

"Ron and I have known each other for some time…Just as we were getting ready to shoot the campaign, I heard about his situation and contacted him about the opportunity immediately."… Joining Artest and as the stars at his new job are Dash, Karolina Kurkova, Naomi Campbell and Kevin Bacon in addition to Rachel Roy, Cam' Ron, Charlotte Ronson, Samantha Ronson and Seven among others. Created by Lipman NYC and shot by world renowned photographer, Mario Testino, the campaign incorporates the many aspects of 'The Roc' lifestyle and its products/

companies. Those include: Clothing lines Rocawear, the Damon Dash Collection, Team Roc, State Property, Rachel Roy and C. Ronson; new MP3 offering, the RocBox; Damon Dash Music Group; and movie production company Dash Films among other initiatives.

The print ad campaign will debut in the March issues of *Details, Elle, GQ, Teen Vogue, V, Vanity Fair, Vibe, Vogue, W* and *XXL*. Dame also served as an executive-producer on an extremely controversial Kevin Bacon-directed film, in which the actor also starred, about pedophilia, called "The Woodsman", which was critically-panned, but commercially too touchy for most of the movie-going public.

Dash—who reportedly put up most of the film's backing, for his part, explained his decision to bankroll the film as one in which "It was about two-weeks before the movie started filming. I was eating in Mr. Chows and an associate of mine said he knew of a good film project I might be interested in…I said, 'Gimme the script.' I read it, saw who was attached, and I just cut the cheque…I'm into realistic things, the truth. It was a no-brainer for me…Where I'm from, a pedophile is considered to be the scum of the earth and even if he goes to jail he's gonna get his ass kicked…"

"But when I was presented with the script I was curious to see how I could have compassion for a pedophile…I read the script and I did feel compassion, so I felt enlightened to a degree." Producer Lee Daniels recalled that "he didn't just cut the cheque. He was very involved. In fact he got sick of me calling him with problems. I made him work for his money." Dash looked at all of his entrepreneurial expansions through the lens of being "a businessman by nature, so the point of business is to build equity…If it makes financial sense, I'm open to be hearing (about) opportunities, but I will always run Roc-A-Fella."

Dash knew how to personally live the image he sold as well, wherein, according to an article written by fashion journalist John Spinner during Traidcraft week in early 2004, he reported that "Damon Dash won't wear the same clothes twice. 'I've got to have fresh clothes at all times…I've gotta look fresh to death.'…It's been reported that the 32-year-old Harlem-born boss of Roc-A-Fella record label and Rocawear clothing label needs 200 towels, 20 pairs of box-fresh trainers and numerous sets of brand new boxers, shirts and suits each day." Dame was definitely living large as 2004 began, and the only downside for Dash publicity-wise came in late January when he was sued by an ex-model Kristie Thompson for $15 million on the charge that Dash had raped her following a New Year's Eve party in Brazil in 2002.

Dash's spokeswoman commented that "these are ludicrous allegations. Damon hasn't been charged with anything." The allegation came and went quickly in the press, as Dash kept generating headlines with new venture after new venture amid wide media speculation over what the state of Roc-A-Fella Enterprises would be following Jay-Z's retirement. For Dash personally, the news of Jay's desire to retire came as no surprise, with Dame half-joking that "Jay has been retiring since Reasonable Doubt…So, I have been preparing for that since then. We have 21 acts signed to Roc-A-Fella, so we're ready. Also, I am expanding beyond hip-hop; we have R&B and rock acts now, too."

"Jay has been talking about retiring every year. So he keeps me nervous and he keeps me on my toes…I was doing mix tapes. I was doing other businesses and I was constantly re-inventing Roc-A-Fella and doing this beyond the scope of what a hip-hop person would do. I kept doing different clothing lines. Creating a magazine. We just are showing everybody that there is so much money to be made in hip-hop…In hustling, you're just trying to get a buck, you're trying to stay ahead…You have to capitalize off every opportunity, so I'm hustling now…I'm always a little paranoid about going broke…If I'm going to stay in this business…I gotta have some fun with it. I gotta keep doing some new things...I'm always working. I'm always up to something. While you go to movies, I'm plotting, I'm planning while you're sleeping, I'm planning to take over the planet...It's time to take it to another level on every level."

Addressing rumors that Jay's retirement was stemming in part out of a falling-out with Dash, Dame was quick to shoot back that "those are just rumors...If Jay-Z leaves, he leaves...He's my son's godfather...I'm not mad at him at all." Jay-Z also went out of his way to make sure his fans knew—possibly in the interest both of his friendship with Dash and of the Roc-A-Fella name brand— that "I hate that the media has created a story that Dame and I have beef. It makes us look like bitches, like we're out here squabbling over something when it couldn't be further from the truth."

"The three of us made a lot of money together, we got nothing to be mad about, period...We don't hang out as much as we did before, but it's no problem. It's just like people do different things. And when other people around us see that, then it'll get cliquish, and then it'll start creating space for someone on my squad, who are basically the dudes I grew up with from Marcy and my family, to say something like, 'I don't fuck with Dame.'...As far as Dame and I go, I liken our current situation to LA Reid and Babyface. We created wealth and musical dynasty together. When we see each other, we laugh and kick it like we did before. We just don't hang out everyday. When we were building the label we used to hang out every single day. We were going to clubs every night, buying the whole bar out. We'd go to Atlanta, to Freaknik or something, frontin'. We would wear the jackets with the logo, we'd rent limousines and put Roc-A-Fella on the license plate. Our hangout was driven to promote the company. So everything we did from the moment we woke up to the moment we went to sleep was -dedicated to Roc-A-Fella."

"We all still have that same ambition, but now we'll go in different directions. I have companies I want to build from the ground up. That's the high, to create something from nothing. Dame is doing the same thing with film. It's typical that the media would create a beef where there is none, but we're not typical dudes by any stretch of the imagination. We made history together…Me and him will always be great…We made history—we took a little company (Roc-A-Fella) and ran it for eight years. (But) now we have different things. He sees a Basquiat (painting) and goes and buys it. I'm not into that. We got different tastes. It ran its course." One thing that was clear in all of Dame's movements—that Jay definitely had his own plans for the future.

As the spring unfolded for Jay, he was riding high off the double-platinum success of *The Black Album*. In February, the Grammys were lovin Jay, who won 2 Grammy Awards, for Best R&B Song (songwriter), and for Best Rap/Sung Collaboration, both for 'Crazy in Love', his collaboration with girlfriend Beyoncé. Jay also received 4 additional nominations for Record of the Year for 'Crazy in Love', Best Rap/Song Collaboration for 'Frontin' with the Neptunes and Pharrell, Best Rap Album for 'The Blueprint II: The Gift and the Curse', and Best Rap Song (songwriter) for 'Excuse Me Miss' with Chad Hugo and Pharrell Williams.

That same month, he released his second single, '99 Problems', which became an instant smash on MTV for the old-school black and white feel of its video (which co-starred legendary Def Jam co-founder Rick Rubin—who also produced the track). Jay described it to MTV.com as one in which "I want to say, no rappers were harmed in the making of that video…I really just wanted to do powerful images in Brooklyn. The last two videos, I mean, they're cool, but I was pretty much just going through the motions. (This time) I was like, 'Man, we can't shoot the same old thing.' So I called Mark Romanek, he's like the director's director. Every director is like, 'Mark is the one.' He…did Johnny Cash's 'Hurt' (video), did some work with Lenny Kravitz, the Michael

Jackson joint ('Scream') with him and Janet...I just really wanted him to shoot, like, where I'm from in Brooklyn and shoot the 'hood, but shoot it like art, not shoot just a bunch of dudes or a bunch of cars around it—shoot it like art. And shoot it powerful and strong. So that's basically what we came up with, but at the end, the whole (being) shot thing is just really symbolic to the whole retirement thing and putting the whole Jay-Z thing to rest..."

"We still in the street like, you know, 'What up, Jay-Z?' It's all good. It ain't on that level. It's just like, you know, the artistry, I'm putting that down, to the side...It's just symbolic. It's artsy." In early March, Jay traveled to the United Kingdom to headline the Prince's Trust Concert, spending time with Prince Charles, and proving his international status as one of hip-hop's biggest stars. That same month, Jay released his third single with 'Dirt Off Your Shoulder', and Jay's label, Roc-A-Fella prepped for the late spring release of one of the most highly anticipated albums of 2004, superstar producer Kanye West's 'College Dropout.'

Kanye's album, released in February, debuted at # 2 on the *Billboard* Top 200 Album Chart, moving 441,000 copies in its first week at retail, and going platinum in its first month of release. *Rolling Stone Magazine* hailed the album as a "perfected...warm, almost sentimental brand of hip-hop, using bright, soulful beats and melodic choruses to humanize otherwise chilly gangsters... (West's) debut as a rapper on *College Dropout* might do the same thing for Jigga's Roc-A-Fella label...West has got something to prove on *Dropout*...His ace in the hole is his signature cozy sound—dusty soul samples, gospel hymns, drums that pop as if hit for the very first time. He has also succeeded in showing some vulnerability behind a glossy mainstream hip-hop sheen."

During the spring, things also started to take off with an upscale New York sports club called 40/40 which Jay had launched late the previous year, which a New York Restaurant journalist Dan Glass described as a nightspot where "multi-millionaire athletes flock… Jay-Z's ultra-upscale sports lounge with enormous plasma and projection TVs, modern leather eggcup chairs suspended from the ceiling, and three private rooms (one's a cigar lounge), each equipped with entertainment centers featuring 60-inch plasma screens, PlayStation II and XBox, pool tables, and Italian leather wraparound couches."

"Named after the exclusive coterie of baseball players who can claim both 40 home runs and 40 stolen bases in one season, (there are only three), the club is the venue of choice for big-name draft parties and other events. Barry Bonds (one of the aforementioned trio, along with Alex Rodriguez and Jose Canseco) is a regular, and both WFAN and ESPN Radio broadcast from here once a week, adding to the huge list of star athletes and other celebrities who have made this their 'local' sports bar." The club was such an instant success that Jay planned to open a second location in Atlantic City in later 2004.

Oddly, in February, 2004, a new trend altogether began in the business, in theory an extension of the mix tape phenomenon, wherein DJ Danger Mouse created 'The Grey Album', matching Jay-Z's vocals from the 'The Black Album' up with songs from the Beatles' historic double LP 'The White Album'. Though EMI served the DJ and his record label with a Cease-and-Decist order, the experiment not only bridging musical genres and generations, the mash-up as it were, would become a new craze in hip-hop.

Describing his process, Mouse explained that "a lot of people just assumed I took some Beatles and, you know, threw some Jay-Z on top of it or mixed it up or looped it around, but it's really a decons-truction…It's not an easy thing to do…I was obsessed with the whole project, that's all I was trying to do, see if I could do this…Once I got into it, I didn't think about anything but finish-ing it…I stuck to those two because I thought it would be more challenging and more fun and more of a statement to what you could do with sampling alone…It is an art form. It is music."

"You can do different things, it doesn't have to be just what some people call stealing. It can be a lot more than that…I stuck to those two because I thought it would be more challenging and more fun and more of a statement to what you could do with sampling alone…It is an art form. It is music. You can do different things, it doesn't have to be just what some people call stealing. It can be a lot more than that…My whole thing with this was I didn't want to mess up the Beatles song either…I don't want to disrespect the Beatles. A lot of people thought it was sacrilege in the first place. I knew that would be something, but I didn't know it was going to be (distributed) on a wide scale. I knew my friends wouldn't think it was sacrilege, so I just made sure it was something I would dig myself…I was lucky in a lot of ways…If it had been the Who, we wouldn't be here. If it had been LL Cool J, we wouldn't be here."

MTV.com described the physical process of putting the album together as one in which "the first thing the producer did was listen to *The Black Album* acappella and measure the amount of beats per minute for each track, a common technique for club DJs who seamlessly mix music together. Next, he scoured all 30 songs on *The White Album*, listening for every strike of a drum or cymbal when other instruments or voices were not in the mix. Most were single sounds, which he would later put together to make beats. With the intricate method Burton used for the rhythm tracks on *The Grey Album* he could have easily tossed in a kick drum from another album here or a bass drum there, and no one would have noticed, but that never crossed his mind…After pulling every possible Ringo Starr part from *The White Album*, Burton repeated the process for guitar and bass samples.

Once he felt there was a workable amount of sounds banked, he started with a Jay-Z vocal track and built the music around it using the software Acid Pro, an alternative to ProTools that retails for about $400…The program allows the layering of separate tracks of samples, with the average song on *The Grey Album* being

16 tracks, although some have as many as 25...All together, he worked nearly nonstop for two weeks on the album." The result was 100,000 downloads off of the Grey Tuesday Group website, who distributed the album online for Downhill Music.

Jay-Z, for his part, enthusiastically categorized the project as "flattery to me. I'll promote any type of creativity. You know what I'm saying? I mean I put a acappella album out there so I promote it...I've heard a lot of them. I heard the purple album with all the prince music. I heard jay-zeezer with weezer in the background. I heard, of course, the grey album. I heard the Latin album."

While all of the aforementioned was happening in and around Jay's world, *Fortune Magazine* also released its annual list of the 40 richest Americans under 40, and Jay got a big raise in both his net worth and ranking in the magazine, coming in at $286 million, sandwiched right between Tiger woods at $295 million and P. Diddy at $315 million. Ironically, Damon Dash was nowhere to be found. Jay's star was definitely still on the rise, and right amid the dark falling on one phase of his career, the sun was dawning upon another.

One industry executive described Jay's evolution out of emceeing as one in which "I think Puffy became a businessman so he could become a rapper...Jay-Z became a rapper to become a businessman. That was his way of getting into the game, because who wouldn't want to hire the most popular guy in hip-hop? His face alone would get the deal done. That wouldn't have happened to a kid coming straight out of the ghetto—he never would have had a shot."

Jay, for his part, was clearly at peace with his decision, and had a much more relaxed perspective on the whole subject of his exit, reasoning that "I've read articles where people compare rap to other genres of music like jazz or rock n roll. But it's really most like a sport. Boxing to be exact. The stamina, the one-man army, the combat aspect of it, the ring, the stage, and the fact that boxers never quit when they should. Also, historically, boxers wind up in bad shape financially."

"When I think of athletes who left their game when they were still dominating their sport, I think of Jim Brown and Barry Sanders... Michael Jordan, who, next to Biggie, is the only nigga outside of my family or team whom I absolutely love, did two years too many. When he went to the Washington Wizards, It killed me as a fan. I knew he was trying to fulfill something inside himself. But for me, as a fan, to see him come out of retirement for the first time, after his father was buried, to come back and win championships, there was nothing better in the world."

"In 1998, the Bulls were down, Jordan scored, stole the ball from Karl Malone, scored again, then came down, pushed a guy, hit the winning shot! I could have died. I could have laid down and died after that game. It was too perfect. That's probably why he came back—it was too perfect...I've had moments like that in my career, moments where your skill transcends who you are as a physical being. You almost feel not human. It's what performers or athletes talk about when they say God was working with them. It's scary. It's almost like you have to come back and fuck up to remind yourself and the world you're human..."

"Then there's something I remember Jordan said about feeling uninspired that I can relate to. When he came into the NBA, he was looking forward to playing with Magic Johnson and Larry Bird, and they both retired relatively early in Jordan's career. I feel that way about Big and 'Pac. They're both still very present in hip-hop; Biggie in terms of his influence and the love people have for him as the greatest MC. We all keep Big alive by sampling him; that's my intention when I use his lyrics, to keep him present in the game. But it's not the same. I wish they both were still here...I can honestly say I'm bored with hip-hop. I spend a lot of time feeling uninspired. I guess I'm spoiled. I grew up in a time where you had Ice Cube and Brand Nubian releasing albums the same year.

One was West Coast, stylish, gangsta, and political. Polar opposites but still linked, with crazy support from the same fan."

"Now, no one makes an album anymore. As soon as they walk into their label's office, executives are asking for a single. I know I'm guilty of co-creating that format, but it just gets dimmer every time it's copied. A rapper will do their 'girl' song, the 'club' song, and then their 'gangsta white label.' It's not about the music anymore. It's about reaching for numbers…For me, its from my heart. If that wasn't the case, I would've stopped years ago. People try and throw me in a commercial box now. I've sold a lot of records. I've made anthems. The thing is, I don't necessarily set out to make a hard-core record or a pop record. I don't even believe in going to the studio to make a huge record. Some of my largest records have had the nastiest hooks. Listen to 'Big Pimpin' or 'Can I get A Fuck You'…That was a huge record, but it wasn't 'I love you baby.' That wasn't a formula record. It was just a good record that turned out to be huge…"

"There are artists that still get me excited, like dead prez, who remind me of Cube-they're political and street. 50 Cent benefited from having a compelling life story, a sense of humor, and great timing. He did what I call 'DMX-ed' the game. The 'Excuse Me Miss' and 'Beautiful' kind of records were getting all the love, and he came and made it street again. DMX did the same thing five years ago. Plus, 50 posted first-time numbers like Puff. Now he faces the same challenge we all faced, which is to stay relevant over a period of time…"

"So far at least two years, this is my last album and I'm only saying two years because I already have people coming up to me in the street who swear they're depressed that I'm retiring. It would take something real drastic to get me to make another album. People crying in the streets, or a petition with 3 million names on it, or me in a corner like a junkie, withdrawing from rap. But unless I'm inspired by something, I don't see a full-length album by Jay-Z coming down the pike. But I'm human."

"Ghostwriting for other artists might actually be my creative outlet. I may do collaborations, but not for a year. I read Miles Davis did this—took a break—and I understand it now. It probably got to a point where he felt he just couldn't hear what was being played, and he just had to stop. He didn't play his horn professionally for a couple of years. I truly did this rap game to death. No one can be mad at me for putting it down...(So I'm retiring from making) solo albums, and I don't know. I'm going to take a break from touring but I can't say I won't play another gig again, but mainly from solo albums...If I have withdrawal in three or four years, if I'm in the bathroom, chills on the floor or something, maybe I will make another album...Ten years in hip-hop feels like decades...I hope to continue to live and grow."

As Jay and Beyoncé continued to get more serious, speculation throughout New York's gossip columns also spun wild that Jay and B would settling down soon to start a family. For Jay's part, he admitted that "I don't know, a big boat somewhere, throwing a couple kids in the air...I carry my nephews like my sons, always have and they have filled that void for me. But it has definitely come a time where I want to have my own family. Absolutely... I'm really scared to have kids because I know the way I am with my nephews, I don't think I'll be able to go outside. I'll never want to leave my kids. (Parenthood) puts everything into perspective."

That perspective was at least consistent with Jay's plans for retirement from the hectic schedule of being a rap superstar. While Jay's passion for emceeing had grown weak, even partner Damon Dash acknowledged that it would be logical for Jay to have ambitions toward running his own show completely, warning competitors not to "put it past him...He laid down the blueprint of how an artist should not rely only on the money from the music...He has a lot more compassion than I do…Every time I would fire some-one, he hire them. He's always been that nice of a guy."

While nothing had been said officially on the subject, as the summer of 2004 bloomed, in June, Jay and his girl Beyoncé cleaned up at the BET Awards, won Best Male Hip Hop Artist and Best Collaboration for 'Crazy in Love' with Beyoncé, who took home Best Female R&B Artist, among other awards. At the show, Jay also performed his hit '99 Problems' with an eclectic backing group that included Kid Rock, Dave Navarro, the Roots, Shelia E. and Rick Rubin himself. Roc-A-Fella Records' newest sensation, Kanye West, headed out on a summer-long tour trek with Usher, as his debut album, 'College Dropout' was certified triple platinum, along with his second smash single, 'All Falls Down', which had hit number one on both the Billboard and MTV Top 20 Video charts. Kanye showed the most promise to become Roc-A-Fella's next superstar after Jay's retirement, and he certainly was following the company's formula in that direction, launching a clothing line—Mascott—(including his own Tennis Shoe brand), a religious-themed jewelry brand in partnership with Jacob the Jeweler, and of course, his own record label, called "Getting Out Our Dreams (GOOD)"

His first release was scheduled to be R&B singer John Legend's *Get Lifted* on December 28, 2004, distributed ironically not through Roc-A-Fella Records, rather through competitor Sony Music, with whom he had also signed an independent production deal. In July, Jay announced that he would be sponsoring yet another of his many charity efforts in cooperation with Reebok, wherein between July 19th and 28th, fans were able to go to Reebok's website, and bid on shoes designed personally by supermodels, actresses and musicians including Tyra Banks, Joy Bryant, Fergie, Queen Latifah, and of course Beyoncé, all pro-ceeds of which were donated to the Shawn Carter Scholarship Fund.

Jay had founded his charitable foundation in 2003, through which he sponsored scholarships for impoverished children from his old neighborhood and throughout Brooklyn, explaining that "we're the first generation of hip-hop guys to really make the big money...The generation before us never made this type of cash, so it's on us to keep it going and give it back...You know everyone has their Achilles heel, and everyone had to go through things to become who they are now. You know as a kid you go through things that are just part of life, and you don't come out of the womb perfect. We're all imperfect."

"I really had my mind set on being a boss from the beginning...(Violence in rap and the inner city is) a society problem, nothing to do with hip-hop. They have to fix the 'hood; they've been ignoring it. That's why rap music sells, 'cause we're like the voice that's being ignored...I've seen people killed and it not even be on the news. Nothing!...I guess everything helps, but it's really these neighborhoods. You gotta start feeling like life is important. People feel that life is not important. You have these huge, huge superstars, like 2Pac and Biggie Smalls, that get killed and their murders go unsolved."

"I think people think that life is unimportant. if a politician or a cop gets killed in a violent way like that, you best believe—you better believe—its not going unsolved. I've never even heard of it. Have you ever heard of a cop's murder going unsolved?...People were always telling me, 'Yo, you're good, man,' 'cause it was easy for me...I ain't recognize that it was a gift because my mom always taught me that anything worth having, you gotta work hard for it. But it was easy...I wanted to set them straight on the likelihood of them making it...I broke it down to them by saying that they even had a better chance of being an NBA player than they did a rapper. I was, like, 'Keep it real—there are about 200 or more NBA players getting a check. There are only about 10 to 20 rappers that are in the game making money with album after album. Do the math and get your education.'"

As August began, Jay-Z made history again in real time when he expanded his ownership beyond TEAM Roc to include becoming a part owner in the New Jersey Nets. On August 12th, MTV.com news reported that "Jay-Z's career as part-owner of an NBA franchise has officially begun…The NBA Board of Governors unanimously approved the sale of the New Jersey Nets on Thursday to an ownership group that includes the star rapper…In January, the group, led by developer Bruce Ratner, had its $300 million offer accepted by the New Jersey Nets, though the sale still needed approval from the league.

Ratner recruited Jay-Z and a number of prominent Brooklynites with the idea of moving the franchise from the swamps of New Jersey to downtown Brooklyn. He plans to build a 19,000-seat arena in time for the 2006-2007 NBA season as part of a $2.5 billion development project, although the plan faces community opposition. Jay-Z holds a minority interest in the team. 'When the NBA approved me, I was like, 'This is really happening! This is crazy!' Then came discussion of relocating the team to his native Brooklyn. 'Forget about it', says the star 'That just put steroids on it.' " Later in August, on his quest to tie off all of his obligations as an artist, on August 19th, Jay and R. Kelly decided to take care of some Unfinished Business, making plans to release the second installment of their collaboration, which began with the Best of Both Worlds LP two years earlier.

The pair announced a 2-month tour would kick off in the fall to support the album's release, with Jay ambitiously stating that "we want people to be genuinely shocked and awed, we're on a shock-and-awe campaign." R. Kelly, even more eager to put distance behind the disastrous sales of *Best of Both Worlds*, due entirely to the singer's legal troubles, excitedly declared that "we want to blow up the world…In any arena we go to, we want to give them something they've never seen before. You never know what (can) happen when me and Jay get on that stage—we're spontaneous."

According to MTV.com news, "Jay-Z and R. Kelly are back on the same page and are currently finalizing plans for their long-awaited *Best of Both Worlds* tour. The trek is scheduled to hit more than 40 cities, with the first stop being Kelly's hometown of Chicago on September 30 and the last date being November 28 in Phoenix." As the summer wound down, Jay received 6 MTV Video Music Award nominations, including Video of the Year, Best Male Video, Best Rap Video, Best Direction, Best Editing, and Best Cinematography for '99 Problems.'

Finally, rumors began swirling in late August that Island/Def Jam were pursuing Jay for a high-level executive job following his retirement in December, to which Jay would only confirm that "nothing is concrete yet. There's a bunch of offers from Def Jam as well as from other companies. I'm really excited and flattered about the opportunities but nothing is concrete yet so I don't know what I'm going to do next...(But) I definitely want that to be the next phase of my career; to take on a real executive position."

Elaborating on his general ambitions in the corporate direction, Jay explained that, from his vantage point, "too many times, artists, after they finish their career, wind up on VH1 specials like on 'Where are they now?' and things like that. When you have Hall of Fame sportsmen, they usually end up being great coaches cause the players respect them cause they know they have played the game, they've played hurt, and they will the situations. It should be the same way with artists I believe...I believe that rap has gotten so big from a marketing standpoint that we forget it's the music business and not the business of music."

"The music should come first. I think there's so much pressure coming from the higher ups and it trickles down to the artist to make a hit now. Everything is about making a hit. We're not concentrating on building artists anymore. A perfect example is a guy like Anthony Hamilton. They were already moved away from that project. If the wire record with Jadakiss didn't come out to understand that he's an artist. He's at 900,000 (units sold) now and when he was at 300,000 they were ready to walk away from the project. Had they stuck with it the whole time, who knows where he would be right now. Without the promotion, people just went out and picked out his music and slowly made onto him."

"The same thing happened with Jill Scott. It took a TV appearance, and I don't know if it was on Oprah but one of those TV performances triggered her whole movement but they wasn't on that project like that...(My first piece of advice for any kid would be NOT to get into the record business.) That would weed out all the people that aren't that serious about it. If it's truly your passion and something that you really love, there will be a lot of doors slammed in your face and you have to keep going. You just need that belief in yourself that it's going to happen for you and you need it wholeheartedly. You will hear a lot of different and doors will be slammed. I could have said that this wasn't for me and do something else, but I looked right in the face of the corporation, and told them that they're wrong."

"That's a tough thing to do for someone to do who has never put out an album and tell a record company that's sold millions of records that they are wrong...(For example, with Mos Def), I think he's an extraordinary talent and a very intelligent guy. Absolutely. We have seen Frankie Lyman so many times. We've seen how a person is so successful recording and at the end of the day, everyone is walking away with their masters, and everyone is rich, except for them. We are not prepared to let that happen ever again. With me stepping up to the executive, and I'm an artist, so whatever artist come up through my watch, is going to be taken care of. Every single one of my artists owns their own publishing."

"If they sold it to BMI or someone else, that was their choice, but I don't own their publishing. I encourage them to own other businesses. Beanie Siegel has State Property and Pro-Keds Line and

Memphis Bleek has Get-Low Records, so I encourage them to be entrepreneurs...I think the people that hip-hop artists grew up on, who they are in love with, and emulate, are people who gave in themselves. There are artists who were vulnerable at times; who went crazy and talked about guns and whatever. They had moments, whatever it was, it was them. It was Tupac and Big. They gave themselves. Nowadays, there are people who are trying to make what's popular and whatever is hot, and that's not necessarily a good thing...I'm rock and roll, man. That's not a done deal. We're just talking. We'll see what happens with that situation. I'm an artist across the board. I know what good music is no matter what. I believe in good music and bad music, and that's it. Bad music is bad in rock, is bad in bluegrass, or whatever...Def Jam started out in the college dorm room. I've been hanging out with Def Jam co-founder Rick Rubin so I know this story very well. They created Def Jam because the music people were listening to it in the clubs, they wanted to hear it outside of the club. They wanted to hear it in their car and in the dorm room. They had to go to clubs to hear the music because the DJ had the vinyl. It started out making this music so they can hear it and so at a college dorm room, the people there wanted to hear it too and they would buy a tape off of them and that started the whole thing."

"They didn't start it with the idea of making a business. They started it as a need. I want to hear music and that was it. My focus as President would be to create artists again. It's very simple to focus back on artists. Hopefully, whatever position I take, if they allow me that lead time so I can be an artist instead of making great records. We make good singles and that's good cause I'll listen to it in clubs and I may even buy 'Now 18' or whatever number they are up to with all the good singles on it, but I don't buy into you as an artist. My focus would be on building artists." Jay would spend the rest of the year showing why he was the Professor of Platinum, racking up two more top 10 albums, and countless awards.

As the fall began, Roc-A-Fella was riding high off both Jay-Z and new ROC-superstar Kanye West's wildly successful year, which continued with 6 MTV Music Award Nominations including Best Male Video, Best Hip Hop Video, Best New Artist in a Video, and Breakthrough Video for 'All Fall Down.' When the American Music Awards were announced, West was also blessed with 3 nods for Breakthrough Artist, Favorite Male Artist, alongside label boss Jay-Z, and Favorite Album, also competing with Jay-Z for the *Black Album*.

At the MTV Music Awards ceremony, Roc-A-Fella proved once again to be a dominant force, as Jay-Z cleaned up with awards for Best Rap Video, Best Direction, Best Editing, Best Cinematography for '99 Problems.' As the month continued, Jay was nominated for four Source Award nominations, including Artist of the Year, Male Solo, Lyricist of the Year and Album of the Year, along with Kanye West, who racked up 7 nominations for Breakthrough Artist of the Year, Album of the Year, Lyricist of the Year, Live Performer of the Year, Producer of the Year, and Video of the Year for 'Through the Wire'.

In October, Kanye West cleaned house at the Source Awards, racking up wins for Breakthrough Artist of the Year, Album of the Year for The College Dropout and Video of the Year for "Through the Wire," which he co-directed. Jay, meanwhile, took home the Lyricist of the Year award. That same month, more tour dates were announced for the Jay-Z/R. Kelly Unfinished Business album, due in December. Roc-A-Fella Records announced the tour's first-leg dates as 9/30—Rosemont, IL @ Allstate Arena, 10/1— Cincinnati, OH @ U.S. Bank Arena, 10/2—Columbus, OH @ Value City Arena, 10/3—Cleveland, OH @ CSU Convocation Center, 10/5—Buffalo, NY @ HSBC Arena, 10/8—Baltimore, MD @ 1st Mariner Arena, 10/9—Greensboro, NC @ Coliseum, 10/10—Nashville, TN @ Gaylord Center, 10/17—Memphis, TN @ FedEx Forum, 10/28—Uniondale, NY @

Nassau Coliseum, 10/31—East Rutherford, NJ @ Continental Airlines Arena, and 11/28—Phoenix, AZ @ TBA.

In an attempt to pre-empt hungry bootleggers, Jay and Kelly, according to MTV.com News, "filed a federal lawsuit on Thursday with the hope of preventing bootleggers from selling counterfeit merchandise in advance of the Best of Both Worlds tour that starts next week in Chicago. The suit asks that federal, state and local law enforcement be allowed to seize merchandise from the unlicensed sellers expected to hawk goods outside venues on the tour."

The tour kicked off—as far as the public was told—without a hitch, with Kelly feeling so confident that he even mocked his pending legal charges onstage, wherein, according to MTV.com news, "in a review called 'R. Kelly Flouting His Foes' that ran on October 1, Sun-Times writer Jim DeRogatis—who has been investigating Kelly's alleged predilection for young girls since 2000—took Kelly to task for blurring 'the line between art and obsession.'

Although Kelly didn't refer to the charges directly, DeRogatis wrote that they '(hung) over the concert,' since the singer referred to them indirectly, playing the alleged crimes for laughs and sympathy... His examples included a show-opening video depicting Kelly's tour bus followed by police cars; an e-mail message displayed on a giant video screen in which Kelly (who is married and has three young children) seeks a female companion who is 'at least 19 or over'; dancers wearing orange prison-style jumpsuits in a mock jail cell; and a video backdrop of 'flowing yellow water or rain' (some of the charges Kelly faces involve urination during a sex act)."

Kelly's behavior became stranger as October wore on, with cancelled shows at the Bradley Center in Milwaukee, and the Civic Center in Hartford, Connecticut due to what was being spun as 'technical difficulties', and in perhaps the oddest single act of Kelly's career, one instance on October 26th in which the singer skipped the show altogether, and showed up instead at a

McDonald's Drive-Thru serving fans. Kelly's spokesmen Allan Mayer claimed that "He just loves working behind the counter...He gets a kick out of it, I guess as a way to interact with fans without it being totally crazy." The whole incident made R. Kelly look crazier than anyone else.

By the end of the month, one day prior to Halloween, on October 30th, things turned especially freaky when Kelly abruptly left the stage during the duo's Madison Square Garden date, claiming that he'd seen a gun in the audience, despite the fact that the facility had a 0% record of weapon discovery or violence in the 20 years prior due to their extremely strict metal detector search of each audience member prior to entering the arena.

As MTV.com News reported "The plug has been pulled on Jay-Z and R. Kelly's *Best of Both Worlds* tour after a bizarre show at New York's Madison Square Garden on Friday night that sent Kelly to the hospital and both artists to the media to tell very different stories...A brief statement issued on Saturday (October 30) by tour organizers announced that Kelly would not perform that evening at Madison Square Garden, on Sunday at the Continental Airlines Arena or on Monday, again at Madison Square Garden. The statement indicated that the shows would now feature 'Jay-Z and special guests.'...In his own statement, Kelly expressed his disappointment at the move and noted that he is ready and willing to perform as part of the tour. 'The fans deserve better than this...I'd like the show to go on. It's really disappointing that Jay-Z and the promoter don't.'"

"The tour hit Madison Square Garden Friday night for the first of three shows (the duo performed without incident on Thursday at Long Island's Nassau Coliseum). However, thousands of fans were left disappointed as Kelly abruptly bolted from the show, claiming that his life was in jeopardy. Kelly told the crowd that while he was trying to perform, 'two people were waving guns at me,' and declined to perform further. Shortly after, Jay told the crowd, 'I don't need that nigga!' and, accompanied by Mary J. Blige, Usher and Ja Rule, delivered a hit-filled set."

"In an interview on New York radio station Hot 97 early Saturday morning, Jay called Kelly's actions 'foolery' and said that the 'insecure' Kelly was jealous of the crowds' love for Jay. In a separate interview, Kelly admitted to Hot 97 that he panicked, but said in a statement that he tried to return to the stage, only to be pepper-sprayed by a member of Jay-Z's entourage—an attack that sent him to New York's St. Vincent's Hospital. He said he had been ready and eager to perform on Friday night, but that he was not allowed to do so."

"Friday's show started normally, with the two headliners rocking the stage together during the first set. Shortly after, Jay-Z came back for his solo turn, followed by one from Kelly. The show then went back to Jay's hand with another Jiggaman set…Just before the R's second solo set was to begin, Kelly, dressed in the same black-and-white vest he donned on the cover of his 12 Play LP, came out onstage and began talking somberly. It sounded like he was holding back tears."

"He told the audience that he was originally going to send security out to relay a message to the crowd. He thanked his fans for their support, then said he was about to do one of the hardest things he ever had to do. He said that while he was trying to perform, 'two people were waving guns at me.' As the bewildered Garden audience looked on, Kelly said, 'I can't do no show like that …This shit is over.'" For Kelly it was, as Jay-Z—clearly the true headliner—fired him off the tour.

That night however, Kelly had left Jay holding the bag with a capacity crowd, and being the consummate professional, Jay-Z gave the crowd their money's worth, and then some. As Jigga explained in the aftermath of the whole crisis, "Me, I don't need much—give me a mike and a beat and I'll connect with people… (But Kelly is) a perfectionist. If they miss one lighting cue, he'll be upset. His problems with the lighting and sound guys forced us to miss some shows. Which made me think, 'Why am I out here? I could be doing something else.'…"

"Out of every negative situation, you know what I'm saying, positive things happen. So that happened that night and it so happened that a lot of people were in the audience—Usher being one of them—and, you know, we just put it together. He ran out the audience—'What you need me to do? What you need me to do?' So we had these laptops, so we started burning CD's right on the spot. Burning down CD's for—this is good, this is good downloading…We burnt CD tracks…(Then Usher) got on stage and he performed to—and that was really a big thing for me. To see him do that, 'cause he's a superstar in his own right…He performed with no back music, no anything. He just grabbed the mike, it sounded just like the record…I just really wanted to give the people more than they paid for. I wanted to make sure—you know they paid to see two people. You know what I'm saying… Two all-star talents. And I just wanted to make sure they got more than their money's worth…(With Kelly), I mean, I'm not a lighting guy for one. You know what I'm saying. And I'm not his daddy…So if he thought like his lights were messed up, he should've got a lighting guy."

"The whole thing was supposed to be the best of both worlds. So we had one lighting guy. You know, everything was supposed to be—you know, you do the best at what you do…I do the best at what I do. It wasn't a competition, at least in my eyes. Now that everything has come to fruition, I see it was a competition." In a follow-up report, MTV.com News reported that "(after) Kelly… dropped his microphone and walked off the stage. After several perplexing minutes, Jay yelled from backstage, 'Fuck that! I got this shit myself, New York. Give me my old-school shit! I got hits.'"

"With fans yelling 'Hova!' Jigga came out with Memphis Bleek and continued the concert. He rocked the crowd with verses from

Mya's 'Best of Me' remix, then went into 'Ain't No Nigga.' The song's co-star, Foxy Brown, came out for a surprise guest spot that was met with a loud roar...'I got some good news and bad news...R. Kelly is not coming back. If y'all waiting to see him, go home. The good news is that I got a lot of records—and I got y'all.' He then asked for a few minutes to put a set together."

"'OK, I got it together,' Jay's voice emerged after the break. 'I promise you, you're gonna love it. I found a couple of people.' The first of Jay's 11th-hour guest performers joined him. Ja Rule came out in a gray hoodie for 'Can I Get A ...' It felt like 1998 again as Ja let loose that passionate roar, rapping to cheers. After the next jam, 'Excuse Me Miss,' Mary J. Blige came out with Hov for 'Can't Knock the Hustle.'...Then Usher, who some fans had been screaming for when Kelly made his startling announcement, came out for 'Caught Up.'"

"The singer had come to the show as a spectator. 'This is for the big homie,' Usher said while he was singing. 'I got something special for New York, and I got something special for you (Jay),' Usher said after an a cappella rendition of his 'Confessions' remix. 'You know we should have done this together.'...There was an intermission—during what would have been another Kelly set—and then Jay came back on with a few more surprises. Memphis Bleek and T.I. performed 'Round Here,' then Tip went into 'Rubber Band Man.' Freeway and the Young Gunz came out with Jay and Bleek toward the end of the show and did some of their Roc-A-Fella familiar hits to close out. 'I did the best I could,' Jay told the crowd. 'I love each and every one of y'all.'"

The fallout from Kelly's bouncing was most damaging for Kelly in both financial and fan terms, as Jay quickly announced he would continue the tour based on the blueprint from the show Kelly had bounced on. The industry's elite showed who they were backing when Jay introduced his guest roster to rescue the Saturday, October 30th show, which included P. Diddy, Mase, Black Rob, Busta

Rhymes, Mariah Carey, Mary J. Blige, Method Man, Redman, Doug E. Fresh, Lil Vicious, Memphis Bleek, State Property and Foxy Brown. At the Continental Airlines Arena show in New Jersey on Sunday October 31, Jay continued to fan the fires with a line up boasting Mary J. Blige, Busta Rhymes, P. Diddy, Doug E. Fresh, Foxy Brown Kanye West, Talib Kweli, Q-Tip, Slick Rick, and Pharrell Williams of the Neptunes.

Jay decided that the show could, in fact, go on for the sake of the fans. Calling the newly repackaged tour 'Jay-Z and Friends', Jay, according to MTV.com News, "Just 24 hours after announcing that the 'Jay-Z and Friends' tour would last at least one more date, a spokesperson for Jay said the rapper will, indeed, complete the remainder of the canceled tour...There has been no announcement detailing exactly who will be joining Jay for the remaining 16 dates; however, P. Diddy and Mary J. Blige have been announced for Friday's show at Miami's American Airlines Arena..."

"Several members of the hip-hop community, including Diddy, Mary, Usher, Busta Rhymes and Snoop Dogg, rallied around Hov, helping him to finish the show at the Garden and the remaining three dates he had scheduled in the New York /New Jersey area."

Meanwhile, both performers put their own spins on whose fault it had been that Kelly left the show, with Jay arguing to Angie Martinez on Hot 97 that Kelly's assertion about a gun was ridiculous given that "that's Madison Square Garden. You cannot get a gun into Madison Square Garden. Does he know where he's at?...It's very frustrating to cancel shows...Because I wanna see every single person. I don't want somebody to be holding their ticket for 29 days and on the 30th day it gets cancelled."

"But (the tour) is living up to my expectations when I get out there and I see people and connect with people. I'm like, 'This is the reason I'm here.' When I first step off the bus and I turn that corner and they throwing up Roc signs, I'm like, 'This is why I'm here.' " Kelly, for his part, gave an interview to the same station and DJ, claiming that "I love performing, I'm very secure (with) who I am…Dude opened up his coat—I can't say dude had a gun, I don't know what I saw…I wasn't going to take any chances when I saw what I saw. I'm not crazy."

Jay-Z released a subsequent statement on Monday, November 1, stating that "R. Kelly's lack of professionalism and unpredictable behavior has prevented the *Best of Both Worlds* tour from continuing…Mr. Kelly has cancelled three performances with less than 24 hours' notice and has delayed multiple shows by hours. On Friday, October 29, at a sold-out Madison Square Garden show, Mr. Kelly made a statement from the stage claiming members of the audience were waving guns."

"Jay-Z sees that statement as the equivalent of screaming 'Fire' in a crowded theater and was unable to continue with someone whose actions could potentially create a dangerous situation…Based on his actions on the tour to this point, the statement from R. Kelly's publicist (released on Saturday) suggesting that Robert was not 'ready, willing and able' to continue the tour lacks any credibility. In Chicago and Baltimore, R. Kelly was not 'ready.' In Cincinnati, Milwaukee and Hartford, R. Kelly was not 'willing.' In St. Louis and New York, R. Kelly was not 'able.'"

Sadly, Kelly's behavior for weeks prior to the tour's collapse, as it would later be outlined in litigation, was painted to be at the least eccentric, and at the worst, outright nuts. To no one's surprise, following Jay and the promoter's decision to fire Kelly off the tour, the embattled R&B star responded by filing a $75 million lawsuit against on November 1st, claiming that "the historic and highly anticipated tour quickly turned into a nightmare as Jay-Z and his associates, motivated by spite and jealousy, not only failed to perform their obligations under the relevant agreements but also engaged in conduct intentionally designed to exclude R. Kelly from the tour, including threats and acts of violence…As a result of Jay-Z's conduct, R. Kelly has been excluded from certain past tour performances and will be excluded from future performances as well. Such conduct amounts to breach of contract by the concert promoter and tortious interference with that contract by Jay-Z and his business entity."

The suit sought $60 million in punitive damages, and $15 million in lost income. Jay-Z, to no surprise, counter-sued in short time over what he termed in his legal filing to be a 'nightmare odyssey', wherein, according to the Smoking Gun.com, "Kelly is a weepy, emotional wreck whose bizarre behavior sabotaged a recent concert tour with Jay-Z, according to a blistering court filing. Firing back at the R&B singer (full name: Robert Kelly), who filed a $90 million breach of contract lawsuit last November, the 35-year-old rapper (real name: Shawn Carter) claims that Kelly was the one responsible for the October collapse of the duo's 'Best of Both Worlds' tour."

"In answering Kelly's complaint, Jay-Z describes the 36-year-old singer as prone to crying fits and, in light of his 'precarious financial and legal circumstances,' desperate for money. Below you'll find an excerpt from Jay-Z's January 24 legal response, which includes two counterclaims against Kelly. Along with a remembrance of Kelly once 'crying hysterically,' Jay-Z's filing contains many delights for the urban music fan. Our favorite passage regards the conclusion of a disastrous R. Kelly set in St. Louis: After leaving the stage to assault the lighting director, 'without explanation or apology, R. Kelly returned to the stage, bowed to the audience, changed his outfit, hopped onto a waiting People Mover, and left the venue before the concert was completed…R. Kelly then went to a local McDonald's where he began to serve food to patrons at the drive-thru.'"

COUNTERCLAIMS AGAINST PLAINTIFFS

108. This counter-suit is commenced by the Marcy Parties to recover damages against plaintiffs for tortious interference with contract and fraudulent inducement, necessitated by R. Kelly's flagrant and unjustified misconduct, as well as his repeated histrionics, both before and during the Tour.

109. R. Kelly's material defaults, and unsafe and unpredictable behavior, examples of which are recounted below, destroyed the Tour and forced Jeff Sharp of Atlanta Worldwide (hereafter sometimes referred to as, the "Promoter") and the Marcy Parties to attempt to mitigate their damages by pursuing a new concert tour involving Jay-Z and an all-star cast of hip-hop artists and musical acts.

Jay-Z

110. Jay-Z is a celebrated recording artist and performer who has sold millions of records. He has been awarded the most coveted accolades in the music business, including the Grammy, MTV, Source, Billboard, BET and Soul Train awards. Jay-Z's success as a musical artist arises in part from a combination of artistic credibility and broad commercial appeal. For almost a decade, Jay-Z has toured extensively throughout the world, performing in live concerts before sold-out crowds.

111. Jay-Z also is an internationally respected entrepreneur. He is the co-founder of Roc-A-Fella Records, which includes a roster of popular artists and producers, such as, Beanie Sigel, Cam' Ron, M.O.P., Just Blaze, and Kanye West. His successes also include part ownership of the Roca Wear clothing line. The diversity and magnitude of Jay-Z's built-in fan base has made Roca Wear a highly successful apparel company with a broad demographic base. In addition, Jay-Z has created other branding opportunities, including

18

Reebok's "S. Carter" sneaker collection. Furthermore, Jay-Z has ownership interests in an NBA basketball team, the New Jersey Nets, and an upscale sports club, the 40/40 Club.

112. Jay-Z's artistic credibility and popularity have created strong demand for his participation in tour and musical collaborations with other well-known artists and musical acts. For example, Jay-Z has successfully toured with 50 Cent in the *Rock The Mike Tour* and with DMX in the *Hard Knock Life Tour*.

113. In early 2002, Jay-Z collaborated with R. Kelly on the album *Best of Both Worlds*. During the recording of that album, the artists first discussed the possibility of participating in a personal appearance tour. However, in February 2002, the *Chicago Sun Times* reported that videotape existed depicting R. Kelly having illicit sexual relations with a 14 year-old girl. This startling allegation dampened for many months further discussion of a tour involving Jay-Z and R. Kelly.

114. In June 2002, R. Kelly was arrested in Florida based on an Illinois arrest warrant. Upon information and belief, the warrant charged R. Kelly with twenty-one counts of child pornography based on his alleged illicit sex with an underage girl, which was captured on video.

115. The controversy and public condemnation that arose after R. Kelly's arrest, together with other salacious allegations concerning R. Kelly's sexual proclivities, curtailed any further discussion of a possible tour with Jay-Z.

116. In the fall of 2003, Jay-Z performed in a concert at the Garden that was reported by the media as his farewell live performance. At the concert, Jay-Z performed with a number of guest artists, including R. Kelly, Beyonce, Foxy Brown, and Missy Elliot.

19

R. Kelly demanded a substantial appearance fee for his performance, as he revealed his mounting financial difficulties and legal troubles.

The Best of Both Worlds Tour

117. The audience's tremendous response to a duet performance by Jay-Z and R. Kelly re-ignited discussions of a possible tour collaboration. Intermittent discussions continued until the summer of 2004 when Jay-Z and R. Kelly agreed to record a second album.

118. In the course of those discussions, R. Kelly's representatives represented to Jay-Z that R. Kelly could and would commit to producing a live performance for the proposed Tour, and that he could and would deliver a first-class performance at each concert. The Marcy Parties relied upon those representations in proceeding to negotiate and enter into a contract with Atlanta Worldwide to co-headline the Tour with R. Kelly.

119. In negotiating acceptable financial terms, R. Kelly told Jay-Z and his representatives that he desperately needed money and that he would require substantial compensation to participate in the Tour. He reiterated to them his precarious financial and legal circumstances. Because Jay-Z was highly motivated to tour, he willingly agreed to accept a smaller guaranty and percentage of Atlanta Worldwide's profits in order to accommodate R. Kelly's financial needs.

120. To accommodate R. Kelly's financial needs, the Promoter was compelled to increase the number of concert dates. Ordinarily that would not be a problem, but in this case, upon information and belief, the court presiding over R. Kelly's criminal case granted only two months for R. Kelly to travel outside Illinois. Thus, Atlanta Worldwide's sole option was to begin the Tour in Chicago before the two-month window began. By doing so,

it shortened much needed rehearsal time and violated the rudimentary principle that a tour not begin in a major venue before solving the performance and technical issues that generally arise.

121. Compounding the unnecessary scheduling problems caused by R. Kelly's needs, R. Kelly insisted on selecting the production manager for the Tour. His selection, Chris Weathers, was relatively unknown and lacked the requisite experience to manage a multi-city tour of the Tour's sophistication. R. Kelly's production manager then hired a lighting director who was a no-show, necessitating the hiring of Gary Wescott – a veteran director of such acts as Guns N' Roses, David Bowie, and Bon Jovi.

122. Jay-Z and R. Kelly were individually responsible for coordinating their musical numbers with Gary Wescott as well as insuring that the concert was ready by the start of Tour rehearsals.

R. Kelly's Absences

123. Jay-Z and R. Kelly agreed to meet in Chicago approximately ten days before the Tour's start for the specific purpose of reviewing the material for the show and rehearsing. Jay-Z arrived timely, but R. Kelly's whereabouts was unknown. When he finally materialized several days later, insufficient time remained to rehearse adequately.

124. Because of R. Kelly's absence, rehearsals were initially cancelled at the Northern Illinois Convocation Center, a venue selected by R. Kelly's Tour manager. Moreover, the venue was plagued with electrical issues, leaving only three production days to squeeze in rehearsals and to complete tasks normally requiring considerable amounts of time.

21

206

125. During the first of those three remaining days, Jay-Z scheduled a rehearsal with R. Kelly. Although Jay-Z timely appeared for the rehearsal, R. Kelly was late by more than two hours, and then he squandered the remaining time by playing basketball. Consequently, no meaningful rehearsal occurred that day – let alone during the remaining days.

126. On the last scheduled rehearsal day, R. Kelly panicked, motivating him to attempt to rehearse. However, he spent considerable time laboring over innocuous issues pertaining to his sexually-laden skits, which prevented him from attending important rehearsals with the lighting director, Jay-Z, the dancers, and other critical aspects of the show. R. Kelly's failure and refusal to participate in those rehearsals hindered the lighting director, who needed time to review cues and other lighting issues with R. Kelly and his dancers.

127. R. Kelly concentrated his time on a simulated sex skit involving a "ménage a trois" inside a cage. R. Kelly also rehearsed a skit involving simulated text messaging with a female audience member. That skit concerned the audience member's age, inappropriately prompting reminders of R. Kelly's criminal matter involving an underage girl.

128. Moreover, R. Kelly failed to provide required video elements for the concert. Jay-Z's manager, John Meneilly, volunteered to assist R. Kelly, inasmuch as R. Kelly came empty-handed. Working night and day, Meneilly pieced together video fragments from a variety of sources to meet the deadline for the first concert. R. Kelly belatedly hired a firm to create additional video, but the finished product was delivered late.

22

Chicago

129. The first concert went as well as could be expected given the circumstances of R. Kelly's material defaults and misconduct. The Chicago crowd responded enthusiastically to Jay-Z's performance. R. Kelly's performance was noticeably mediocre, as it reflected his lack of preparation and rehearsal. Throughout this hometown performance, R. Kelly appeared uneasy and lethargic.

130. The Chicago media decried R. Kelly's inclusion of the sexually-laden skits, viewing them as inappropriate and callous in light of the pending felony charges against him. Public outcry ultimately forced R. Kelly to remove the skits from the show. The public's reaction intensified R. Kelly's sullen and unenthusiastic attitude about the Tour.

131. Because the music and vocals for R. Kelly and Jay-Z were pre-programmed in a computer, any changes to R. Kelly's vocals required time-consuming reprogramming. Without telling anyone, R. Kelly instructed a technician that he personally hired to reprogram his musical numbers between the first and second concerts. Those changes necessitated the lighting director, Gary Wescott, to make changes, but he was not provided with R. Kelly's reprogrammed vocals.

132. For the second Chicago concert, the performers were directed to arrive by 7 p.m., and the concert was scheduled to begin at 8 p.m. Jay-Z timely arrived. However, R. Kelly was inexplicably absent. He arrived after 8:15 p.m., but refused to leave his tour bus. R. Kelly's representatives would not approach or even telephone him while he was in the bus. Jay-Z was informed only that R. Kelly refused to exit his bus. Unbeknownst to Jay-Z

23

and the Promoter, R. Kelly was waiting for his personal technician to deliver his re-programmed vocals.

133. After more than a 1-1/2 hour delay, concertgoers became unruly and violent. The police threatened to employ a riot squad to prevent further violence, believing that the concert would be cancelled because of R. Kelly's absence. At approximately 10 p.m., Kelly exited the bus, as his reprogrammed vocals were finally delivered. The entire fiasco could have been avoided had R. Kelly informed the Promoter or Jay-Z of his predicament so concertgoers could have been pacified.

134. Since R. Kelly substantially modified his show, without coordinating with Gary Wescott or anyone else, snags arose in his performance. Appearing frustrated and depressed, R. Kelly abandoned the concert before its end, leaving Jay-Z on stage to perform their grand finale alone.

Cincinnati and Other Venues

135. Due to R. Kelly's unexpected and disruptive delay at the second Chicago concert, the next scheduled concert in Cincinnati, Ohio, was cancelled because it was logistically impossible to travel there and set up in time. Cincinnati ticket-holders were provided less than 24-hour notice of the concert's cancellation. The last-minute cancellation was embarrassing to the Tour and was damaging to Jay-Z's reputation. R. Kelly's conduct impacted box office receipts and thus prevented Jay-Z from increased earnings.

136. In Columbus, Ohio, Jay-Z called a meeting with R. Kelly to discuss, in particular, Jay-Z's distress over and dissatisfaction with R. Kelly's general attitude, conduct and performances. R. Kelly explained that he was dissatisfied with the lighting direction

24

and that he intended to hire his own director. Jay-Z responded that R. Kelly should hire whomever he liked. However, R. Kelly did nothing.

137. In Baltimore, Maryland, R. Kelly sat down with members of the Tour, including Gary Wescott, to review concert video footage so that he could air his complaints. Displeased to hear that he was the source of his own problems, R. Kelly verbally exploded, hurling objects, and shouting that he was "going home." He abruptly left the meeting seeking sanctuary in his tour bus.

138. R. Kelly's violent outburst occurred before the start of the sold-out Baltimore concert, which he had delayed for more than 1-1/2 hours. With the Chicago incident still fresh in mind, the Promoter and others were concerned that audience members would become violent if the concert was cancelled. A parked van blocked R. Kelly from leaving the venue enabling the Promoter to speak with R. Kelly, who by then was a weeping emotional wreck. The Promoter ultimately convinced R. Kelly to perform that night.

139. Following the Baltimore concert, R. Kelly demanded two additional days of rehearsal before the next concert in Greensboro, North Carolina. The Promoter and Jay-Z were informed that R. Kelly would abandon the Tour if his demand was not met. R. Kelly ultimately backed down, agreeing to perform. He also recanted his threat to cancel future shows.

140. Following the concert in Nashville, Tennessee, R. Kelly hired Curtis Battle as his personal production consultant, along with a lighting assistant named "Root." To support R. Kelly, the Promoter set aside a full day to permit R. Kelly to work on more changes to his ever-changing show. However, R. Kelly did not begin rehearsals until well into the evening of that day.

25

141. R. Kelly's next battleground was St. Louis, Missouri. Although he made minor changes to his performance, R. Kelly also added a skit that he had used on occasion during the Tour. In the skit, R. Kelly appeared to strip in silhouette to the song "Strip For You," while a group of dancers sauntered on stage carrying the removed clothing. R. Kelly then emerged from behind the screen wearing a trench coat. At the end of the song, as the lyrics "I'll strip for you" were sung, R. Kelly appeared opening his coat (so as to appear to flash the audience) at the moment the lights went black. Unfortunately, an unintended miscue arose that caused the lights to go black at the wrong moment. R. Kelly left the stage in a rage.

142. In another performance later that same evening, without warning, R. Kelly left the stage with his personal cameraman and bodyguards, all of whom raced through the audience to the back of the venue. Once there, R. Kelly ripped down the divider separating the stage lighting equipment from the concertgoers, kicking over a computer, at which point he first threatened and then assaulted Gary Wescott while cameras were rolling and displaying the scene on video screens.

143. Without explanation or apology, R. Kelly returned to the stage, bowed to the audience, changed his outfit, hopped onto a waiting "People Mover," and left the venue before the concert was completed. The entire incident appeared on video screens in the arena. R. Kelly then went to a local McDonald's where he began serving food to patrons at the drive-thru. The concert's grand finale could not be performed in his absence.

144. After that concert, R. Kelly renewed his threat to cancel the Tour and to return permanently to Chicago. He demanded that concerts in Milwaukee, Wisconsin, and

26

Jay-Z…and the Roc-A-Fella Dynasty

Hartford, Connecticut, be cancelled so that he could rehearse for the upcoming concerts at the Garden in New York City. The Promoter acquiesced to keep the Tour alive.

145. On October 29, 2004, Jay-Z and R. Kelly appeared at the Garden for the first of three scheduled concerts. However, that evening became R. Kelly's final curtain call. Stating that he observed two men at separate times brandishing firearms, R. Kelly announced to the audience that he would not continue his performance. He threw his mike to the ground and exited the stage while crying hysterically. Although a search was conducted by Garden security and, upon information and belief, the New York City Police, no weapons were found in the arena. However, by that time, concertgoers were raucous and impatient for the continuation of the show.

146. Recognizing that R. Kelly was not returning, Jay-Z appeared on stage and performed a number of songs. He then stopped and announced to the audience that if they indulged him, he would put together a show. Jay-Z left the stage and within a short time enlisted a number of well-known performers, who were present that evening in the audience or as guests of the artists, to perform, including P. Diddy, Usher, Foxy Brown, Ja Rule, and Mary J. Blige. That show was one of the most historic evenings in music.

147. Because of R. Kelly's material defaults and misconduct, including unsafe and unpredictable behavior, Atlanta Worldwide terminated R. Kelly from the Tour. His termination left the Tour operationally and economically unfeasible. However, due to the enormous response to the quickly assembled concert that was presented the night before (which was akin to a hip-hop Woodstock), the Promoter discussed with Jay-Z and the other artists the creation of a new tour. Atlanta Worldwide and the Marcy Parties hoped to mitigate some of their damages arising from R. Kelly's material defaults and misconduct.

27

212

148. Thereafter, R. Kelly maliciously attacked Jay-Z and Jeff Sharp in the media, relying on patently false information and rank innuendo. However, upon information and belief, in an interview on Hot 97 FM, R. Kelly admitted that he never observed anyone with a firearm at the Garden on October 29th. Instead, his revised cover story became that his behavior that night was prompted by a threatening telephone call that he received earlier on the same day.

FIRST COUNTERCLAIM
(Tortious Interference With Contract)

149. The Marcy Parties repeat and reallege the allegations set forth in paragraphs 108 through 148 as if set forth fully herein.

150. R. Kelly was fully aware of the agreement between Jay-Z and Atlanta Worldwide for the Tour.

151. R. Kelly was knowledgeable and informed of the principal terms of the agreement between Jay-Z and Atlanta Worldwide.

152. R. Kelly was knowledgeable and informed that the success of the Tour was dependent in part upon his full performance of his agreements with Atlanta Worldwide and his representations to Jay-Z that he would perform in a competent and professional manner throughout the Tour.

153. Jay-Z performed all of his obligations pursuant to his agreement with Atlanta Worldwide.

154. R. Kelly's material defaults and misconduct, prior to and during the Tour, his unruly tantrums, threatening behavior, lack of preparation, and lax performances disrupted the Tour, leading to his warranted and necessary termination by Atlanta Worldwide.

28

213

Despite all of R. Kelly's wining, his antics could not sabotage hova from wrapping up his 'Unfinished Business', the second in a pair of collaboration albums with Kelly, and Jay's 12th album in 8 years debuting atop the Top 200 Billboard Album Charts on November 3rd, scanning 214,000 copies in its first week of release. While the album did debut atop the Billboard Top 200 Album Chart, its numbers were no doubt affected—AGAIN—by Kelly's unprofessionalism and personal problems, just as they had two years earlier.

Seeking to move—AGAIN—past Kelly's negative press and karma, Jay-Z, for the duration of November—in addition to continuing his wildly successful 'Jay-Z and Friends' trek—also turned his focus to promoting his forthcoming 'Fade to Black' documentary. Chronicling the making of The Black Album, and the historic Madison Square Garden in November, 2003, which had ironically inspired Jay and R. Kelly to reunite in the first place, the film was due— through Paramount Classics—to hit theatres November 5, 2004.

In support of the film's release, Jay-Z undertook a massive media campaign, appearing in interviews with everyone from MTV to Carson Daley to Charlie Rose and Newsweek. *The New York Times'* review of the film proclaimed that "its hip-hop splendor proves hype-worthy," while Chicago's Metromix Magazine raved that "it captures the electricity, camaraderie and bravura—backstage, on stage and in the crowd—with sophistication and energetic camera work."

The *New York Daily News*, meanwhile, called the film "a loving tribute to one of the most important figures in hip-hop." Jay, for his part, described the film as a tour behind the scenes "back stage, and also the recording process of 'The Black Album.' So it started as a concert film, and then it turned into this journey, like a young kid from Brooklyn, you know, who gets to play the biggest stage in the world, Madison Square Garden…We knew something special was going to happen. We had the tapes in the building and we were going to make a DVD; but after I got the first 15 minutes of it, I was like, 'This is bigger than just a DVD…I've always had that in my mind…(that) I was going to make one album, foolishly. I thought I would make one album and that would be it. I thought I'd be an executive from there."

"Then the reality of the business came down on me. I was the only artist on Roc-A-Fella at the time, and we were moving situations from priority. Our first deal was with Priority Records from the West coast and then when we made the deal with Def Jam I was the only asset on the label so I had to sign for a certain amount of years so that killed that dream. It's been coming for a while and it just happened that night at the Garden…I hope it serves as somewhat inspirational for some cause I didn't get discovered at Radio City Music Hall or at a fancy TV special…Giants Stadium (for instance), is not the great place to play."

"Madison Square Garden is the perfect place to play. Giants Stadium because of the acoustics, its outdoors, and it's huge, so the sound is hitting you back. It's echoing and you don't feel it in your heart as much. When you're in an arena, you feel the music in your heart and the lighting is perfect. There's nothing like Madison Square Garden…I couldn't get a deal. Just to come so far and full circle from not having a deal to performing on the biggest stage in the world. I hope it's somewhat inspirational…(When I perform), I like to leave that feeling that you can mess up any second, like every time I rehearse the shows…Not after the first song. I get butterflies, but by that time, I'm still thinking about the execution of what I'm going to do. I'm preoccupied. And then when the first note hits, I'm in it. I'm so far in it, I'm not nervous at all…"

"I did *Unplugged*, that album for MTV, we rehearsed Saturday and we recorded Sunday. As far as the preparation for the show, getting people there was longer than the rehearsal time. I hadn't rehearsed with R. Kelly, I did two rehearsals with Mary J. Blige and I hadn't rehearsed with Foxy Brown. I hadn't rehearsed with Beyonce. You can add that up. It's very short...The recording of the CD was supposed to be for an extra bonus on the album, some DVD footage, but of course we missed that...I couldn't feel it at the time."

"It took for me to watch the movie to really say like 'Wow, that was huge'. Because at the time, like I said, with such little rehearsal time, I'm focused on what's coming on next. I was just focused on what was going on, the technical aspect of it, the emotional aspect kicked in later when I looked at it. I was like, 'This is crazy'. When I saw the first 15 minutes, that's when I was blown away...Who else could tell that story? That's how I felt. It had to be in my voice. This is one of the most personal things I put out. I never allow people in the studio during my recording process or listen to my conversations with friends. I'm not that type of person, so I figured it had to be in my voice..."

"When I (watched) the film, my backstage favorite moment was Slick Rick passing Ghostface (Killa) the chain. That's a huge hip-hop moment right there. But I didn't see that live, I was too busy running back and forth. Like when I wasn't on stage, I was changing, so I was in the change booth. When I come out, I run back on stage, so I didn't really get in on the act too much backstage. But when I seen the film, seen that moment, I was like, 'Wow, you caught that?'...And also you get to see the making of *The Black Album* for the most part. You know, it's cut with that type of footage of me creating the songs with pharall and Timbaland and all those guys."

Those parts of the film which focused on Jay's recording of *The Black Album* shed light for the first time on the genius of Jay's recording method, namely that he DOESN'T WRITE DOWN ANY OF HIS RHYMES. While this was a widely-known phenomenon of Jay's within the industry, earning him the nickname of 'Hova' among producers and peers, the public would learn the secret behind Jay's method largely for the first time through the documentary on the making of *The Black Album.*

As Jay explained the evolution of his writing and recording method, "because I don't write, they was like, 'You like a god, man. You Like Hov.' That name was given to me…I took 'Jay' off of 'Hova' because I don't want people to think that I think I'm God. I don't think that. I guess every man has God in him, but not in the way where I could split the Red Sea or nothing…I don't write…so everything's basically a freestyle for me. It's just organized; I think about it a little more. I never wrote a lyric since my first album…I think it was just a God-given talent, because I don't write anything when I'm recording, I don't write lyrics, I just listen to the music and I formulate the song, like just off the top of my head. I just go over the lyrics again and again until I have the song, and then I just go on in and I record it."

"So it's definitely a God-given talent, and it was drive also. It was drive. I mean, it was tough. I mean, we toured the whole Eastern seaboard, because that's where our record would get played…So we would tour all the way up to North Carolina, just hit that area, not even Atlanta, just all the way up to North Carolina, we would tour, just jump in the van and just drive ourselves and just do endless, endless shows, I mean, with 20 people in the building sometimes…I used to get ideas and I used to be running around. I used to be outside. I wasn't nowhere where I could write. Sometimes I used to run in the store, write them on a paper bag, put them in my pocket…so I had to start memorizing…I say, like—like, if you had—here's—here's the melody…Me, I'll rhyme…so I'm so in sync with the beat, like, when the music's going…I'm going… with words, though…That's flow…"

"See, what happened was I used to write so much as a kid. Growing up, I would write everyday, everyday. I had this green notebook and I would write so much that when I started getting out, growing up, and I was in the houses, I would have these ideas and they would come to me. And then I would look around. I would go in the bodega. That's the store for people who don't—going to the stationary store. And I would get this paper bag and I would just write them and stuff the lyrics in my pocket. So I would go home, I would have all these lyrics on paper bags. But then, you know, as I started standing out more and more—I started memorizing one line and then two songs. You know, it's like exercising. You do five pushups one day. The next day you'll be able to do ten. And I just started memorizing."

As December began, Roc-A-Fella Records superstar Kayne dominated the Grammy Award nominations, with a record 10 nominations, including Album of the Year and Best Rap Album nominations for *College Dropout*, Song of the Year for *Jesus Walks*, Best New Artist, and among other nominations, a producer nod on Best R&B Song for '*You Don't Know My Name*,' which he produced for Alicia Keys.

Jay also received nominations for Best Rap Solo Performance and Best Rap Song for '99 Problems,' and Best Rap Album for 'The Black Album.' Not quite done with his commercial release schedule, Jay issued album number 13 on December 8th, on another collaborative effort, this time with multi-platinum rock band Linkin Park, introducing yet another new phenomenon called the *Mash-Up*. Under this formula, according to MTV.com News, the style "blends Jigga's rhymes and beats with the grinding guitars, explosive choruses and anguished lyrics of the Nu-metal band." Debuting atop the Top 200 Billboard Album Chart after moving 368,000 copies in its first week, the LP stemmed out of an MTV special called 'Ultimate Mash-Ups.'

Jay-Z's month would get even bigger when his retirement became official, and to no one's great surprise—within the industry at least—Jay-Z, Dame and Biggs sold their remaining 50% stake in Roc-A-Fella Records to Def Jam for somewhere in the neighborhood of $30 million (despite the silly press rumors of a $10 million price tag, implausible considering the value of Jay-Z's catalog alone, not counting Kanye West, Cam'ron, Beanie Sigel, etc). The sale made way for Jay-Z to make his next major move in the game: being named PRESIDENT of Def Jam Records.

It was both a logical and natural ascension, with Island Def Jam Music Group Chairman L.A. Reid, in a press statement announcing the deal, proclaiming that "after 10 years of successfully running Roc-A-Fella. Shawn has proven himself to be an astute businessman, in addition to the brilliant artistic talent that the world sees and hears…I can think of no one more relevant and credible in the hip-hop community to build upon Def Jam's fantastic legacy and move the company into its next groundbreaking era." The statement was a gracious gesture, but no one needed convincing that Jay was qualified for the position.

Jay, for his own part, summed up his decision to take the position as part of a larger "drive…to succeed and open up doors for the next generation just like Russell Simmons opened up the doors for me as far as fashion and music. I don't have any secret obsession…It's just so that I can open up doors like on the executive level. There's a need for that. While I'm in this position, I feel that it's my duty…it's just another thing, like to challenge myself. I made—I want to say—10 CDs, or I don't know how many CDs…I think we've just seen the guys before as the guys who laid the blueprint for recording, and we've seen how their lives, how it ended up, and most times they end up with nothing, you know, for all the fruits of their labor, for all their hard work, they didn't end up with anything…I was doing so much, that I felt like I had to challenge myself in other areas, and there's also a void on black executive side, you know. They have like head of black music, which is great, and things like that, but you know, just wanted to take it to the next level…I have inherited two of the most important brands in hip-hop, Def Jam and Roc-a-Fella…I feel this is a giant step for me and the entire artistic community."

Unique within Jay's composition as an executive was his unique ability to command the attention and respect of his artists both as an executive and musician, such that "I'm just really procreative. If people want to be creative, I encourage that and if I can help a person sound good on a track album, and make a suggestion, or if I think the hook should sound like that, like I said, I'll make a suggestion. Like Memphis Bleek benefited from that and Destiny's Child has benefited from that. I'm just a person that likes to create with people…Hopefully into new artists, maybe I can channel that through new artists and teach them how to be artists instead of making the hot club record or just one record. Make albums and have lengthy careers…I have this opportunity to open doors for the next generation of artists on the executive level. Why not at least try?…That's my goal right there."

"All the real artists and the people that these guys look up to growing up have their vulnerable moments, Tupac with 'Dear Momma', Biggie Smalls. Right now, it's so much pressure to get the hot single now and get the audience. No one is concentrating on the album…I think artists will relate to me 'cause I know their story…I share some of the same struggles they have, possibly more. These people were signed. I never got signed to a major label. I had to start my own label. I been through all those hardships, from not being able to get a deal to putting out a record that didn't work. I worked around all that. I see it more as being a coach who's been on the field and the players will respect me 'cause I'm speaking their language."

Jay-Z ended 2004 on a high note with the announcement of his appointment to the position of President at Def Jam Records. He spent the holidays vacationing with Beyoncé and his family, and at peace with the legacy he'd left behind as one of hip's greatest emcees historically, and—aside from perhaps Eminem or Dr. Dre—one of its only true living legends. Regarding the future of Jay-Z and Damon Dash as partners, their joint decision to sell

Roc-A-Fella Records outright to Def Jam seemed primarily fueled by Jay's desire to run his own show completely.

Dash rationalized the sale of Roc-A-Fella as business as usual, commenting that "the purpose of business is to build equity in it, and sell it, and start another one." Still, Dash's impersonalization of Roc-A-Fella was out of step with how proudly and loyally he'd embraced the company's brand name in past press releases of any sort, painting the picture of a team, and at times, a family that could never be broken up. Perhaps nothing had come between Jay and Dame, that's the way they both painted it in their own interviews with the media in the wake of Jay-Z's retirement.

Both men had been handsomely compensated when they sold the remaining 50% stake in Roc-A-Fella back to Def Jam, each man, along with their third partner Biggs, taking around $10 million away from the deal. Dash had plenty of independent business interests to occupy him, as did Jay, so the split seemed logical in one light as Dame's greatest single responsibility—managing Jay-Z's career— was now over by default due to the rapper's retirement.

With 2005 approaching fast, both men had gone in a decade from a struggling independent to rap's most premium brand name, and as one era of greatness ended, another was sure to begin for both men as they sought to accomplish their greatest mutual challenge—to attain the same success they had together independent of one another.

Conclusion
2005 and Beyond...

What can you say when the man who has done it all still feels there's more to do? Follow him. Seas of fans do (30 million and counting to be exact), like disciples. Industry insiders do, eager to ride even a little bit of the coat-tail of whatever his next great innovation of the hip-hop game will be. If New York truly does have a Teflon Don, it is Jay-Z.

He made his climb from the Marcy Projects to the peak of the pop charts—all the way to the top floor boardroom, and beyond. Now officially retired as an artist, his position as hip-hop's Emperor is secure. Still, even as he takes his throne ruling over a new empire, he's not starting over by any means. Rather continuing a legacy that began simultaneously with his astral rap career.

As 2005 began, with Jay-Z just settling into his new role as President of Def Jam Records, he was still receiving the derivative accolades from his wildly successful 2004. While he had royalties coming for years as an artist from catalog sales of his 12 platinum and multi-platinum albums released between 1996 and 2004, Jay was already looking to the future of hip-hop, beyond the bar he had set as an artist, seeking to raise it as an executive for all emcees who would come up at Def Jam under his watch.

Jay personally felt he had been bestowed a huge responsibility, and intended to rise up to the challenge, remarking that "I'm looking for a situation where I have a real meaningful role and break the glass ceiling for black executives."

While Jay's early moves included signing free agent Foxy Brown to Def Jam, things were much less locked down for the Roc-A-Fella camp. Kanye West remained signed under both the Roc-A-Fella and Def Jam umbrellas as an artist, but was now working and reporting directly to Jay-Z. Cam'ron and his Diplomats crew had been released from their contract with Roc-A-Fella, after Cam felt the label had put little effort into promoting his December, 2004 sophomore release, 'Purple Haze', which had gone Gold only by the start of the new year.

Beanie Sigel's position was much more precarious in general as he was facing a year in Federal Prison on a Federal Gun Charge, as well as awaiting trial for Attempted Murder in early 2005, and a 1st Degree Assault charge dating back to 2003—although he had a new album, entitled 'The B. Coming', slated for release in the later spring of 2005—despite his incarceration.

As for Damon Dash and the rest of the Team-ROC, L.A. Reid had diplomatically worked out a pact with Dash that kept him under the Island/Def Jam Umbrella, but that gave Dame a new joint-venture label, which, according to the Associated Press statement from L.A. Reid, was "a great new beginning for Damon, Biggs, and all the artists involved…We are casting our sights on the future with Damon Dash Music Group, while respecting the impact and recognition that RAF has built up within the hip-hop community. What has been accomplished over the past decade with the careers of Jay-Z, Kanye West, Beanie Sigel, Young Gunz, Memphis Bleek, and many others, has set an entirely new standard of achievement throughout the industry. The popularization and mainstreaming of rap and hip-hop into the pop world owes a monumental debt to the vision and courage that RAF put forward on behalf of its roster of artists. Now, a new generation of performers will benefit from their trailblazing. Everyone at Island

Def Jam is enthusiastic over the opportunity to continue working with Damon Dash and Kareem Burke."

For his part, Dash commented that "I am so very proud of what we built in Roc-A-Fella Records,' said Mr. Dash. It was an amazing, fulfilling ten years. Now, with the launch of Damon Dash Music Group, my partner Kareem 'Biggs' Burke and I have the unique opportunity to develop, distill, and nurture our vision for another great record company. Damon Dash Music Group will be dedicated, of course, to producing the hottest, most cutting-edge music on the market, but will also be unique in its encouragement and development of entrepreneurship in its artists, executives and staff. We will continue to advise and consult the artists whose careers we helped launch and watched flourish, but we also welcome the challenge of working with a new family of artists both new and established to build Damon Dash Music Group into one of the industry's finest."

Reid was also keeping Dash on in a consulting capacity with Roc-A-Fella artists Cam'ron, Beanie Sigel, and N.O.R.E., among others. In February, Jay won what may (or may not) be his final Grammy Award for Best Rap Solo Performance for '99 Problems,' showing Roc-A-Fella Records was still alive and well, not to mention the Grammys that Kanye West took home.

Outside of the recording realm, Dash, Jay and Biggs continued to co-own the rest of Roc-A-Fella Enterprises' various subsidiaries, most notably including Roc-A-Wear. Though the day-to-day operations of the latter company, along with most of Roc-A-Fella Enterprises' other ventures, were handled by executives through which Jay and Dame communicated on major money and product line decisions, the foundation and chemistry for the aforementioned corporation remained intact.

In effect, by Jay-Z retiring, all three men had retired from Roc-A-Fella Records. It seemed the only appropriate move, given how all three had been so inextricably tied to and identified with the brand name. Jay-Z had paid Dash and Biggs an undisclosed amount to buy exclusive rights to Roc-A-Fella Records, but Dash had retained—through license from Jay for his ownership stake—the rights to use the 'ROC' prefix for a variety of independent ventures that Dash invested in with his own money.

Jay and Dame even competed against one another on occasion—in a friendly fashion—for example, when Jay, in late 2004, launched his own line of cognac with Grey Goose, which the media attempted to portray as proof of a rivalry. Dash's spokeswoman commented that "they started a business together and they hope each other's deals go really well. There is no animosity."

As far as Jay having any comment on Dame's new company, he's showed little interest, perhaps being completely engrossed in his new duties as President of one of hip-hop's biggest record labels, commenting only that "(Dame) has a situation of his own. I don't know what they named it. Same building." Dash, for his part, has been attempting to remain more diplomatic, stating that "I'm sure in life or in business, there's a bunch of people that start off doing business together for one thing and then they branch off. Why do we have to have a beef?...People need to know we are not enemies...Its not the end of a dynasty. We're all still together. There's a certain way of living and there's a certain way of life. We live by a certain code of honor that still exists."

Whether that code continues to be communicated through the ROC label—no matter how its divided up corporately—it wouldn't be fair to hate on Damon Dash because he's been cut throat, but it would be easier than acknowledging the significant role he's played in helping Jay-Z get to where he is today. Jay-Z is famous in an entirely different way than Damon Dash, despite any number of photo ops they take together, or any number of business ventures Dash announces.

Suge Knight only became notorious because of his literal criminal record, and Sean Combs only became P. Diddy after he forced himself upon the public in enough guest appearances, remixes and outright albums that he became part of the pop mainstream by default. Damon Dash has a LOUD personality, and his talent for hype has played a substantial role in building Roc-A-Fella's name as a brand. He's also undeniably a brilliant business mind, by the sheer net worth of his company.

Because Jay is less boisterous than Dame, its also easier to point fingers at Dash for his arrogance, which is possibly rooted in some insecurity stemming from concern over life without Jay-Z's record sales to rely on. Or in the past for some sub-conscious knowledge that Jay would desire to retire one day. The bottom line is simple: Jay-Z would never have become who he has as an entrepreneur today, with the net worth he has accrued, without Damon Dash, and conversely, Damon Dash would never have attained the reputation and wealth as an entrepreneur he has without Jay-Z as a partner.

Lord only knows the silent role Biggs played, since he was only ever identified as a silent partner. The fact that Biggs stayed part-nered with Dame in their new venture with Island/Def Jam probably speaks quiet volumes, but we'll leave that between the triage that has now gone their separate ways. From where each man started, the world can only envy and respect their positions today, and with the tireless work ethic of both Jay-Z and Damon Dash, no one can say they don't deserve to be where they are. Both men are examples of what anyone—no matter their class, economic level, race, environment, social status, or adversities—can achieve with hard work, and hustle. What Jay-Z and Damon Dash have most importantly accomplished for many generations of African Americans to come is to redefine the definition of hustler as it has been traditionally interpreted—where rap in the past had glori-fied the image of a hustler primarily as a crack dealer in the past, Jay-Z and Damon Dash made it cool to be legitimate businessmen.

By showing those young, African Americans growing up in the projects of Harlem and Brooklyn that there were other roads out other than just rap or basketball stardom, perhaps Roc-A-Fella has awakened a new generation to the beginning of the next American Dream…

Jay-Z Complete
Chart/Singles/Awards History

1995

▼ Jay-Z began a different career as a solo rapper with the single "In My Lifetime" which eventually led to a distribution deal.

1996

April

▼ Jay-Z topped the Billboard Dance Music Maxi-Singles Sales chart for 5 weeks with "Ain't No.../Dead Presidents."

June

▼ Jay-Z released Reasonable Doubt with the tracks "Can't Knock The Hustle,""Feelin' It," "Dead Presidents," and "Brooklyn's Finest."

▼ The single "Dead Presidents" was certified gold.

September

▼ Reasonable Doubt was certified gold.

1997

▼ # 141 Singles Artist of the Year

September

▼ Jay-Z released *Volume 1... In My Lifetime* with tracks "The City Is Mine" and "Sunshine."

1998
▼ # 44 Singles Artist of the Year

January

▼ *Volume 1... In My Lifetime* was certified gold.

May

▼ Jay-Z appeared in the film *Streets Is Watching* and appeared on the soundtrack with the tracks "It's Alright," "Love For Free," "Only A Customer," "In My Lifetime" (remix), and "Celebration."

September

▼ *Volume 2... Hard Knock Life* was released. Jay-Z could be heard on rap and even pop radio with his hits "Hard Knock Life" and "*Can I Get A...*" and his videos became a staple on MTV.

October

▼ *Volume 2... Hard Knock Life* topped the Billboard 200 Albums chart for 5 weeks and the R&B Albums chart for 6 weeks.

December

▼ *Volume 2... Hard Knock Life* was certified 3x platinum.

▼ Jay-Z hit the Top 40 with "Can I Get A..."

▼ Rolling Stone named Jay-Z the Best Hip-Hop Artist of the Year.

▼ Jay-Z topped the Billboard Year-End Charts as the Top R&B Album Artist and Top R&B Album Artist—Male.

1999
▼ # 26 Singles Artist of the Year

February

▼ Jay-Z won a Grammy Award for Best Rap Album (*Volume 2... Hard Knock Life*) and was nominated for Best Rap Solo Performance ("Hard Knock Life") and Best Rap Performance by a Duo or Group ("Money Ain't A Thang" with Jermaine Dupri). Jay-Z boycotted the awards ceremony "...because too many major rap artists continue to be overlooked... Rappers deserve more attention from the Grammy committee and from the whole world. If it's got a gun everybody knows about it, but if we go on a world tour, no one know." A spokesperson for

Jay-Z said after the awards: "If they want to give us awards, we'll take them. But we aren't gonna drop everything and run to the show to get a small pat on the head when they don't even air the award he won."

▼ *Volume 2... Hard Knock Life* was certified 4x platinum and *Volume 1... In My Lifetime* was certified platinum.

March

▼ The single "Hard Knock Life" was certified gold.

April

▼ Jay-Z and DMX donated 1-night's worth of concert profits to the families of the Columbine victims when their Hard Knock Life tour hit Denver. Jay-Z told MTV: "We decided to donate the proceeds from this show as soon as we saw the date on the schedule."

▼ Jay-Z returned to the Top 40 with "Can I Get A..."

May

▼ Jay-Z hit the Top 10 with "Can I Get A..."

August

▼ Jay-Z was named Lyricist of the Year, Solo at the Source Hip-Hip Music Awards.

▼ Jay-Z could be heard on the soundtrack for *Blue Streak* soundtrack with "Girls' Best Friend."

September

▼ Jay-Z won a MTV Video Music Award for Best Rap Video Can I Get A...") and was nominated for Best Video from a Film and Viewer's Choice ("Can I Get A...").

▼ Jay-Z hit the Top 40 by helping out Mariah Carey on her hit "Heartbreaker."

▼ Jay-Z topped the Billboard Rap Singles chart with "Jigga My..." for 2 weeks.

October

▼ Jay-Z won a WB Radio Music Award for Song of the Year (Rhythm/Urban) ("Can I Get A...").

▼ Jay-Z hit the Top 10 with his contribution to Mariah Carey's "Heartbreaker" (which topped the Billboard Hot 100 for 2 weeks and the Billboard Hot 100 Singles Sales chart for 2 weeks and the Billboard R&B/Hip-Hop Singles & Tracks chart for 2 weeks, the Billboard

231

R&B/Hip-Hop Singles & Tracks chart for 2 weeks, and the Billboard Maxi-Singles Sales chart for 8 weeks.

December

▼ Jay-Z was arrested after turning himself in in New York for charges related to a stabbing the night before—he was later charged with 4 counts of assault, but maintained his plea of innocence.

▼ Jay-Z released Volume 3... *The Life & Times Of Shawn Carter* at the end of the month with anticipation of selling over 1 million copies in the first week of release.

▼ Jay-Z won a Billboard Music Award for Rap Artist of the Year.

▼ Jay-Z hit #1 on Mariah Carey's hit "Heartbreaker."

▼ Jay-Z topped the Billboard Year-End Chart-Toppers as the Top Hot Rap Artist.

2000

▼ # 39 Singles Artist of the Year

January

▼ Jay-Z was nominated for an American Music Award for Favorite Rap/Hip Hop Artist.

▼ *Volume 3... The Life & Times Of Shawn Carter* debuted at #1 on the LP charts selling less than half a million copies in its first week of release in the U.S. and topped the Billboard R&B Album chart for 2 weeks.

▼ By the end of the month, a grand jury in New York indicted Jay-Z on 2 counts of attempted assault related to the alleged stabbing last December.

February

▼ Volume 3... The Life & Times Of Shawn Carter was certified 2x platinum.

March

▼ Volume 2... Hard Knock Life was certified 5x platinum.

April

▼ Jay-Z won an Online Hip-Hop Award for Artist of the Year.

May

▼ Jay-Z hit th e Top 40 with "Big Pimpin'."

June

▼ Jay-Z could be heard on the soundtrack for *Nutty Professor II: The Klumps* soundtrack with "Hey Papi."

▼ Jay-Z could be heard on Busta Rhymes' LP, *Anarchy*, on the track "Why We Die."

September

▼ The video "Big Pimpin'" was nominated for a MTV Video Music Award for Best Rap Video.

October

▼ Jay-Z released his next LP, *The Dynasty Rock La Familia 2000*, on the last day of the month.

November

▼ Jay-Z won a Radio Music Award for Artist of the Year: Hip Hop/Rhythmic. *The Dynasty Rock La Familia 2000* debuted at #1 on the Pop and R&B/Hip-Hop LP charts.

▼ Jay-Z hit the Top 40 with with "I Just Wanna Love U (Give It To Me)."

December

▼ Jay-Z hit #1 on the Billboard R&B/Hip-Hop Singles & Tracks chart with "I Just Wanna Love U (Give It To Me)" for 3 weeks.

▼ *The Dynasty Rock La Familia 2000* was certified 2x platinum.

2001

▼ # 29 Singles Artist of the Year

January

▼ Jay-Z hit #1 on the Billboard R&B/Hip-Hop Airplay chart for a week with "I Just Wanna Love U (Give It To Me)."

February

▼ Jay-Z was nominated for 2 Grammy Awards for Best Rap Performance by a Duo or Group ("Big Pimpin'") and Best Rap Album (*Volume 3... The Life & Times Of Shawn Carter*).

▼ *Volume 3... The Life & Times Of Shawn Carter* was certified 3x platinum. Jay-Z was nominated for a Soul Train Music Award for Best R&B/Soul or Rap Album (*The Dynasty Rock La Familia 2000*).

April

▼ Jay-Z was nominated for a Blockbuster Entertainment Award for Favorite Artist—Rap.

May

▼ Jay-Z hit the Top 40 helping out R. Kelly with "Fiesta."

June

▼ Jay-Z hit #1 on the Billboard R&B/Hip-Hop Singles & Tracks chart for 5 weeks and the R&B/Hip-Hop Airplay chart for a week with "Fiesta" (with R. Kelly).

▼ Jay-Z won a BET Award for Best Male Hip-Hop Artist.

September

▼ Jay-Z hit the Top 40 with "Izzo (H.O.V.A.)."

▼ Jay-Z's video for "I Just Wanna Love U (Give It To Me)" was nominated for a MTV Video Music Award for Best Rap Video. Jay-Z also performed at the ceremony.

▼ Jay-Z won a Source Award for Artist of the Year—Solo.

▼ Jay-Z released *The Blueprint.*

▼ *The Blueprint* topped the Billboard 200 LP chart for 3 weeks and the R&B/Hip-Hop Albums chart for 3 weeks—selling over 426,000 copies in its 1st week of release in the US.

▼ Jay-Z topped the MTV Top 20 Video Countdown with "Izzo (H.O.V.A.)."

October

▼ *The Blueprint* was certified platinum.

▼ Jay-Z performed at *The Concert For New York City* benefit concert in New York City (later released as an LP) with proceeds going to 9/11 charities.

November

▼ Jay-Z hit the Top 40 with "Girls, Girls, Girls."

December

▼ Jay-Z released *Unplugged.*

▼ Jay-Z topped Billboard Year-End Charts with the Top Hot R&B/Hip-Hop Singles & Tracks ("Fiesta" with R. Kelly) and as the Top Hot R&B/Hip-Hop Singles & Tracks Artist and the Top Hot R&B/Hip-Hop Singles & Tracks Artist—Male.

▼ Readers and critics of Rolling Stone voted Jay-Z as Best Hip-Hop Artist of the Year.

2002

▼ # 59 Singles Artist of the Year

February

▼ Jay-Z was nominated for 3 Grammy Awards for Best Rap Solo Performance ("Izzo (H.O.V.A.)"), Best Rap Performance by a Duo or Group ("Change The Game" featuring Beanie Sigel & Memphis Bleek), and Best Rap Album (The Blueprint).

March

▼ *Reasonable Doubt* was certified platinum.

▼ Jay-Z won a Soul Train Award for R&B/Soul or Rap Album of the Year (*The Blueprint*).

▼ Jay-Z teamed up with R. Kelly for the LP *The Best Of Both Worlds.*

April

▼ *The Best Of Both Worlds* topped the Billboard Hot R&B/ Hip-Hop Album chart.

▼ The hits collection *Chapter One: Greatest Hits* was released overseas.

May

▼ *The Blueprint* was certified 2x platinum and *The Best Of Both Worlds* was certified platinum.

October

▼ Jay-Z appeared on the *8 Mile* soundtrack with the track "8 Miles And Runnin."

November

▼ Jay-Z released a 2-CD set, *The Blueprint 2: The Gift And The Curse.*

▼ Jay-Z hit the Top 40 with help from Beyoncé Knowles on "'03 Bonnie & Clyde

▼ Jay-Z topped the Billboard Top 200 LP chart for a week and the Hot R&B/Hip-Hop Albums chart for 2 weeks with *The Blueprint 2: The Gift And The Curse* selling over 545,000 copies its first week of release in the US.

December

▼ *The Blueprint 2: The Gift And The Curse* was certified 3x platinum.

▼ Jay-Z had moderate R&B and rap hits with the tracks "People Talking," "Jigga," "Take You Home With Me a.k.a. Body" (with R. Kelly), "Get This Money" (with R. Kelly), "Song Cry," "Somebody's Girl" (with R. Kelly), "Shake Ya Body" (with R. Kelly and Lil' Kim), and "Hovi Baby."

2003

▼ # 12 Singles Artist of the Year

January

▼ Jay-Z hit the Top 10 with "'03 Bonnie & Clyde."

February

▼ Jay-Z was nominated for a Soul Train Music Award with R. Kelly for R&B/Soul Album Group, Band or Duo (*The Best Of Both Worlds*).

▼ Jay-Z was nominated for a Grammy Award for Best Rap Solo Performance—Male ("Song Cry").

April

▼ Jay-Z hit the Top 40 with "Excuse Me Miss."

▼ Jay-Z released *Blueprint 2.1: Gift & Curse*—the LP was shorter version of *The Blueprint 2: The Gift And The Curse* with 2 additional unreleased tracks.

▼ Jay-Z topped the Billboard R&B/Hip-Hop Singles & Tracks chart for a week and the R&B/Hip-Hop Airplay chart with "Excuse Me Miss."

▼ VH1: 50 Greatest Hip Hop Artists includes Jay-Z at # 10.

▼ Jay-Z brought his viewpoints against the US war with Iraq with a remix of Panjabi MC's single "Beware Of The Boys (Mundian To Bach Ke)."

May

▼ Panjabi MC and Jay-Z topped the Billboard R&B/Hip-Hop Singles Sales chart for a week with "Beware Of The Boys (Mundian To Bach Ke)."

June

▼ Jay-Z hit the Top 40 and then the Top 10 helping out Beyoncé Knowles on "Crazy In Love" from her LP *Dangerously In Love*.

▼ Jay-Z and 50 Cent started touring together as part of the 'Rock The Mic Tour' kicking off in Connecticut.

July

▼ Jay-Z topped the Billboard Hot 100 Singles chart for 8 weeks, the Hot 100 Airplay chart for 8 weeks, the Top 40 Tracks chart, the Hot R&B/Hip-Hop Singles & Tracks chart for 3 weeks, the Hot R&B/Hip-Hop Airplay chart for 4 weeks, the Hot Digital Tracks chart for 6 weeks, and the UK singles chart for 3 weeks helping out Beyoncé Knowles on "Crazy In Love."

▼ Jay-Z could be heard on the *Bad Boys 2* soundtrack with the track "La, La, La."

▼ Jay-Z hit #1 for 7 weeks helping out Beyoncé Knowles on "Crazy In Love."

August

▼ Jay-Z topped the Billboard Rhythmic Top 40 chart and Mainstream Top 40 chart with Beyoncé Knowles on "Crazy In Love."

▼ Jay-Z's video for "'03 Bonnie & Clyde" was nominated for a MTV Video Music Award for Best Hip-Hop Video. His contribution to Beyoncé Knowles' "Crazy In Love" won for Best Female Video, Best Choreography (Frank Gatson, Jr.), and Best R&B Video, and was nominated for Viewer's Choice. Jay-Z also performed at the ceremony.

▼ Jay-Z topped the Billboard Hot R&B/Hip-Hop Singles & Tracks chart for 6 weeks and Hot R&B/Hip-Hop Airplay chart for 5 weeks helping out Pharrell on "Frontin'" from *The Neptunes Presents... The Clones* compilation.

▼ Jay-Z could be heard on Mary J. Blige's LP, *Love & Life*, on the track "Love & Life."

September

▼ Jay-Z hit the Top 40 helping out Pharrell on "Frontin'."

▼ Jay-Z topped the Billboard Hot Dance Music / Club Play chart helping out Beyoncé Knowles on "Crazy In Love."

November

▼ Jay-Z released *The Black Album.*

▼ Jay-Z topped the Billboard 200 LP chart for 2 weeks and Top R&B/Hip-Hop Album chart for 3 weeks with *The Black Album.* The LP sold over 463,000 copies in the US during its first shortened week of release.

▼ Jay-Z was honored at the Vibe Awards with the TuBig Award. Jay-Z also won an award for Coolest Collabo along with Beyoncé Knowles for "Crazy In Love."

▼ Jay-Z could heard on Missy Elliott's LP *This Is Not A Test* on the track "Wake Up."

▼ Jay-Z hit the Top 40 with "Change Clothes."

December

▼ Jay-Z topped the ARC Top Songs of 2003 along with Beyoncé Knowles with "Crazy In Love."

▼ Rolling Stone: The 500 Greatest Albums of All Time: # 248: *Reasonable Doubt*, # 464: *The Blueprint.*

2004

▼ 16 Singles Artist of the Year

February

▼ *The Black Album* was certified 2x platinum.

▼ Jay-Z won 2 Grammy Awards for Best R&B Song (awarded to the songwriter) ("Crazy In Love" with Rich Harrison, Beyoncé Knowles and Eugene Record) and Best Rap/Sung Collaboration ("Crazy In Love" with Beyoncé Knowles), and was also nominated for Record of the Year, Best Rap/Sung Collaboration ("Frontin'" with The Neptunes and Pharrell), Best Rap Album (*The Blueprint 2: The Gift And The Curse*), and Best Rap Song (songwriter) ("Excuse Me Miss" with Chad Hugo and Pharrell Williams

March

▼ Jay-Z hit the Top 40 with "Dirt Off Your Shoulder."

May

▼ Jay-Z released *The Black Album: Acappella* (Billboard peak: 106).

June

▼ Jay-Z hit the Top 40 with "99 Problems."

▼ Jay-Z won 2 BET Awards for Best Male Hip-Hop Artist and Best Collaboration ("Crazy In Love").

August

▼ The video for "99 Problems" won 4 MTV Video Music Awards for Best Rap Video, Best Direction (Mark Romanek), Best Cinematography, and Best Editing, and was also nominated for Video of the Year, and Best Male Video.

October

▼ Jay-Z won a Source Award for Lyricist of the Year.

▼ Jay-Z released *The Best Of Both Worlds: Unfinished Business* with R. Kelly.

▼ The single "Dirt Off Your Shoulder" was certified gold.

November

▼ Jay-Z topped the Billboard 200 LP chart with *The Best Of Both Worlds: Unfinished Business* with R. Kelly selling over 215,000 copies in the US its first week of release.

▼ Jay-Z won an American Music Award for Favorite Rap Male Artist and was nominated for Favorite Rap/Hip-Hop Album.

▼ Jay-Z collaborated with Linkin Park on *MTV Ultimate Mash-Ups Presents Jay-Z / Linkin Park: Collision Course* with the track "Numb/Encore."

▼ Jay-Z and Linkin Park topped the Billboard Hot Digital Tracks chart with "Numb/Encore."

December

▼ *MTV Ultimate Mash-Ups Presents Jay-Z / Linkin Park: Collision Course* topped the Billboard 200 LP chart selling over 368,000 copies its first week of release.

▼ Jay-Z was named president and CEO of Def Jam Records.

▼ *The Best Of Both Worlds: Unfinished Business* was certified platinum.

▼ Jay-Z's "99 Problems" was chosen by *Rolling Stone* magazine's critics as the best single of the year.

▼   # 92 on the Top Pop Artists of the Past 25 Years chart.

2005

February

▼   Jay-Z won a Grammy Award for Best Rap Solo Performance ("99 Problems") and was nominated for Best Rap Album (The Black Album), and Best Rap Song (awarded to the songwriter) ("99 Problems").

▼   Jay-Z won a Soul Train Music Award for R&B/Soul or Rap Music Video ("99 Problems").

▼   The single "Numb/Encore" was certified gold.

March

▼   The single "Numb/Encore" was certified platinum.

About the Author

Jake Brown resides in Nashville, Tennessee. An avid writer, Jake has penned several books, including the best-sellers: *SUGE KNIGHT – The Rise, Fall & Rise of Death Row Records*; *Your Body's Calling Me: The Life and Times of Robert "R" Kelly – Music Love, Sex & Money* and *Ready to Die: The*  *Story of Biggie—Notorious B.I.G.* Upcoming titles on Colossus Books are: *50 Cent: No Holds Barred* and *Tupac SHAKUR (2-PAC) in the Studio: The Studio Years* (1987-1996).

ORDER FORM

WWW.AMBERBOOKS.COM

Fax Orders: 480-283-0991   Telephone Orders: 480-460-1660
Postal Orders: Send Checks & Money Orders to:
  Amber Books
  1334 E. Chandler Blvd., Suite 5-D67, Phoenix, AZ 85048
Online Orders: E-mail: Amberbk@aol.com

_____*Jay-Z...and the Roc-A-Fella Dynasty*, ISBN#: 0-9749779-1-8, $16.95
_____*Your Body's Calling Me: The Life & Times of "Robert" R. Kelly*, ISBN#: 0-9727519-5-52, $16.95
_____*Ready to Die: Notorious B.I.G.*, ISBN#: 0-9749779-3-4, $16.95
_____*Suge Knight: The Rise, Fall, and Rise of Death Row Records*, ISBN#: 0-9702224-7-5, $21.95
_____*50 Cent: No Holds Barred*, ISBN#: 0-9767735-2-X, $16.95
_____*Aaliyah—An R&B Princess in Words and Pictures*, ISBN#: 0-9702224-3-2, $10.95
_____*You Forgot About Dre: Dr. Dre & Eminem*, ISBN#: 0-9702224-9-1, $10.95
_____*Divas of the New Millenium*, ISBN#: 0-9749779-6-9, $16.95
_____*Michael Jackson: The King of Pop*, ISBN#: 0-9749779-0-X, $29.95
_____*The House that Jack Built (Hal Jackson Story)*, ISBN#: 0-9727519-4-7, $16.95

Name:_____

Company Name:_____

Address:_____

City:_____State:_____Zip:_____

Telephone: (____) _____E-mail:_____

Jay-Z...	$16.95	❑ Check ❑ Money Order ❑ Cashiers Check
Your Body's Calling Me:	$16.95	❑ Credit Card: ❑ MC ❑ Visa ❑ Amex ❑
Ready to Die: Notorious B.I.G.,	$16.95	Discover
Suge Knight:	$21.95	
50 Cent: No Holds Barred,	$16.95	
Aaliyah—An R&B Princess	$10.95	CC#_____
Dr. Dre & Eminem	$10.95	
Divas of the New Millenium,	$16.95	Expiration Date:_____
Michael Jackson: The King of Pop	$29.95	**Payable to:**
The House that Jack Built	$16.95	Amber Books

        1334 E. Chandler Blvd., Suite 5-D67
        Phoenix, AZ 85048

Shipping: $5.00 per book. Allow 7 days for delivery.
Sales Tax: Add 7.05% to books shipped to Arizona addresses.

Total enclosed: $_____

For Bulk Rates Call: **480-460-1660**   **ORDER NOW**